The Ore Knob
Mine Murders

CONTRIBUTIONS TO SOUTHERN APPALACHIAN STUDIES

1. *Memoirs of Grassy Creek: Growing Up in the Mountains
on the Virginia–North Carolina Line.* Zetta Barker Hamby. 1998

2. *The Pond Mountain Chronicle: Self-Portrait of a Southern
Appalachian Community.* Edited by Leland R. Cooper and Mary Lee Cooper. 1998

3. *Traditional Musicians of the Central Blue Ridge: Old Time, Early Country, Folk
and Bluegrass Label Recording Artists, with Discographies.* Marty McGee. 2000

4. *W.R. Trivett, Appalachian Pictureman: Photographs of a Bygone Time.* Ralph E. Lentz II. 2001

5. *The People of the New River: Oral Histories from the Ashe, Alleghany and Watauga Counties
of North Carolina.* Edited by Leland R. Cooper and Mary Lee Cooper. 2001

6. *John Fox, Jr., Appalachian Author.* Bill York. 2003

7. *The Thistle and the Brier: Historical Links and Cultural Parallels
Between Scotland and Appalachia.* Richard Blaustein. 2003

8. *Tales from Sacred Wind: Coming of Age in Appalachia.
The Cratis Williams Chronicles.* Cratis D. Williams.
Edited by David Cratis Williams and Patricia D. Beaver. 2003

9. *Willard Gayheart, Appalachian Artist.* Willard Gayheart and Donia S. Eley. 2003

10. *The Forest City Lynching of 1900: Populism, Racism, and White Supremacy
in Rutherford County, North Carolina.* J. Timothy Cole. 2003

11. *The Brevard Rosenwald School: Black Education and Community Building
in a Southern Appalachian Town, 1920–1966.* Betty J. Reed. 2004

12. *The Bristol Sessions: Writings About the Big Bang of Country Music.*
Edited by Charles K. Wolfe and Ted Olson. 2005

13. *Community and Change in the North Carolina Mountains:
Oral Histories and Profiles of People from Western Watauga County.*
Compiled by Nannie Greene and Catherine Stokes Sheppard. 2006

14. *Ashe County: A History; A New Edition.* Arthur Lloyd Fletcher. 2009 [2006]

15. *The New River Controversy; A New Edition.*
Thomas J. Schoenbaum. Epilogue by R. Seth Woodard. 2007

16. *The Blue Ridge Parkway by Foot: A Park Ranger's Memoir.* Tim Pegram. 2007

17. *James Still: Critical Essays on the Dean of Appalachian Literature.*
Edited by Ted Olson and Kathy H. Olson. 2008

18. *Owsley County, Kentucky, and the Perpetuation of Poverty.* John R. Burch, Jr. 2008

19. *Asheville: A History.* Nan K. Chase. 2007

20. *Southern Appalachian Poetry: An Anthology of Works by 37 Poets.*
Edited by Marita Garin. 2008

21. *Ball, Bat and Bitumen: A History
of Coalfield Baseball in the Appalachian South.* L.M. Sutter. 2009

22. *The Frontier Nursing Service: America's First Rural
Nurse-Midwife Service and School.* Marie Bartlett. 2009

23. *James Still in Interviews, Oral Histories and Memoirs.* Edited by Ted Olson. 2009

24. *The Millstone Quarries of Powell County, Kentucky.* Charles D. Hockensmith. 2009

25. *The Bibliography of Appalachia: More Than 4,700 Books, Articles, Monographs
and Dissertations, Topically Arranged and Indexed.* Compiled by John R. Burch, Jr. 2009

The Ore Knob Mine Murders

The Crimes, the Investigation and the Trials

ROSE M. HAYNES

Foreword by
Barbara Moore Pless

CONTRIBUTIONS TO SOUTHERN APPALACHIAN STUDIES, 33

McFarland & Company, Inc., Publishers
Jefferson, North Carolina, and London

LIBRARY OF CONGRESS CATALOGUING-IN-PUBLICATION DATA

Haynes, Rose M., 1934–
    The Ore Knob mine murders : the crimes, the investigation
and the trials / Rose M. Haynes ; foreword by Barbara Moore
Pless.
        p.   cm. — (Contributions to Southern Appalachian
studies ; 33)
    Includes bibliographical references and index.

    ISBN 978-0-7864-7316-8
    softcover : acid free paper ∞

    1. Murder—North Carolina—Ashe County—Case studies.
I. Title.
HV6534.A784H396 2013
364.152'309756835—dc23   2013032598

BRITISH LIBRARY CATALOGUING DATA ARE AVAILABLE

© 2013 Rose M. Haynes. All rights reserved

*No part of this book may be reproduced or transmitted in any form
or by any means, electronic or mechanical, including photocopying
or recording, or by any information storage and retrieval system,
without permission in writing from the publisher.*

On the cover: The gate at the fenced Ore Knob mineshaft on
January 8, 1982 (courtesy of Gene Goss); (inset) the location
of the former Ore Knob Mine (EPA).

Manufactured in the United States of America

McFarland & Company, Inc., Publishers
  Box 611, Jefferson, North Carolina 28640
  www.mcfarlandpub.com

To retired Sheriff Eugene Goss, who served Ashe County, North Carolina, for many years. He was instrumental in arresting some of the criminals described in this book; he descended into the mine to help retrieve the bodies; and he guarded Joseph Vines during the Paul Wilson Bare trial. He shared his personal scrapbooks containing pictures and news articles, as well as his copy of the Ashe County Oral History Project related to the Bare trial. The photographs in this book came from his personal collection. He answered my many questions during the numerous interviews I conducted with him over our 30-year friendship. Gene has freely shared his personal experiences with me, and he made it possible for me to write this book.

Thank you, my friend.

Table of Contents

Acknowledgments

In 1982 when I began chronicling this tale of illegal drugs and related crimes, I had no conception of how long the journey would be or how far afield it would take me in both time and distance. Nor did I know how many people would help and encourage me. Nor did I dream of how many friends I would gain on this trip. Nor did I realize that it would span thirty years!

1982–1990

I would like to say a heartfelt thanks to the following people: Susan Andrews, Fay Byrd, Patsy Howard, and retired Sheriff Gene Goss of Ashe County, for interviews, suggestions, and materials shared over the years; John Downey, for his help during the Joseph Vines trial in Asheville and the Chicago trial, as well as for his kindness to my Aunt Selma Wiles and myself while we attended the Asheville trial of Joseph Vines; my teacher, Dr. Barbara Pless, for her patience while I was working and taking classes to help my writing career; Jule Hubbard of the *Wilkes Journal-Patriot* for giving me the chance to get my name in print and for his patience in re-writing my copy; David Johnson, the musician who co-wrote "The Mine Song" words and music and recorded it; and Aunt Selma Wiles, who was so supportive and spent two weeks in Asheville with me while I reported on the Joseph Vines trial for *The The Journal-Patriot* in 1984.

2009–2012

Others who continued to help me when I resumed writing in earnest included my sister, Betty Brothers, now deceased, who typed and mailed my copy back and forth from Ohio over the years while I re-worked this book; Jim, my husband, for all of the crackers and viennas he ate for lunch because

I was busy with the book; my son Mike and his wife, Pat Gambill (Pat drove me across three counties to continue my research and took great pictures to include in my book); my daughter Terre Combs for continuous support and encouragement; my grandson, Josh Sparks, for never giving up on me; and, especially my granddaughter, Jessica Griffin, for taking my "hen-scratching" and transcribing it to computer files; and her husband Cody for transporting the flash drive back and forth; and last, to Bailee and Carson, my great-grand children, for a break in life when I needed it most.

Other people helped by making valuable records available and giving me permission to use them — Sheriff James Williams of Ashe County, who loaned the official statements included in the Paul Wilson Bare trial, and Carolyn Gentry Lee, who retrieved those records from the archives; retired ATF Agent Thomas Chapman, who proofread portions of the manuscript for accuracy; Lindsay Wagner, who enhanced a photograph; Terrence Byrd, on-scene coordinator, Emergency Response and Removal Branch of the Environmental Protection Agency, who provided a copy of the final report on the Ore Knob Mine Reclamation Project and gave me the "grand tour" of the site — an appropriate finale for the Ore Knob Mine saga.

I am especially grateful to Joseph Vines for his help via personal and telephone interviews over the years, and his permission to use the interviews.

My thanks go to the newspapers— the *Jefferson Post* and Editor Clifton Clark's permission to use whatever I needed for the book; The *Wilkes Journal-Patriot* and Jule Hubbard's permission to use the articles for whatever I needed as well; the *Winston-Salem Journal* and editor Carol Hanner for limited permission to use articles; the *Lenoir News*, Chicago UPI, the Associated Press and the Catawba Valley Bureau for brief comments used from various articles printed from 1982 to 1986. Also, many thanks go to the public libraries in North Wilkesboro and West Jefferson, and the Wilkes Community College Library for locating many needed materials; and to Dr. Fay Byrd, who never stopped encouraging me over the years. The same goes for my friend, retired Sheriff Gene Goss, whose help truly made the book possible. Special acknowledgment goes to Judge Michael Helms for a call on my behalf.

Most of all, many thanks go to my friend Dr. Barbara Pless, who has edited the contents and formatted the book, coming to my home and working tirelessly over the past three years. It is impossible to say how much help Dr. Pless has been in converting *Shadow Over the Mountain* into *The Ore Knob Mine Murders*. I do know that her knowledge of computers has been invaluable in editing and formatting my book. The long hours we have spent together over the last three years has included talking, planning, agreeing, disagreeing, and laughing. Through it all, we have remained friends and have had only one goal in mind — getting the book to the publisher on time! We might have made it if I had not kept unearthing more fabulous materials—the latest in the final week. Barbara has been right there with me all the way helping me reach my goal.

I am deeply grateful for all of the help from my friends and family and many other people I became acquainted with over the years while writing the book.

Foreword

BARBARA MOORE PLESS

It is difficult to say which is more astounding, remarkable, or surreal, the story or the author. It is my privilege to write this foreword because there is no one better qualified to enlighten the reader on both. I was part of her educational journey, and I have been a part of the final process—editing her manuscript.

Rose Haynes picked up the newspaper on a January morning some thirty years ago to stare at the headlines about a kidnapping and murder purported to have occurred in neighboring Ashe County. Her first reaction was one of horror. Her second was that someone needed to write a book to expose this drug-related event, followed quickly by her decision to be that person. Thus her goal was born. She immediately began collecting the articles published in the local and regional newspapers and making notes on the daily newscasts.

She realized that she did not have the skills needed to write a book, so she set out on an educational journey to prepare herself by taking classes at Wilkes Community College and completing correspondence courses. In the meantime, she continued collecting news articles. She also began writing feature articles for the local newspaper. When asked if she could take pictures, she admitted to not owning a camera and having very little photography experience. The newspaper provided her with a camera, and out the door she went!

During the days after the Paul Bare trial, Rose began interviewing persons connected to the trial. This also marked the beginning of her friendship with Eugene Goss, who has been instrumental in the accomplishment of her goal in so many ways. In her preface, she describes the great effort it took to obtain an interview with Joseph Vines within prison walls.

Another example of her determination is she laboriously hand-copied the entire court transcript of the Paul Bare trial for the kidnapping and murder of Lonnie Gamboa. This endeavor took her over two years. This book could not have been written otherwise because the original transcript was destroyed. Her perseverance and ability to gather information have been phenomenal.

To make a long story short, she was able to produce reference after reference from her boundless collection of news articles and court documents. In the process, she uncovered even more material to enhance this tale, and the book is even better than before.

Her personal qualities, courage, and determination have enabled her to complete a monumental task and produce a highly professional, well-written, thought-provoking, and interesting book. Where there's a will, there's a way.

Barbara Moore Pless, Ed.D., is a management consultant specializing in oral and written communications, supervisory and management skills training, and team-building and problem-solving skills training. She lives in Wilkesboro, North Carolina.

Preface

The Ore Knob Mine Murders tells the true story of events that led to the horrific death of a drug dealer on an isolated mountaintop in Ashe County, North Carolina, early on a windy Christmas Eve morning. Joseph Vines, a former teenage drug dealer who made a conscious decision to turn informant after seeing the tragic results of drugs on close friends, had served as a government informant for the last eleven years. On this particular night, he was forced at gunpoint to push Lonnie Gamboa into an old mine shaft alive or be killed himself.

I will never forget those headlines: "Man Pushed Alive into Ore Knob Mine Shaft — 23 Bodies Rumored to Be in Mine." I was horrified that one person could do that to another person. My next thought was that someone needed to write a book to expose the magnitude of our illegal drug problem. This story broke on January 8, 1982. For the next several months this crime was featured daily in newspapers and on television news shows, and I knew I had to write this book. During this time, the issue became even more personal because several people close to me became involved with illegal drugs. When I began my research, I had no concept of where this would lead me or how much I would learn about the inner workings of the illegal drug trade and the legal system itself.

My data collection grew by leaps and bounds. Through sheer determination I was able to interview key figures in these events. I conducted interviews in Ashe County, Wilkes County and Buncombe County. I visited the mine site and other sites connected to the story. I spent many hours on the telephone tracking down individuals involved. My greatest challenge came in tracking down and interviewing Joseph Vines, who was under a protective alias after he was convicted of murder and sentenced to life in prison. I obtained permission to interview him after promising complete secrecy, flew to an undisclosed location, audiotaped the interview, and returned home. This information allowed me to incorporate his innermost thoughts and feelings authentically.

I followed this true story through four major court trials, even transcribing in long-hand the entire court transcript for the Paul Bare trial. I also obtained a copy of an official court document from the Chicago trial. The sources of information on the third trial came from newspaper accounts. I attended the fourth two-week trial to report for my local newspaper. I consider my research sources to be factual and accurate.

Just recently I gained access to the remaining court records for the Paul Bare trial that are archived at the Ashe County Sheriff's Department. Again, I must express gratitude to my friend Gene Goss who made this possible. He accompanied me to the office and introduced me to Sheriff James Williams, who provided copies of documents for use in writing my book. This necessitated another re-write.

A second reason for writing this book is to highlight the importance of the undercover informant in solving major crimes and the personal risks taken by the informant. A third reason is to raise the questions about the legal rights of that informant. A fourth related point that I became aware of as I gathered information was the evidence of many inconsistencies within the legal system in the handling of factual information.

Included in the book are copies of the original photographs taken during the retrieval of the bodies at the Ore Knob mine shaft, loaned to me by retired Sheriff Eugene Goss. The images are stark and gruesome. I have also included a "List of Persons," a "Timeline," and several charts and maps.

I have included a section on the history of the Ore Knob Mine in Laurel Springs, North Carolina, and a section on the reclamation of the land surrounding the mine. The positive impact for the area was that it was an active mine for over one hundred years and provided employment for many people through that time. The negative impact was the poisoning of the land and water supply over time. Fish and wildlife suffered from the leaching of sulfuric acid into the water supply. The federal Environmental Protection Agency Reclamation Project is now completed, and the water supply is now safe. Terrence Byrd, Project Manager, generously shared documents and pictures with me.

One of the advantages of the length of time spent writing my book is that I have continued to uncover powerful resources that have enriched the telling of this dramatic series of events. Over the last thirty years, I have been able to remain in touch with several of the major characters in this saga and am including a section that gives updates on their lives.

My recommendation is to first read for the story to get the full impact of the crimes committed and the far-reaching effects of drug trafficking on a community, region, and nation. A second reading with attention to the documentation of the content through the references will further enhance appreciation for the efforts necessary to build the credibility that is needed to validate a true crime story.

Introduction

It has been almost 30 years since the last trial for the Ore Knob Mine murders of Thomas Forester and Lonnie Gamboa were held in 1984. Many people in the small communities of Jefferson and Laurel Springs have forgotten details about the tragedy of the past. Only the older generations recall much about those events. My book has taken many twists and turns since I first began writing it. To begin with, it was a story that focused on a single murder that occurred early on the morning of December 24, 1981, that came to light on January 5, 1982, when Joseph Vines was finally able to get in touch with Agent Thomas Chapman, a law man he knew and trusted and with whom he worked as an undercover informant.

This book began as a true crime story that I named *Shadow Over the Mountain*. In late May, 2012, it evolved into this book. It is the story of a former teenage drug dealer who became an undercover informant after the sad experiences of two young friends on drugs. Readers will follow Joseph Vines through his involvement in a kidnapping and a murder where he is forced at gunpoint to shove the blindfolded victim into a mine shaft in Ashe County, North Carolina. Vines lives in fear of being exposed as an informant, but successfully manages to maintain his cover, even to the point of receiving the infamous kisses on each cheek from his boss, a man rumored to be a member of the Mafia.

The crime trail stretches from Florida to Atlanta to Asheville to Ashe County to Tennessee to Chicago and includes coverage of four major trials. Apparently unrelated events are all a part of the bigger picture of the same drug scene. As the story unfolds from the Christmas Eve morning murder of Lonnie Gamboa to the discovery of a second body in the mineshaft, the facts begin connecting the seemingly unrelated actions in Asheville, Ashe County, and Boone, NC. The connection to the crime scene in Chicago is also revealed.

But back to my story of how the book came to be. I began working as a free-lance writer for the *The Journal-Patriot* in North Wilkesboro, North Carolina, in 1981 before the kidnappings and murders occurred. I will never forget the horror of hearing and watching the breaking news about the murder on the TV evening newscast. I decided that night to write a book about this as my way of fighting illegal drugs.

I began collecting information from television and newspaper reports, doing interviews and even attended one of the trials. I personally interviewed a number of people in Ashe County, and I followed the Paul Bare trial closely. The trial of Paul Wilson Bare for the kidnapping and murder of Lonnie Gamboa occurred in June 1982 in Jefferson, the county seat of Ashe County.

The trial for a related kidnapping and forced prostitution case brought forth many details related to the murder that occurred in Ashe County. I obtained a copy of court documents from the 1982 Chicago trial of Gary Miller, Alan Hattaway, Marty Curran, George Burroughs and Thomas Stimac. This document was important because of the direct connections to the Ashe County kidnappings and murders.

In June 1984, Miller and Hattaway were allowed to plead guilty to second-degree kidnapping and murder charges related to the deaths of Forester and Gamboa because the police could not find Vines to testify against them. In October, I covered the Vines trial for *The Journal-Patriot*, where Joseph Vines was found guilty of kidnapping and murdering Lonnie Gamboa.

I spent many hours at the Ashe County Courthouse copying the testimony of the Paul Bare trial word-for-word. I felt this was important since Paul Bare was convicted on the testimony of Joseph Vines. I attended the Joseph Vines trial in Asheville, North Carolina, in 1984 to cover this trial for *The Journal-Patriot*. I had hoped to speak with Vines, but security was so tight that I could not even take a picture of him. After the trial, I continued to work on the book in my spare time.

I soon realized that I really needed to talk with Joseph Vines personally. I phoned the Wilkesboro police station to see if I could work something out and was referred to the N.C. Department of Corrections in Raleigh. They gave me very limited information. I explained that I was writing a book about the murders. The officer was very polite and transferred me to someone else who informed me that Joseph Vines was still in protective custody within the prison system. He agreed to try to contact Vines to see if he would allow an interview. A few weeks later, I received a letter from Raleigh saying that, if Vines agreed to an interview, I was not to reveal where he was in prison, and I was to go alone and not tell anyone where I was going. This was to protect Vines. About a week later, I received a letter from Vines agreeing to talk to me and also asking for security reasons that I not tell anyone where I was going. I would receive a letter from Raleigh telling me the place and time for the interview. To this day I have never revealed this information to anyone.

My appointment with Vines was for 2:00 P.M. The prison was a well-kept but cold-looking place, but once I was inside, the guards and personnel were very friendly. I was asked to wait for a few minutes; then I was taken through some doors that locked behind us, sending a chill up my spine. I was shown into a small, neat room. A few minutes later the guard returned followed by a large man with a full beard and long hair. I could not tell what he really looked like under all that hair, but when he spoke, his voice was soft and self-assured.

"They told me I could bring a tape-recorder if you don't mind." He nodded and added politely, "I will ask that you not use anything that would put my security in jeopardy." I promised I would keep his secret. He answered my questions calmly. We talked for about an hour while I recorded our conversation. I realized how tired I was when I sat down for the flight back home. I arrived home to an angry spouse, who demanded to know where I had been. I kept my promise to Joseph Vines, but my husband was very unhappy for a few days. Vines had trusted me with his life, and I could not betray his trust.

One of my own greatest learning moments came as I read ATF Agent Thomas Chapman's official statement where he revealed the many links in the chain of ownership changes of the pistol found in the search of the Paul Bare residence. He was able to discover through the paper trail from the gun manufacturer to the first gun dealership through numerous ownership changes that circled back to Lonnie Gamboa.

Over the years, I continued to rewrite portions of this book. In recent years the mine openings have all been filled in, forever sealing the fate of those 21 other unknown bodies never recovered. The Environmental Protection Agency has rebuilt the dam where the sludge from the mines had leached into the Peak Creek area. They also re-routed the streams in the sludge area.

After living with the characters in my book for these 30 years, I am now ready to put them to rest with a brief update. Paul Bare died in prison in 1989. Gary Miller was released from prison but soon returned to prison. There is no record on the Internet of Alan Hattaway's having been released from prison.

Joseph Vines served his sentence in prison under an alias. After he was released, he completed a five-year probation term. While in prison, he earned three college degrees but, because he is a felon, he has been unable to find work in those fields. I have been in touch with him by phone, and he has continued to contribute additional information to be used in my book. I have no knowledge about where he is living in accordance with his wishes.

Thomas Chapman has retired from the ATF and is pursuing other interests. I have been in touch with him several times over the past three years. Richard R. Waddell retired as sheriff of Ashe County in 1982. He enjoyed his family and his retirement before his death in 2009.

I have been in touch with Eugene Goss, Ashe County chief deputy who was elected sheriff in 1982 and re-elected in 1986. He established an outstanding reputation as a capable law enforcement officer, receiving numerous awards, some across state boundaries, for his exemplary performance and fair treatment of people. Later, he moved to Myrtle Beach, South Carolina, where he worked for Santee Cooper, a state-owned electric company. After the death of his wife, he moved to Statesville, North Carolina, for a couple of years. In 2004, he returned to his beloved mountains and bought a home with a fantastic view in Jefferson near his family. He has continued to open doors that have provided additional resources for my book.

Carolyn Gentry Lee, a former deputy under Sheriff Goss, at this writing works in "Records" in Sheriff James Williams' office. Goss fondly refers to her as his "right-hand man." She dug through the archives to retrieve the Paul Bare trial records for me. Many moral and ethical issues are exposed. What are the rights of an informant? What are the boundaries? Should an informant be tried in court for actions taken while performing the role of informant? Can you commit murder in order to save your own life without being prosecuted? Could those criminals have been successfully captured and found guilty of drug-dealing, forced prostitution, kidnapping, and murder without the aid of a single informant? Should that informant have been sent to prison? There are many other questions unanswered. Who traded information and received special consideration? Who had been paid off?

Questions linger not just in this case, but in the general role of informants in solving crimes and the security (or lack thereof) for those who dare to risk their own lives as they help law enforcement agencies. The informant is the key to infiltrating active elements of the crime world.

Readers will emerge with a clearer understanding of the devastating effects that can arise from a single decision to experiment with illegal drugs.

One word describes my journey as an author: serendipity. I never cease to be amazed at how many of the resources used in documenting the true story of Joseph Vines have fallen into my hands as I followed where my "news" nose has led me these past 30 years.

List of Persons

Not every person mentioned in the book is included in this listing.

Absher, James— Ashe County deputy sheriff.

Annarino, William— Asheville policeman who arrested Gary Miller, but not Joseph Vines.

Ashburn, Michael— Wilkes/Alleghany District Attorney; prosecutor in Bare trial.

Bare, Paul Wilson— aka "Papa Bare," Ashe County mechanic and drug dealer; tried and convicted of kidnapping and murdering Lonnie Gamboa; sentenced to life imprisonment; died in prison.

Barton, Richard— Sheriff's Department, Martin County, FL; first employed Vines as an informant; detective in Lenoir, NC.

Beaver, C. R.— Asheville police captain.

Bluxon, Garth— member of Chicago Outlaw Club; tried in Chicago on multiple charges; sentenced to life imprisonment.

Boggess, Anthony— drug dealer in Asheville, NC, involved in the Moffitt Branch shootout at Gary Miller's home before the kidnappings and murders occurred.

Brewer, Charles S.— U.S. Attorney for Western District of NC, Charlotte, NC; involved in custody dispute with D.A. Ron Brown of Buncombe County, NC, over the Miller-Hattaway trial after the Chicago trials.

Broughton, Sallie— Garth Bluxon's girlfriend.

Brown, Ronald— district attorney for Buncombe County, NC; prosecuted Hattaway, Miller, and Vines in the kidnapping of Forester, Colby, and Gamboa.

Bueker, Ernest— SBI agent stationed in Raleigh, NC.

Buckner, Roger— Asheville policeman who helped Eugene Goss retrieve the bodies from the mine shaft.

Burroughs, Robert George "Snoopy"— Canadian drug dealer associated with the Chicago Outlaw Club; sentenced in the Chicago trials to five years in prison.

Butts, Dr. John— assistant medical examiner, Chapel Hill, NC.

Cabe, Steve— State Bureau of Investigation agent.

Callahan, Betty Darlene— girlfriend of Thomas Forester; kidnapped and taken to Chicago, where she was forced to work as a prostitute for the Outlaw Motorcycle Club.

Calloway, Michael— detective, Asheville Police Department, Asheville, NC.

Cameron, Bradley— Wilkes County assistant district attorney. Recommended that Vines be put in the witness protection program.

Cash, Gary— defense attorney for Joseph Vines in Asheville trial.

Chambers, Charlie— director of the Hickory, NC, SBI office.

Chapman, Thomas— ATF officer, Asheville, NC; engaged Vines in the undercover operation to infiltrate an Asheville drug ring operating out of Sarge's Lounge; Chapman was trusted by Vines.

Cole, Donald—criminal investigator for the Buncombe County Sheriff's Department, Asheville, NC; investigated "Moffitt Branch" shootout.

Coulson, William R.— assistant U.S. district attorney, Chicago, IL; assisted in Chicago trials of Outlaw Motorcycle Club.

Crouse, Becky— Ashe County medical examiner's office, Jefferson, NC.

Curran, Marty— aka "Scarface"; Chicago Outlaw Motorcycle Club member; sentenced to 20 years in prison in Chicago trials.

Dowdy, John— special agent for the Florida Department of Law Enforcement.

Edwards, Sgt. Ernest— Asheville Police Department.

Elmhorst, Deborah— lived with Thomas Stimac; killed by Jocko Rey.

Fagel, Jay— involved in kidnapping Callahan and Forester, but not prosecuted.

Fernandes, Terry— special agent for the DEA in Florida.

Forester, Thomas— Asheville drug dealer; kidnapped and murdered by Bare, Miller, and Hattaway at the Ore Knob Mine; body retrieved in January 1982.

Frye, Thomas— FBI, Asheville, NC; asked Vines to "check out" Paul Harris for drug dealing.

Gamboa, Lonnie— Asheville drug dealer; kidnapped and murdered on December 24, 1981, when Vines was forced at gunpoint by Bare and Miller to push him into the mine shaft.

Gamboa, Sharon— wife of Lonnie Gamboa; testified at Bare's trial in Ashe County.

Ghassenieh, Morrey— manager of In Town Motel, Tunnel Road, Asheville, NC.

Goss, Eugene—chief deputy, Ashe County Sheriff's Department; one of three men who descended into the mine shaft to retrieve the bodies; guarded Vines during the Bare trial in Ashe County.

Gozdecki, Stop— Chicago Outlaw member; witnessed Elmhorst murder.

Greer, Eugene— Ashe County deputy.

Greer, Jimmy— West Palm Beach, FL, Sheriff's Department; former employer of Joseph E. Vines.

Haller, Clifford—inmate at the Metropolitan Correctional Center; contacted by Gary Miller to help him find a "hit" man to kill Darlene Callahan and Joseph Vines, who were in the witness protection program; he called the attorney general's office and reported Miller.

Harris, Paul "Sarge"— owner of Sarge's Lounge in Asheville, NC.

Hattaway, Alan Ray "Red"—drug dealer, Outlaw Motorcycle Club "hit" man; convicted on kidnapping and murder charges; sentenced to life imprisonment.

Hay, Edward C.—attorney for Joseph E. Vines in 1984 trial; assisted Gary Cash.

Hays, Edward—assistant district attorney, Asheville, NC.

Hegarty, Edward D.—head of Chicago FBI, Chicago, IL.

Henderson, Wayne—West Palm Beach, FL, DEA; former employer of Vines.

Holliday, Bob—West Palm Beach, FL, DEA; former employer of Vines.

Howell, Ronald W.—Superior Court judge, Asheville, NC. Stated that U.S. Attorney Charles Brewer must assure that Alan Hattaway would appear in court in Buncombe County or Brewer be cited for contempt.

Hudson, Page, M.D., chief medical examiner, Chapel Hill, NC.

Jennings, Virginia—witness, Fairview Road, Asheville, NC.

Jurjovec, Maureen—lived with Stimac; worked at the Algiers Club and Club Taray; witnessed Elmhorst's murder.

Juso, Ed—mining inspector, Raleigh, NC.

Kalas, Kimberly—17-year-old dancer at Club Algiers; found murdered; was to have been a witness against Stimac.

Keel, Stan—aka "The Indian"; FBI, North Carolina.

Keener, Jeffrey—surprise witness (of dubious credibility) against Vines in Asheville trial in 1984; long prison record.

Kiser, Robert (Bob)—State Bureau of Investigation, Asheville, NC.

Kilby, John—judge, Ashe County; presided at Bare's pre-trial hearing.

Kirkpatrick, John—undercover policeman; testified against Vines in 1984.

Klimes, John—aka "Burrito," Chicago Outlaw Motorcycle Club member; committed suicide before the Chicago trials.

Kravitz, Jeffrey—Department of Mining Safety and Health.

Lewis, Robert L.—Asheville judge in Vines' 1984 trial.

Lockwood, Glenn—Martin County, FL, Sheriff's Department, former employer of Vines.

Marger, Edwin—notorious Atlanta defense lawyer who defended Bare and lost.

McKing, Philip—witness, Tanglewood Mobile Park, Lenoir, NC.

Miller, Gary Hansford—Drug dealer, murder suspect, Asheville, NC; convicted on kidnapping and murder charges; sentenced to life imprisonment.

Miller, Lowell—Tampa, FL; special agent, DEA; former employer of Vines.

Miller, Jr., Richard L.—Assistant District Attorney, Chicago, IL.

Morrow, Robert Lewis—witness in Moffitt Branch shootout.

Myers, Jim—Florida Department of Law Enforcement; former Vines employer.

Parnell, Larry—assistant district attorney for Western District, Charlotte, NC; involved in jurisdictional squabble with Asheville D.A. Ron Brown over handing Hattaway over for trial for the murders of Forester and Gamboa.

Parsons, J.D.— Ashe County sheriff's deputy.

Powell, Charlie— sheriff's department, Caldwell County, NC; former Vines employer.

Ramer, Phil— Department of Law Enforcement, Florida; former Vines employer.

Redding, William— retired FBI agent who had previously used Vines as an informant; trusted by Vines.

Rey, Jocko— Chicago Outlaw biker; found dead in May 1982.

Rhew, William— police officer in Asheville.

Robinson, Ross— detective, Asheville Police Department.

Rousseau, Julius— Superior Court judge, Wilkes County; refused bond for Bare initially.

Sands, Johnny— aka "The Nashville Flame," Nashville, TN; stunt man, country singer; volunteered to enter mine shaft to search for bodies.

Sheridan, Paul— Detective, Boynton Beach, FL; former Vines employer.

Shockley, Ken— ATF Agent, Ohio; former Vines employer.

Siskind, John— Ashe County, NC, lawyer; defended Bare.

Smith, Donald L.— Superior Court judge, Ashe County; presided over Bare's trial.

Stimac, Thomas— aka "Westside Tommy"; head of Chicago Outlaw Club; involved in drug dealing, prostitution rings, and numerous crimes; received 30-year prison term in Chicago, IL.

Summers, Toni— prostitute; Stimac's "old lady," later married Stimac.

Vines, Joseph— aka Kojak, Jojo, Satan; paid informant whose testimony convicted Bare; later tried and sentenced to life in prison.

Waddell, Richard— Ashe County sheriff at the time of the murders of Forester and Gamboa.

Webb, Dan K.— U.S. District Attorney, Chicago, IL; prosecutor for the Chicago Outlaw trials.

Whitman, Charles— deputy, Ashe County Sheriff's Department

Williams, James— deputy, Ashe County Sheriff's Department; at this writing Ashe County sheriff.

Winner, Dennis— attorney for Paul "Sarge" Harris and Gary Miller.

Wolfe, Bill— Department of Law Enforcement, Temple Terrace, FL; former Vines employer.

Timeline

July 1981	Vines meets Tommy Chapman, Thomas Frye.
August 1981	Vines began frequenting Sarge's Lounge.
November 7, 1981	Moffitt Branch shootout.
December 1, 1981	"Sarge" Harris hires Vines as a bouncer.
December 12–13, 1981	Forester and Callahan are kidnapped by Hattaway and Miller and taken to Ashe County; Forester killed by Hattaway and Bare, and Callahan transported to Chicago and forced into prostitution.
December 20, 1981	Harris introduces Vines to Miller and Hattaway.
December 21, 1981	Gamboa, Hattaway, and Vines drive to Atlanta to get rings, drive to Candler to pick up drugs.
December 23, 1981	Gamboa kidnapped by Miller, Hattaway, and Vines, taken to Ashe County.
December 24, 1981	Gamboa killed at mine.
December 24, 1981	Vines and Miller return to Asheville.
December 24, 1981	Vines tries to get in touch with Thomas Chapman.
December 28, 1981	Vines leaves message for Redding, which he gets on the 31st.
January 5, 1982	Vines reaches Thomas Chapman by phone. Miller arrested and charged with kidnapping Forester and Callahan and released on $10,000 bond. Vines is not arrested. Miller had contacted Vines for another "job" in Ashe County.
	Chapman, Keel, and Kiser meet Vines; Chapman advises him to be ready to leave town.
January 6, 1982	Vines and wife travel to Virginia to her sister's home.
January 7, 1982	Chapman and Vines met Sheriff Waddell in Virginia; official statement made to Waddell; Vines leads tour of mine site; Waddell contacts MSHA to assist at mine shaft.
January 8, 1982	Waddell, Vines, and Chapman go to Wilkesboro; warrant for Bare issued; search warrant issued; search conducted; Bare booked, arrested for kidnapping Gamboa; released on bond.

January 9, 1982	Gamboa's wallet discovered.
January 12, 1982	Camera search for bodies is abandoned.
January 25, 1982	Mine entered, bodies retrieved.
	Callahan escapes captors in Chicago and phones home.
January 26, 1982	Bare turns himself in; charged with kidnapping and murder.
February 8, 1982	Probable cause hearing for Bare on murder charges; bound over to Superior Court.
May 27, 1982	Hattaway and Miller charged in Chicago by a federal grand jury for kidnapping and inter-state prostitution in the Betty Callahan case; also indicted were Stimac, Curran, and Burroughs.
June 2, 1982	Paul Wilson Bare trial begins at Ashe County Courthouse, Jefferson, NC.
June 11, 1982	Gary H. Miller is captured at a Lenoir, NC, campground. Alan Ray Hattaway surrenders to authorities in Newport, Tennessee.
June 12, 1982	Bare is convicted for the kidnapping and murder of Lonnie Gamboa.
June 14, 1982	Bare sentenced to life in prison.
June 22, 1982	Miller and Hattaway taken to Chicago for arraignment on charges of kidnapping and forced prostitution of Betty Darlene Callahan.
October 1982	Chicago trial.
November 3, 1982	Chicago trial sentencing.
August 18, 1983	The North Carolina Supreme Court upholds the Ore Knob Mine murder verdict against Paul Wilson Bare.
February 14, 1984	A federal fugitive warrant is issued against Joseph Vines for unlawful flight to avoid prosecution.
February 26, 1984	Vines is missing from the witness protection program and can't be located.
March 14, 1984	Vines is located and arrested in Lake Worth, Florida, where he had been since October 1983. Vows to fight extradition back to North Carolina.
March 15, 1984	Vines is dropped from the Witness Protection Program.
September 1984	Paul Bare's lawyers announce plans to ask for a new trial for Bare based on new evidence.
	Vines' trial set for October 15, 1984, in Buncombe County.
October 15, 1984	Vines' trial begins; the first two days of the trial taken up with jury selection.
October 24, 1984	Vines convicted of first degree murder and sentenced to life in prison by a Superior Court jury for the kidnapping and murder of Lonnie Gamboa.
October 25, 1984	Vines is put under protective custody inside the prison system.

1

Christmas Eve

Winter settled early over the small mountain communities of Western North Carolina in 1981. Channel WXII weather reporters warned of a snow storm approaching, and residents were hoping for a white Christmas. In the early hours of December 24, cold, brisk winds swept over the mountains in Ashe County and tugged at the coats of the four intruders stumbling over the rough terrain, making it difficult to walk.

The small man in front had a blindfold over his eyes. When he slipped and fell on the frozen ground, the large man walking along side pulled him to his feet and guided him with a hand on his shoulder. Two other men walking behind them held guns and flashlights in gloved hands. Flashlight beams bounced over boulders and underbrush to a woven wire fence in front of them. The men stopped, and the blindfolded man was pushed through a tear in the fence. The man with the shotgun motioned for the big man to follow. Forced on by the men waiting outside the fence, he pushed his way through the hole. When he scrambled through to the other side, a terrified gasp was the only sound he made as he found himself looking at a huge, gaping hole directly in front of him. One more step and he would have disappeared into blackness. He grabbed the fence behind him as his shocked mind blanked out the whimpering sounds made by the blindfolded man.

Now he knew what the other two wanted from him ... he wished to hell the blindfolded man would take a step forward and fall into the hole on his own. Then, maybe it wouldn't be murder. He knew when he pushed the terrified man beside him, he might be next. He hoped that, if he pushed the man, they might let him live. If he didn't, the men would kill them both.[1]

He remembered hearing somewhere that when you face death, your whole life flashes before you. Born Joseph Vines, he had been eight when his mother moved from Baltimore, Maryland, to West Virginia. He had grown up never knowing his father, but with seventeen brothers, there had always been a house full of people. His mother had become a foster parent to six more kids in West Virginia.[2]

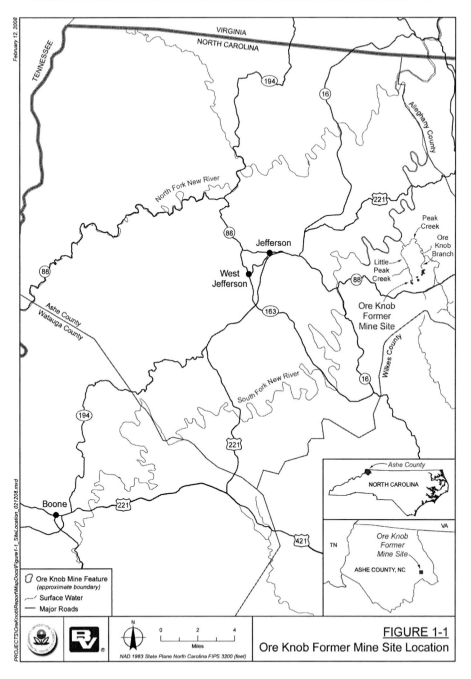

The location of the Ore Knob Mine just north of NC 88 (courtesy Terrence Byrd, EPA On-site Coordinator).

They moved to Florida when Vines was 15. He dropped the name Joseph and became "Joe" to his friends. Most of them were street-wise kids who were mixed up in drugs and stolen goods. That was okay with him. He liked the easy money. He dealt drugs, but played it cool and didn't use them to excess. Too many of his friends spent all of their money on drugs for their own use.

He had really liked Maria Lopez. She was special and something to look at with her dark skin, brown eyes, and long black hair. Vines had tried to get her off drugs, but she was hooked. He gave her money when she was broke, admitting to himself that he cared too much to let her work the streets. He remembered clearly the day a dealer sold her STP for mescaline. He could still see her drug-glazed eyes pleading for the help he couldn't give. At seventeen, she would spend the rest of her life in a mental institution. That same day he watched an 11-year-old boy vomit to death from an overdose of drugs.

Vines wrestled with his conscience for days afterward. He had always hated informers, but he knew what he had to do. He turned the dealer's name in to the police and helped set him up for a drug bust. He owed Maria and the kid that much. At that point, the police had offered him a deal working as an informant. That was eleven years ago. It had taken a few years to get accustomed to living the life of half-crook, half-cop, but he had earned his reputation as a reliable informant.[3]

The case he was working on now wasn't supposed to have taken him to the edge. His mind raced back over the past few months to that day in May when he first drove into North Carolina. The mountains were a dismal gray in the morning fog, matching his depressed mood. He was on his way to pick up a check from Agent Thomas Chapman at the Alcohol, Tobacco and Firearms (ATF) office in Asheville. He dug into his shirt pocket to make sure he had the address. The pocket was empty. "Where the hell did I put that damn address?" Vines muttered, as he pulled the old car into a parking space at the courthouse. They would know where the ATF office was. Wiping his bald head, he glanced into the mirror. Cold, blue eyes stared back at him. He yawned, stretched his six-and-a-half-foot frame, and ambled toward the double doors that looked like something out of the 18th century.

The receptionist looked up from her typing as Vines walked in. "Hi. I'm Joseph Vines. I'm looking for the ATF office. I need to see Thomas Chapman."

"That office is in the Federal Building." The woman smiled at him, jotting down something on a piece of paper. "Here's the address."

"Thanks. I'm new here. What's the best way to get there?" As Vines spoke, he leaned closer to see the directions she was outlining. After looking over the directions, he headed toward the Federal Building. This time he was expected when he pushed open the door labeled "Alcohol, Tobacco and Firearms." A tall, dark-haired man stood up as Vines entered.

"I'm Thomas Chapman. You must be Joe Vines. The girl called from the courthouse." Vines had heard of Chapman's reputation of always getting his man. Looking at the tall, self-assured man in front of him, he could believe the things he had heard. "Yeah, I'm supposed to pick up a check here." Vines shook hands and sat down.

"I'll get it." The ATF agent deftly plucked a brown envelope from a desk drawer. "You better verify the amount." Vines looked at the check, nodded and headed for the door. Chapman called after him, "Listen, if you need some work, I have a few connections at the police department."

Vines replied, "I guess I wouldn't mind talking to a few people. I'm not tied up right now."

"If you have time, we can ride over there now," Chapman offered.

Vines replied, "Yeah, might as well." They went out to Chapman's car. After a short drive, Chapman pulled up in front of the police station. He introduced Vines to two officers standing in front of the building and asked them if Frye was around.

One of the officers replied, "In the office. Is he expecting you?" Chapman shook his head, "Nope, we just took a chance on catching him here."[4]

Thomas Frye was a short, stocky man with piercing blue eyes that looked Vines over carefully. Chapman introduced Vines and identified him as an experienced, reliable government informer. Frye was silent for a moment, then told them that he could use an informer on a case he was working on now. Frye pulled a pad closer, telling Vines that he needed some information from him. He asked Vines for information regarding his previous employment as an informer. As they left, Frye told Vines to give him a call within the next couple of days.

Vines rented a room at the EconoLodge and spent some time looking over the small city of Asheville, shooting pool and drinking beer. Spring was just beginning to appear in the higher elevations. The people of Asheville were friendly, and Vines found himself relaxing with the slower pace of life in this mountain country. Two days later, he called Frye at his office.

"Frye, this is Vines. We talked when I was in with Chapman the other day." Frye said that he remembered and asked him to come to headquarters the following morning at 10 o'clock. The meeting was brief. Frye told him that he needed something on a guy named Paul Harris whose nickname was "Sarge." He said Harris had been in the Army but was now running a bar called Sarge's Lounge. He asked Vines to see if he could set up some drug buys and get information on the bikers hanging out there.

"Anything in particular?" asked Vines.

Frye replied, "Anything that is big enough to make a bust and involve Sarge. We especially want two guys, Alan Hattaway and Gary Miller. Both work out of Sarge's."

"I've heard of Harris' operation and that he's mixed up with the Mafia," replied Vines.

Frye commented, "We've never been able to prove anything. Not much use picking him up just to turn him loose again. You know where Sarge's is located?" Vines said that he would find the lounge and stop by to get a feel for the place, and that he would be in touch.[5]

Finding Sarge's Lounge was no problem. Located on the Swannanoa River Road, the small, ugly, white building squatted in front of an embankment covered with scrub pines. A small stream ran behind the building, separating the parking lot and the steep hill. The graveled parking lot drifted into a dirt road that led up an incline to an X-rated drive-in theater.

Vines paused outside the lounge. Then, with an arrogant swagger familiar to motorcycle people, he went through the door, stopping just inside for a moment as his eyes adjusted to the dark. The overwhelming stench of sweat, beer and pot assailed his nostrils. Two girls sitting at the bar glanced his way. With his jeans, boots, tattoos, bald head, and beard, he blended right in. Vines knew that the overweight man behind the bar eyeing him was Sarge. Chapman had described the six-foot-plus retired military man with wavy salt-and-pepper hair and a mustache. The white in his hair blended into white sideburns.

Sarge's voice was gruff as he spoke. "What'll it be?"

"Schlitz." Vines finished a second beer before the bartender spoke again. Sarge asked him, "You new around here?"

Vines replied, "Yeah, come in from Florida last week."

"I'm Sarge. I own this joint. What's your handle?"

Vines replied, "Jojo—Joe for short." Bogus names were nothing new to Vines. In his line of work, he had a list of them. He had used Jojo as an alias before in Florida.

Vines could tell that Sarge was looking him over. Although the bar wasn't a large place, there was usually a crowd, most of them bikers, drug dealers, and ex-cons. Sarge's bar was well-known in places where it counted moneywise. Vines knew that it wasn't always easy to keep things under control in bars where bikers hung out, especially on weekends. He hoped that Sarge might need a bouncer. He knew his size and appearance might appeal to Sarge. He was 6'6" tall and weighed 240 pounds. The bald head, drooping brown mustache, beard and cold blue eyes gave him the look of the devil himself. If he checked out with the right people, Sarge might offer him a job.[6]

The following week, Vines called his wife to join him in Asheville. She was his fourth wife. They had met when she was working as a stripper in a night spot in Chicago where Vines was investigating the Hells Angels Motorcycle Club. He helped her out of a dangerous spot when she had been pulled into the investigation. They had been attracted to each other and shacked up together a few months before getting married. She was a handsome woman, and they understood each other's needs. His wife arrived two days later, and they found a furnished two-room apartment. After doing some shopping, paying the rent, and having a mechanic work on his old car, Vines' reward check was dwindling. He would have to find a job somewhere soon.[7]

Vines spent part of each day hanging around Sarge's Lounge, hoping Sarge would check him out. His drug-dealing record in Florida would help establish him as one of the boys.

On Friday evening Vines eased his big frame onto a bar stool, and Sarge slid a cold beer in front of him, commenting, "How come your head is so bald, you shave it or what?"

"That's my business about my head," grunted Vines.

Sarge asked, "Jojo, do you ever use aliases?"

Vines replied, "Sometimes. Why the questions?"

"How would you like to go to work for me as a bouncer?" Sarge was still eyeing him intently as he stated, "I'm going to call you Kojak."

"I've been called worse," Vines replied. Kojak was a recent popular television series character, a bald New York City police detective. "Let me think about the job. My old lady's looking for work, too."

"The factory in town is hiring." Sarge suggested that she might try there.

"Yeah, I'll let you know something in a couple of days." His wife was hired on at the factory. The following Friday, Vines began working at Sarge's Lounge.[8]

2
Working Undercover

During the first few months at Sarge's, Vines was able to set up a few small drug buys. None resulted in arrests. He noticed a lot of backroom conferences between Sarge, Miller, and Hattaway that included no one else. He hadn't been introduced to them yet, but he knew who they were from Agent Frye's descriptions. Vines could feel something big was about to go down, but Sarge obviously didn't trust him enough to tell him anything yet. He caught snatches of conversation with names like Tommy Forester, Callahan, and Laurel Springs, but was unable to piece anything together. He could tell somebody was in trouble for not paying up. No one could buy drugs from somebody like Sarge without paying for them.[1]

During the week of December 13, Hattaway and Miller didn't show up at the Lounge. When Vines casually inquired where they were, Sarge just grunted, "Out of town." The last time Vines remembered seeing the two, they were with a short, dark-haired man in an off-white van.[2]

When they showed up again, two weeks later, Sarge called Vines into the back room. "Listen, Kojak, I need a little help with a local fellow who owes me money. Are you willing to back me up?" When Vines asked him what kind of back-up he meant, Sarge replied, "I just want to scare the guy."

"Just scare him, huh? Hell, yes, count me in." Vines knew he had found his way in. If he helped, Sarge would trust him more. Maybe things were coming together at last.

After talking with Vines, Sarge called Miller and Hattaway into the back room. "Boys, this is Jojo, but I'm calling him 'Kojak.' He'll be working with us from now on and may become one of the family — we'll see. I want you to use him as muscle to scare some of the boys into paying up. You know who to start with. I'll see you tomorrow."[3] As Sarge left, Hattaway was still looking Vines over. "I've seen you somewhere before."

Vines shook his head. "I don't think so, but I hung out with some bikers in Florida a few years back."[4]

After picking up a six-pack, Vines left for his apartment. It wasn't much, but then most motel apartments never were. His wife wasn't home. Flipping on the TV, Vines opened a beer and stretched out on the couch. They were beginning to accept him. He felt good about that, but he didn't much like Hattaway with his scraggly, red beard, long hair and foul mouth. Vines knew from the redhead's reaction that he was suspicious of him. Miller was a different sort — tall, clean-shaven and with a quieter manner. But they both shared common goals of selling as many drugs and making as much money as possible.[5]

The next day, Miller and Hattaway gave Vines his first job. "Kojak, take my car," ordered Hattaway. "Go to the Pizza Hut at the shopping mall on Highway 70. Park at the back door, and go inside. Wait for an Italian-looking fellow. He'll join you. Name's Lonnie Gamboa. We're going to teach the son-of-a-bitch a lesson."

Vines asked, "Is this the fellow we're going to scare?"

Hattaway replied, "Yeah, sure, just go inside. We'll be watching from the parking lot and join you after he gets there."

Vines had been given a .38 Special to carry since he had begun working for Sarge. He had an uneasy feeling about it and hoped it was just for show. He hoped he wouldn't have to find out if that gun really worked.[6]

Finding the pizza place was easy. He parked and went inside, glad to be out of the cold air. This weather was sure different from the Florida sunshine where he had been living. He ordered a pitcher of beer to help pass the time. Watching the Christmas shoppers pour into the restaurant was amusing. Their tired faces didn't go with the gaily wrapped packages. Children were being scolded, the men looked bored, and most of the women had their shoes off under the tables. He glanced at the clock — 5:30 P.M. They hadn't said how long to wait. Just then, Hattaway strode through the door and sat down with Vines. A few minutes later, a well-dressed young fellow joined them. He could have passed for a business executive.[7]

Hattaway growled, "Lonnie, you're late. Where you been?"

"That traffic's a mess. The holidays, you know," Gamboa replied. To Vines, the voice was smooth, soft, and well-educated. He guessed the man to be in his 20s.

Hattaway gestured, "This is Kojak. He's working with us now. This is Lonnie Gamboa. Sit down, Lonnie. You want to order something?" Gamboa stated that he had already eaten. Hattaway said, "Let's get down to business then. Where are the rings I gave you to be sized?"

Gamboa responded, "I gave them to a girl named Kathy in Atlanta. We can pick them up anytime."

Hattaway then asked, "How about the $380,000 worth of drugs brought into town? No money has been paid on that debt yet."

"I only owe you $30,000," argued the Italian. His voice began to have an edge. Hattaway snapped, "You're crazy as hell! One hundred and twenty thousand dollars is what you owe us. I know who owes the rest of it and I'll get it all. You have any property or vehicles to help pay off the debt? My people want their money." Hattaway took a drink of beer, wiping his mouth with the back of his hand.

Gamboa replied, "I have two acres of land, a trailer, and a van I can give."

"How much did you pay down on your drugs?" Hattaway demanded angrily.

"Two thousand. I don't have any money, but I'll make arrangements to pay some every month," offered Gamboa.

"Damn it Lonnie, you know that's not good enough. Do you have any of the drugs left?" demanded Hattaway. When Gamboa told him that he knew where 4,500 of the Canadian Blues were, Hattaway challenged, "Let's see if you do! We'll pick them up now."[8]

Vines glanced at the clock again — 6:15 P.M. Everything appeared to be going all right. The fellow was cooperating. They followed Gamboa to his house in Hattaway's car. There they got into Gamboa's 4-wheel drive Jeep. Gamboa told them they would have to drive to Candler to get the drugs.

Hattaway answered, "Just get them."

As they drove toward Candler, Vines took note of the odd collection of people this business threw together: Gamboa, a young, handsome well-educated Italian; Hattaway with the foul mouth, a true outlaw motorcycle type; Miller, big and quiet; and then himself. When working undercover, he had been compared to the devil. He wished the arguing would stop. The alcohol and drugs they were using were making the situation worse.

Gamboa drove to two separate locations in Candler before giving Hattaway a bag containing 4,500 of the Canadian Valium known as "Blues." Turning the Jeep around, they started the trip back to Gamboa's house. The cold wind and crooked roads made Vines shiver. This must be the coldest place in the world. Even the fifth of liquor they were sharing didn't help.[9]

As he turned into his driveway, Gamboa, calmer now, invited them in. "My wife will have supper ready if you want to stay. You can count the pills."

Hattaway commented, "Yeah, it's 9:00 now. I'm hungry. How about you, Kojak?"

"Okay, sounds good," Vines agreed. Inside, he noticed the house was expensively furnished. A young attractive woman in her 20s was introduced as Sharon, Lonnie's wife. Vines was surprised to see a small child. No one had told him Gamboa was a family man. Gamboa's wife served the meal and left the room. The four men ate and talked.

When the clock chimed 10:00, Hattaway stood and motioned to Vines, "Let's ride." Vines drove in silence. Hattaway offered no information on the way back to Sarge's Lounge as to whether the scare had worked or if he expected anything else of Vines. As Hattaway got out of the car, he paused, "Be ready to go to Atlanta with us in the morning to get the rings. We'll leave by 9:00."[10]

The next morning Gamboa drove the Jeep to Atlanta. There was little conversation despite the lengthy trip. That afternoon, they pulled up in front of a Ham House restaurant in the suburbs of Atlanta where a sign proclaimed the "Best Ham in the South."

"This is it." Gamboa got out as he spoke. "I'll be back with the girl." A few minutes later, he emerged alongside a chunky-built teenager with long brown hair. As she got into the back with Vines, he felt the warmth of her body as she settled into the seat.

"Kojak, this is Kathy. I think you already know Alan Hattaway." The girl nodded as she handed two rings to Hattaway. One identified him as a member of the Ku Klux Klan. The other was a skull and crossbones ring outlined in diamonds. Hattaway nodded as he put the rings on. Then he told Kathy not to come back to Asheville to go to court for the Moffitt Branch Shootout case. Kathy stated that she had to come back to Asheville for the trial because she had signed an extradition waiver. Hattaway, again, told Kathy, "Don't come back to Asheville."

Gamboa commented nervously, "Okay, Kathy, the rings look fine. If I need you again, I'll call you."[11]

The five-hour drive back to Gamboa's house was quiet. Gamboa commented, "It's been a hell of a winter so far." Vines, half asleep, only grunted. As Gamboa pulled into his drive, Hattaway asked him about the deed to his land and trailer. Gamboa stated that his lawyer had been in court all morning, and he couldn't get the deeds signed but that he would get it done the next morning.

"Okay," Hattaway nodded. "I won't be around, but Kojak will call you in the morning."

Vines started the car and headed for Sarge's on Hattaway's promise of buying a beer while they talked to Miller. Back at the lounge, Hattaway filled Miller in on the day's happenings. While Vines listened, they argued whether Gamboa was telling the truth about the land and trailer. "That damn wop better be straight." Miller's voice was threatening.

Hattaway then told Vines, "Kojak, we'll call you in the morning and give you a name for Gamboa to have put on the deeds."

"I thought you told Gamboa you would be in Virginia tomorrow," a puzzled Vines said. Hattaway nodded and explained that he told Gamboa that so he could not be "set up" by Gamboa because they had warrants for him (Hattaway) at the Asheville Police Department, and he needed to be careful.

The next morning, the insistent ringing of the phone woke Vines. The phone fell to the floor as he fumbled to get it. "Kojak, you awake?"

"Yeah, Hattaway."

"Listen carefully. Call Gamboa and tell him to put the deeds in the name of Alan Hattaway. Also ask him if he got the trial transcript of the Moffitt Branch shootout from the courthouse for me."

"That all?" grunted Vines.

Hattaway said, "For now. I'll be in touch later today."[12]

Vines touched the cut-off button and dialed Gamboa while the instructions were fresh in his mind. Gamboa answered, "Hello."

"This is Kojak. The name you are to put on the deed is Alan Hattaway. Also, he wanted to know if you got the transcript from the courthouse."

Gamboa answered, "Yes. The bastards charged me $370 for it. I can't get the property transferred because the courthouse is closed this morning." Vines replied that he would give the message to Hattaway.

When Hattaway called back, Vines relayed the message from Gamboa. There was silence at Hattaway's end of the line.

Vines spoke again, "You there?"

"Yeah, I'm here. Listen, Kojak, I want you to pick Gamboa up at his house. Make sure he has the transcript. It's a record of a trial on a shootout between Gamboa and Miller that happened on the Moffitt Branch Road back in November. There were a lot of drugs, money and guns taken from Miller's home by the Asheville Police. I need to read it and see who's lying — Miller or Gamboa. I think one of them made a deal to talk. Call him back and tell him you are picking him up. Meet me at the River Lounge. You know where it is?"

Kojak replied, "Yeah. We'll be there."[13]

Vines pulled up in front of Gamboa's house, waited a few minutes, then beeped the horn. When nothing happened, he beeped the horn again and started to get out. Gamboa opened the door and yelled, "I'll be out in a few minutes."

Vines closed the car door and waited. Gamboa appeared a few minutes later and slid into the passenger side. Reaching into the back of his pants, the Italian pulled out a .44 Magnum and laid it carefully on the front seat between Vines and himself. He clutched a brown manila envelope in his hand. They drove to the River Lounge in silence. Hattaway's car was in the parking lot, but there was no sign of the redhead. As they got out of the car, Gamboa picked up the gun and stuck it under his belt. Inside, they both ordered beers. When Hattaway came in, the three sat down at a nearby table. Gamboa handed Hattaway the brown envelope.

"Let's go for a ride. I don't want to read this in here," Hattaway nodded at Vines. As the three walked toward the parking lot, Hattaway handed Vines his keys. "Here, drive toward Sarge's. I'll sit in the back with Gamboa and read over the transcript."

As Vines parked the car at Sarge's, a tan car pulled alongside them. Miller jumped out, opened the passenger's side of Hattaway's car and slid in.

"Lonnie, why are you telling all of these lies about me," snapped Miller. "You shouldn't do that." With those words, Miller jerked a gun up to where Gamboa could see it. Hearing a click, Gamboa jerked his head around to look at Hattaway, who was also holding a gun on him.

"Kojak, hold his hands together," snapped Miller as he took the .44 out from under Gamboa's leg and slid it under the driver's seat. As Vines held the Italian's hands, Miller got a roll of tape out and bound Gamboa's hands together.

"All right, let's get him out of the car and into the trunk." Miller was giving the orders now.

"Where are you taking me?" Gamboa's voice trembled.

"To Virginia, to the big man, to see what can be worked out on this deal." Miller replied as he unlocked the car trunk, and Vines shoved the helpless man inside.[14]

Hattaway and Vines left the parking lot in the black Cordoba. Miller followed in his car. They drove on Interstate-40 to Morganton and took Highway 18 to the Blue Ridge Parkway, where they turned left onto the Parkway. They proceeded on the Parkway traveling for ten minutes before making a right turn onto an old paved rural road. Following this road a mile or so, the cars turned onto a dirt road leading past a big wooden house with three motorcycles on the porch in Laurel Springs, NC. Farther down the road after passing two mailboxes, they turned right on another dirt road. The driveway led past a house and through the middle of a junkyard to a garage. An old trailer sat to the left. Three men stood outside where a tractor was being repaired by a tall bearded man.[15]

"There's Papa Bare now." Hattaway was looking at the bearded man.

"Who is Papa Bare?" There was curiosity in Vines' voice.

Hattaway replied, "Papa Bare is a friend of mine. You'll meet him later. You wait in the car. He don't like strangers."

Vines parked near the trailer. After talking to Bare, Miller returned and took Gamboa from the trunk, ordering Vines to hold a gun on him. Miller removed the tape from his hands and put a handcuff on one arm before they walked him up a hill to a wooded area behind the garage. Gamboa was told to put his arms around a tree, where Miller locked him securely in place. In spite of the bitter cold weather, he was left in that position for six hours while the others discussed his fate inside the garage.[16]

The tape in the foreground was removed before Lonnie Gamboa's arms were placed around the tree and his hands were handcuffed together. The picture was taken by Roger Buckner on the morning after Paul Bare's house was searched (courtesy Gene Goss).

Back at the garage, Miller asked Bare to trace some names for him: the names of two girls who wanted to trade cocaine for Quaaludes and the name Joseph Vines. Vines felt a chill go through him at the mention of his real name. He knew someone was getting close to identifying him. Bare made a phone call, and Vines heard him repeating the names over the phone.

"It will be a while before I can get you anything on the names," Bare informed Miller. "The machine is down." Vines couldn't believe his luck. The machine was on his side.

After making sure Gamboa was secure, the four drove to a small country store called Stop and Shop on Highway 88 because no one had eaten all day. They ordered sandwiches and coffee. After taking one bite, Vines felt nauseated and headed outside to wait in the car.[17]

When they returned to the garage, Bare and Miller left again to check on some business. Hattaway and Vines stayed at the garage. When the two men returned around 9:00 P.M., Miller and Vines went to get Gamboa. When Miller unlocked the shivering man from the tree, he accidentally knocked some leaves back, uncovering Gamboa's wallet and a bag containing marijuana and a chunk of hashish. Vines picked the things up, and the two men walked back to the garage, dragging Gamboa between them.

Gamboa was offered a snack before the questioning began. He refused the food, but took some hot coffee in shaking hands, spilling some on his numb legs. Miller demanded, "Where is your list of drug customers?"

"In my wallet," replied Gamboa.

"Where's the rest of the drugs you still owe for?"

Gamboa's voice was shaking from fear and cold. "I only have fifty pounds of marijuana left." Miller ordered Gamboa to call his wife in Asheville and tell her to deliver the marijuana to the Country Food Store parking lot. Gamboa called his wife, who agreed to deliver the marijuana to the designated spot.[18]

After Gamboa hung up, the phone rang. Bare answered it, talking low. Vines strained to hear the conversations, but couldn't. As Bare hung the phone up, he looked at Vines strangely. "Kojak, have you ever heard of anyone by the name of Joseph Vines?"

Vines felt a shock go through his body. "I don't think so," he mumbled, as he turned away trying to control the fear he felt. "Do they know?" he thought desperately. "If so, they will kill me."[19]

At 11:30 that night Bare told Gamboa they were taking him to see the "big boss." "You come, too, Kojak. We'll take the back roads, but we'll have to walk part of the way through some brush and stuff. We might need you."

"I'm about sick," Vines hedged. "Do you really need me?"

"You aren't going soft on me are you?" growled Hattaway. "Sarge said we could count on you."

Vines mumbled, "Yeah, I just thought if you ... never mind, hell, I'll go."

The scared man was blindfolded and put in the truck with Bare, Miller and Vines. Hattaway followed in his car, but stopped at the entrance to a rough dirt road to keep a lookout. The others continued on the dirt road. Minutes later, they stopped. Gamboa was taken from the truck and led along a path that ended at an open air shaft enclosed by a woven wire fence. Bare pushed Gamboa through a tear in the fence and ordered Vines to follow.[20]

3

Murder at the Mine

Cold, stinging wind jerked Vines back to a reality he didn't want to face. Even in his worst times, he had never taken a life. He knew now that the men outside the fence had lied to him, telling him they only wanted to scare the man into paying the money he owed them for drugs. They had backed him into a corner. Now he would have to kill.[1]

When a dark outline motioned with a shotgun, Vines took a deep breath and pushed the blindfolded man. He watched as the figure disappeared into the hole. It was done. Vines wondered if he would be next. Had they found out he was a paid informant? But suddenly he realized it wasn't over. The terrified man had been snagged by something in the hole and was dangling helplessly a few feet below. Vines heard a voice yelling from behind.

"Kojak, reach down and pull him back up," Bare yelled.

"I can't reach him. He's too far down." Vines' voice was high pitched with fear as he backed against the fence.

"Here, tell him to grab this." Bare shoved a small limb through the tear in the fence. Vines, bracing himself, took it with shaking hands in case Bare decided to push him into the hole. Bare let go of the branch, and Vines carefully edged toward the hole, sliding the limb down to the sobbing man.

"Grab this and I'll pull you up," Vines shouted.

"I can't!" shrieked the terrified Gamboa. "I think I broke my leg."

"Damn you, you better try!" screamed Bare.

The blindfolded man grabbed the limb and hung on. Vines pulled slowly, cursing as he felt the limb tearing his hands. With a last desperate jerk, he fell backward against the fence, pulling the man onto the edge of the hole. Vines helped the terrified Gamboa to his feet and looked at Bare, who was standing outside the fence. The dark figure motioned with the shotgun a second time, and Vines put his hand on Gamboa's back a second time and pushed, sending him down into the hole. The wind swept away the screams of the man as he fell to the bottom of the shaft. Vines felt numb. He heard nothing. This had to be a nightmare. He wondered if they were going to kill him next.[2]

Vines scrambled quickly back through the hole in the fence, straightened up, and found himself face to face with Bare. He backed against the fence as Bare jerked the limb from his hand and threw it into the hole, listening as it went down.

"Miller, you and Kojak throw some rocks in there. Make sure he went all the way down this time," ordered Bare. The two men pitched rocks into the hole, listening to the thud as they struck the bottom.

"He went down." Miller spoke through chattering teeth. "He went in easier than the one two weeks ago. That makes twenty-two."

"You're wrong, that makes twenty-three," argued Bare. "Let's get out of here before we freeze to death in this damn wind." When they reached the truck, Bare barked at Vines, "Pull that cap back down over your eyes. What you don't see can't hurt you."[3]

The truck crept off of the mountaintop onto a narrow dirt road, passing houses that were dark and tightly closed against the weather. The noise from the truck faded, leaving only the sound of the wind and the barking of dogs on the road leading to the old abandoned copper mine. As they drove onto a paved highway, Hattaway, who had been standing guard, pulled in front of them and led the way to the garage they had left only a short time before.

Inside the truck, Vines slumped against the seat. The Cossack cap he had been ordered to pull over his eyes blocked most of his view so that he just caught glimpses of trees and buildings. None of it was familiar to him. His mind wandered.[4]

Vines had been incorrigible as a boy and a real problem for his mother. He had overheard his mother telling some of her friends it was because he had grown up without a father. He wondered if it would have been any different if his father had stayed — probably not. He wondered if he would have been on the mountaintop this cold Christmas Eve night anyway. He had chosen the life of a paid informant and admitted to himself that he liked the danger of living on the edge of both worlds. At the moment, though, he wasn't sure which world he belonged to. If it was the law, could what had just happened be justified? A man was dead, and he had pushed him. What if he notified the FBI? Would he be arrested? What was the guy's name? Gamboa? Hell, he didn't really know the man he had just killed. All he knew was that Gamboa was a small-time drug dealer who had gotten in debt to the wrong people.

Was it murder? He had been forced to push the man. Vines couldn't shake the uneasy feeling that Bare knew who he really was. If he did, it would only be a matter of time before they would dispose of him too. He had to let Chapman know what was going on, but how? When would they let him out of their sight?[5]

The truck slid to a stop in front of the garage, bringing Vines abruptly back to the present. The three men, shivering from the cold, got out and hurried inside. Miller and Bare were already swilling whiskey from a bottle when Vines reached the warmth of a wood heater in the corner of the garage. Vines glanced around the garage, seeing some used car parts and a calendar turned to December 1981. Circled in red were the dates December 13 and 23. He wondered why. A clock showed 12:30 A.M.[6]

"Damn, Kojak, you done all right!" Bare, over six feet tall himself, nodded as if to emphasize his words. "What do you think, Miller?"

Miller nodded, "He did all right. At least we're rid of one problem, right Hattaway?"

Hattaway had come in last, closing the door behind him. His long, unkempt red hair and scraggly beard set him apart from the others. His pale blue eyes showed no emotion as he spoke.

"I'm glad the bastard's gone," growled Hattaway. "That's what finks

Inside Paul Bare's garage, where Lonnie Gamboa was brought and questioned before he was murdered (courtesy Gene Goss).

deserve." As he reached for the bottle, the light danced coldly on the skull and crossbones ring on his hand. The skull and crossbones were outlined in tiny diamonds with two larger diamonds for eyes, and the large ruby for the mouth glowed blood red — the status symbol of a hit man for the Outlaw Motorcycle Club.[7]

4

Acceptance

When the four men had thawed out from their trip to the mountaintop, Gamboa's wallet was emptied. The credit cards were tossed into the fire and burned. Bare kept the driver's license and the wallet, saying that he said he could use it in a scheme to make the police think that Gamboa was still alive.[1]

"Put on your coat," Bare directed Vines. "I've got something I want to show you up behind the garage. You come, too, Miller."

Vines put on his coat as his mind raced frantically, "If they were going to kill me, they could have easily done it at the mine!" Vines pulled the Cossack cap down over his ears as perspiration rolled down his neck.

As they walked past the old wrecked cars, the wind was already numbing his face. He couldn't make out what Bare was saying. Still sick with the flu, Vines stumbled and fell. "I've got to rest a minute. I'm still sick."

After resting a few minutes, they continued walking up the hill toward a huge, black shape sitting up ahead. Bare stopped and pointed, "I own that airplane. We use it to bring marijuana in. We've got a good set-up if you should need anything. Let's go back. You don't sound so good."[2]

"Yeah, we should be getting back soon, I guess." Vines' voice was only a husky whisper. "I hate this weather. Wish I was back in Florida."

When they returned to the garage, Bare led them over to a big truck parked outside. It looked like a garbage truck. It had some metal garbage cans in the back. Bare got into the back and slid two of the cans to Miller and Vines, who carried them inside the garage where they opened the cans, finding them filled with marijuana. Bare handed two light blue garbage bags to Miller, who transferred the marijuana to them. He then placed the filled blue garbage bags inside green garbage bags and placed them in the trunk of Miller's car.

When they returned to the garage, Miller asked Bare what he wanted to do with the rest of Gamboa's stuff — a small bag of pot, a chunk of hashish, and about $60. Hattaway told him to give Kojak (Vines) the money. He told Kojak that they were short of cash, but he would receive more after the first of the year.

When they were ready to leave, Hattaway took Gamboa's automatic weapon from Miller's car and put it in the front seat of his Monte Carlo. Hattaway told them he was stopping at Myers' Motel to spend the night because he was sick. He told Miller to swap guns with Vines because Vines' gun was too "hot" and would be sent back to the Outlaws.

The two men drove through the small towns of Jefferson and West Jefferson. Miller headed toward Boone, NC. He told Vines that he needed to stop at his home in Boone to leave the pot and swap vehicles.[3]

Vines hadn't dared to ask how the others knew the number of bodies in the mine. He was still surprised to be alive. Papa Bare seemed to know a lot about everything in Laurel Springs. "He went in easier than the one two weeks ago." The words still echoed in Vines' ears. He remembered the talk he had heard about a Forester and his girlfriend disappearing from one of the motels in Asheville. The time would be about right. He felt like he was in a sinking quagmire. He had to get in touch with Tommy Chapman, but how? He knew they would be watching him. He would like to ask if they had found out anything about Joseph Vines, but he didn't want to show too much interest. He would try to call the FBI office ... but with the holiday, he might not have much luck.[4]

As they left Boone, Vines took one last look as the mountains faded into the dusky distance. He drove the Jeep toward Asheville under clouds gray and threatening snow. It had been a long night, fatigue had caught up with them, and talk had stopped.

Vines knew he would have to report the killing as soon as possible. He knew he would also have to be careful to whom he reported this. The call at Bare's garage had come from the police station in Asheville. When they reached Asheville, Miller drove to Vines' apartment and gave him fifty additional dollars, telling him to buy his wife a Christmas present as he left.[5]

When Vines went to Sarge's later that evening, the heat, music, and whiskey were a welcome change from the last twenty-four hours. Vines saw Miller and Sarge disappear into the back room. Hattaway came in the door, nodded at Vines, and went into the back room only to reappear in a few minutes and motion to Vines. "Sarge wants to see you."

Vines rose slowly and followed Hattaway. As he entered the room, Sarge came toward him. Not knowing what to expect, Vines stopped. Sarge caught him by the shoulders. Reaching up, he kissed Vines on each cheek and said, "Welcome to the family, Kojak." He told Vines that he would be making a lot of money from now on.[6]

"So it is true," Vines' thoughts were racing. "They are Mafia." How was he going to get out of this?

When Vines got home, his wife was there with several of her friends.

She had quit work at the factory and was working for Sarge as a waitress. "Where the hell have you been?" she demanded. He ignored her. He had to think of a way to get in touch with Chapman. He could trust him.

The next few days Vines tried to call Chapman but was told he was out of town. Not knowing exactly what to do, he tried to get drunk while waiting for Chapman's return, but the thoughts of Gamboa and the horror of that night haunted him. The weekend crept by. There was no answer at the FBI office.[7]

On January 1, 1982, Vines called the FBI office and asked to talk to Bill Redding. He called the number they gave him, and he asked Redding to set up a meeting with Chapman. Redding promised to set the meeting up. Vines didn't hear from Redding or Chapman.

On January 4, he decided to go with friends to the River Lounge for a few drinks. The phone rang at the River Lounge. The bartender motioned to Vines. Hoping it was Chapman, Vines grabbed the phone. "Hello?" It was Miller. He asked him to meet him outside the River Lounge because he needed to talk to him about something. The beer Vines ordered wasn't helping the bad taste in his mouth or the fear in his heart. Vines could feel the sweat popping out even though the room was cool. What was up now?

When Vines went out to the parking lot, Miller was already there. Miller motioned for him to get into the car. As they headed back toward Sarge's Bar, Miller said, "We've got to go back to Ashe County. We have another contract to fill.[8]

He couldn't murder again, yet he had not been able to reach Chapman. He knew what doing a contract meant; he just didn't know who. Vines didn't want to go back, but he saw no way out. He should have tried harder to get in touch with Chapman. He was silent as Miller drove away from the restaurant.[9]

As they reached the outskirts of Asheville, a blue light flashed behind them. "Damn it," Miller cursed. "I wasn't speeding. What in the hell do they want?" As he slowed to a stop, he threw his gun on the dash and asked Vines where his gun was. Vines told him it was in the trunk.

As the officer came up on the driver's side, Miller's voice changed. "Hello, Officer. What's wrong?"

"Let's see some ID." The patrolman was flashing a light around the inside of the car. Miller fumbled with his wallet and handed the officer a driver's license. After checking his license, the officer said, "Step out of the car, please. I have a warrant for your arrest."

Miller responded, "For what? I haven't done anything."

"Just get out of the car, please." The officer was almost too polite. The second officer patted him down and stated, "Put your hands behind your back." When Miller complied, the cuffs were snapped into place.

The first officer stated, "You are under arrest for the kidnapping of Tom Forester and Betty Callahan. You have the right to remain silent..."

The officer glanced at Vines. "I don't have anything on you. An officer will drive you back to wherever you wish."[10] Vines accepted. On the way back to his apartment, he told the officer he was an informant and needed to get in touch with Tommy Chapman.

His wife was asleep when he got home. Vines sank into a chair and grabbed the phone, dialing with shaking hands and hoping someone would answer.

Thomas Chapman opened his eyes. The phone was ringing insistently. "What could anyone want this early in the morning?"

Almost before he could say hello, Joe Vines' voice came over the phone, "Chapman, this is Joseph Vines. Where have you been? I need to talk to you. It's important," emphasized Vines.

Chapman agreed to meet him in the morning and told Vines, "Look, just say where."

"Pick me up at 8:00 A.M. I'll be walking down Main Street, and bring Stan Keel with you," mumbled Vines.

"We'll be there," Chapman told him as he hung up the phone.[11]

5

The Tale of Murder
at the Mine

On the morning of January 5, 1982, ATF Agent Tommy Chapman, SBI Agent Robert Kiser, and FBI Agent Stan Keel — all assigned to the Asheville office — picked up Vines as he walked down Main Street in Asheville. They drove to a parking lot on the Blue Ridge Parkway where they usually met. The tale Vines told them was enough to chill even the warmest blood. It was a tale of drug dealing, of double dealing, and of man's inhumanity to man.[1]

From there, they returned to the FBI office where Vines was advised to go to a phone located where he could talk freely. Vines went to a friend's house and stayed until about 4:00 P.M. He then took his car to a local gas station where it was repaired by 6:30 P.M. He returned to the friend's house to wait for Chapman's call. Chapman called about 8:30 P.M. and advised him to get his wife and be ready to leave the area. He picked up his wife from work at 1:00 A.M. on January 6.[2]

At 7:30 A.M. on January 6, 1982, Tommy Chapman phoned Sheriff Richard Waddell of Ashe County. Sheriff Waddell picked up the phone impatiently, "Hello?"

"Waddell, this is Tommy Chapman. Can you meet me at 12:00 P.M.?" Waddell replied, "I guess so. What is this about, Chapman?" Chapman told him that he couldn't discuss the matter over the phone but told Waddell, "It's urgent that you meet me." Waddell asked Chapman where they could meet, and Chapman told him to be at Eldreth's Restaurant at noon.

That same morning, when Sheriff Waddell arrived at his office, he found a message to call Lyle West of Channel 13 in Asheville. Waddell dialed the phone, wondering what the TV reporter wanted with him.

"Good morning, Lyle West's office." Waddell identified himself, "This is Sheriff Waddell of Ashe County. I had a message to call Lyle West."

"Just a moment." After a short wait, a voice replied, "This is Lyle West."

"Sheriff Waddell here. You called me?"

"Yes. I'll get right to the point, Sheriff. I have heard some rumors I wanted to check out. Is it true that there are two or more bodies buried in Ashe County?"

Waddell replied, "What are you talking about, bodies? Don't be scaring me like that. I don't know anything about bodies." West responded, "Well, I heard there were two or more bodies buried in Ashe County, and they were connected with some kidnappings that occurred in Asheville. If you don't know anything yet, I'll get in touch with you later when someone has filled you in."[3]

At 11:00 A.M. on January 6 while Sheriff Waddell was still puzzling over the phone call from Lyle West, three SBI officers arrived at his office — Charlie Chambers, director of the Hickory SBI office, Bob Kiser of Asheville, and Ernest Bueker of Raleigh.

"What's this all about?" asked Waddell. Agent Chambers told Waddell the visit concerned some kidnappings that had recently occurred in Asheville and that Bob Kiser and ATF Agent Tommy Chapman would fill him in when Chapman arrived. At that time, Agent Chambers offered Waddell the full support of the SBI.

At noon that day, Waddell met Chapman and Agent Kiser from the Asheville SBI office at Eldreth's Restaurant. Waddell greeted them, "How are you, Tommy? Are you ready to tell me what this is all about?"

Chapman wasted no time. "We have information that there were two kidnappings from a motel in Asheville on December 13, 1981—a man and a woman. And that also, a Lonnie M. Gamboa was kidnapped around 10:00 A.M. on December 23, 1981."

Waddell responded, "What are you talking about?"

"We have an informant," Chapman added. "A man called Kojak. His real name is Joseph Vines, and he told us he brought Gamboa to Paul W. Bare's house in Laurel Springs in the trunk of a car on December 23, 1981. That puts it in your territory."

"What else?" demanded Waddell.

"Vines described Paul Bare and the premises among other homes and landmarks. He also said Bare, Miller, and he took Gamboa to an open air shaft at the Ore Knob Mine where he was forced to push Gamboa into the shaft because Miller and Bare were pointing guns at him, and he was afraid for his own life." Chapman went on, "He also stated that Gamboa hung on a root, that he pulled him back up and pushed him in again. Gamboa was alive when he was pushed into the shaft a second time."

Waddell was shaken, "Go on."

"Vines said Paul Bare stated that Gamboa went in easier than the one did two weeks ago. And also said that made number twenty-three in the mine."

"Do you believe Vines?" questioned Waddell. Chapman replied that he did because everything that Vines had told them had checked out. Waddell then asked where Vines was, and Chapman replied that he was hiding out in Virginia.[4]

At 2:00 P.M. on that same afternoon (January 6), Waddell, Chapman, Bob Kiser and Captain Gene Goss went to the Ore Knob Mine. The chain link fence around the huge mine shaft hole had a tear in it, as Vines had described to Chapman. One hour later, the Ashe County Rescue Squad came to the mine to try to go in and look for the bodies. At 4:30 P.M., the Blue Ridge Electric basket truck also came. Ross Robinson got into the basket and was put out over the opening of the mine shaft, where he took pictures and tried to look down into the dark area of the shaft with spotlights. He could see very little. It was obvious to everyone that professional help was needed before anything could be found, if there was anything to find.

At approximately 7:00 P.M., Sheriff Waddell contacted the federal Mining, Safety and Health Administration (MSHA) and asked them to make an assessment of the mine shaft to see if it was possible to reach the bottom. The MSHA agreed to send people to the mine shaft at 2:00 P.M. on January 7.[5]

By 8:00 P.M. on the evening of January 6, Chapman had set up a meeting for the next day between Vines and Sheriff Waddell at the John Deere Tractor Company in Marion, Virginia.

As Waddell's meeting with Chapman and Kiser was ending, Vines and his wife were driving to Bluefield, West Virginia, where he contacted Chapman from the motel. Shortly after speaking with Chapman, he dropped his wife off at her sister's house, where her parents were staying, and returned to the motel.[6]

On January 7, Chapman and Ashe County Sheriff Richard Waddell met Vines at the John Deere Tractor dealership at 1:30 P.M. where they stored Vines' car. Waddell advised Vines of his rights, and Vines gave him an oral statement about Lonnie Gamboa's kidnapping. Vines told Waddell much of what he had told Tommy Chapman earlier, but in such detail that Sheriff Waddell knew he had been at Paul Bare's house and that he had been at the mine shaft.

They returned to Ashe County and Vines directed them to the mine area and told them where to park — the same place where Paul Bare, Gary Miller, Lonnie Gamboa, and he had parked on December 23, 1981. He walked directly to the mine shaft and said, "That's it." Vines showed them the tear in the fence, the roots, and the pine trees around the area of the mine shaft, just as he had previously described. Vines walked the agents through the events of that cold Christmas Eve. He then directed them to the Paul Bare garage and described what had taken place there.[7]

When interviewed by the Asheville Police on January 7, 1982, by Detectives Ross Robinson and C.M. Calloway, Mrs. Gamboa had filed a missing persons report on her husband, Lonnie Marshall Gamboa. Mrs. Gamboa reported that in the morning hours of December 23, 1981, she had been out to a trailer owned by Lonnie and herself in the Fairview section of Buncombe County, North Carolina, and had completed several other errands, returning home just prior to 9:00 A.M. She said shortly after her return home Lonnie left the house to meet his attorney at the office to obtain a transcript of a recent probable cause hearing which involved the arrest of Gamboa, Gary Miller and several other people in an incident on Moffitt Branch Road. The officers asked why Lonnie would have wanted a transcript of that nature. Mrs. Gamboa said Lonnie wanted to demonstrate to a man known as Red, aka Ron Miller, that he had no part in the arrests on Moffitt Branch Road. Mrs. Gamboa said Red, for some reason, believed Lonnie had given information to law enforcement officers which led to those arrests.[8]

Sheriff Waddell received report at 9:00 P.M. on January 7 from Captain Eugene Goss that Captain Melvin Roberts of the Wilkes County Sheriff's Department had Lonnie M. Gamboa's wallet in his possession. Waddell set up a meeting for 11:45 P.M. with Captain Roberts to take a statement at the Pine Ridge Baptist Church in Wilkes County, where the wallet was found. He took possession of a light brown nylon wallet which contained Gamboa's North Carolina driver's license, two Buncombe Technical Institute I.D. cards, a MasterCharge card, and two spent 9mm shell cases.[9]

On January 8, Sheriff Waddell obtained a sworn statement from Vines in which he related the following information. Vines had worked for various federal, state, and local law enforcement agencies for the past eleven years as an undercover informant. He had previously testified in federal and North Carolina state criminal proceedings. Vines was put into protective custody after stating his life was in danger. Vines was taken to the office of District Attorney Michael Ashburn in Wilkesboro, North Carolina. Ashburn advised Waddell to charge Paul Bare with kidnapping Gamboa and to search his premises.[10]

After leaving the D.A.'s office, Sheriff Waddell, Captain Gene Goss, J.D. Parsons, James Williams, James Absher, Eugene Greer, Steve Cabe, Charles Whitman, Ernest Bueker, and Tommy Chapman proceeded to the Paul Bare residence with search and arrest warrants. They confiscated the following items:

1. .357-caliber pistol — serial number 3845 — found under seat of sofa
2. .22-caliber RG23 pistol — serial number 255993 — found in Patty Simmons' purse

3. Two Quaalude pills—found in the purse
4. Plastic film container containing marijuana—found in Patty Simmons' purse
5. Pack of firecrackers—found in Patty Simmons' purse
6. .44 Magnum Ruger Super Black Hawk pistol—serial # 84-06727—found under cushion of a chair in bedroom
7. Plastic sandwich bag containing marijuana seed—found in a suitcase in back bedroom
8. One-half carton firecrackers—found in a pillowcase in back bedroom
9. Two roman candles
10. Three pieces of scrap paper with telephone numbers—found on the phone table
11. One quart can of marijuana seeds
12. A Mead notebook with telephone numbers in it
13. A 20-gallon garbage can with marijuana residue in bottom—found on the back of an old garbage truck
14. One box of blue garbage bags—found in the dryer in house trailer (14 of those bags, blue in color and reinforced with fiberglass, described before the search by Joseph E. Vines)
15. One pair of work boots—from the living room of Paul W. Bare
16. Several cans of black powder and rifle shells—found in the closet of Paul W. Bare's house.

Thomas Chapman, in his sworn statement, gave a fuller description of the search procedure (the full statement is in Appendix A):

On January 8, 1982, about 8:30 P.M., Chapman was present when a state search warrant was executed at the residence of Paul Wilson Bare. He first went to the old trash truck parked in the junkyard and saw two new metal trash cans containing a vegetable material residue on the truck. When Chapman entered the back door, Sheriff Waddell handed him an H. Schmidt, .357 caliber revolver. Chapman unloaded the pistol and recorded the identifying information. Shortly afterward, Detective Robinson found an RG .22 caliber revolver in Patricia Watson Simmons' purse. Simmons told Chapman that she was living with Bare. He unloaded the pistol and recorded the identifying information. Chapman also found a long-barrel pistol under the seat cushion of a chair in Bare's bedroom and called Waddell to show him the Sturm Ruger .44 magnum revolver. The two men picked up the loaded pistol by the handles and placed it inside two plastic bags.

At 8:40 P.M., in the presence of Waddell and SBI Agent Whitman, Chapman advised Simmons of her constitutional rights. She told them that she understood and waived her rights and claimed ownership of the three firearms found in the Bare home. Simmons told Chapman that she had received the .22 caliber revolver and the .357 caliber revolver from "Pug" Miller (Van Miller, Jr.) of Alleghany County, NC, a friend. Simmons also said that she had a long barrel .22 caliber revolver that she received from Paul Bare's father, Hiram Bare; however, they did not find it, and Simmons did not know where it was. Simmons first told Whitman and Chapman about buying the Sturm Ruger on February 5, 1981, for $150 from a boy known as "Slick" at the Ray parking lot in Sparta, NC. Later, during the interview, "Pug" Miller came to the back door looking for Paul Bare, and Chapman told him that Bare was under arrest. Miller acknowledged that he had let Simmons borrow an RG .22 caliber revolver and a .357 magnum caliber revolver. Chapman showed him the revolvers and Miller claimed ownership. Miller said that he got the .22 caliber revolver from his mother (now deceased) and the .357 revolver from a man from California who used to rent his gas station on Hwy 18 in Wilkes County, NC.

After about an hour, Simmons started crying and told Chapman and Whitman that she would be killed if she told the truth about the Sturm Ruger. Simmons stated that she did not want to get in trouble over something that she did not do, that she had not done anything wrong. She said that the truth was that a couple of days after Christmas 1981, Gary Miller of Asheville, NC, talked with Paul Bare in the garage. Simmons stated that Gary Miller stopped by the house on the way out and came in carrying the Sturm Ruger. Simmons said that she started pleading for the pistol that Miller had and that he finally agreed to let her keep the revolver. She said that Gary Miller told her that she could keep the revolver until he wanted it back. Simmons said that Bob Miller worked for Bare in his shop. When asked, Simmons said that she knew "Red," or Ron Miller, a friend of Gary Miller, and that they had been together on several occasions. Further, she added that "Red"/Ron Miller drove the white Thunderbird parked in the junkyard. Also, Simmons said that "Red" had hepatitis and sometimes drove a Chevrolet pickup. During the interview, Simmons said that she had been in Wilkes County on the evening of January 5, 1982, and that she did hear shots being fired at the parking lot of Piney Ridge Church and that she later returned to the same parking lot along with Bare and law enforcement officers. She says that she knew a man from Asheville, NC, by the name of "Sarge" and that he had been at the Bare premises on at least two occasions. Simmons stated that she remembered some of the events of December 23, 1981. She was driving Paul Bare's old model maroon colored Ford with some friends and saw a bald man in a black car parked at Bare's garage. Simmons had a short conversation with Ron Miller and then left with her friends. She said that Bare did not return home for the evening meal and that she knew that he was at the garage when she went to bed about 11 P.M. Simmons noted that she started drinking about 5 that afternoon.

Later, Waddell showed Chapman a heavy blue trash bag that was woven with white string. Vines, in his statement, described bags that appeared to be similar and stated that Bare got two heavy blue bags on the early morning of December 24, 1981, and that he, Miller, Hattaway, and Bare placed the marijuana from the metal trash cans into the bags.

Early on the morning of January 9, 1982, Waddell and Chapman picked Vines up from a motel in Jefferson, NC. Just before Waddell placed one of the blue bags on the front seat of his patrol vehicle. Vines got into the back seat. When he spotted the bag on the front seat, he said, "You found them." Waddell, Vines, and Chapman returned to the Bare premises, went inside, and there joined Robinson, SBI Agent Bueker, and Simmons in the kitchen. Vines spoke to Simmons, and she asked if he was the bald man she had seen rise up from the back seat of the car that Ron Miller was in. Vines said that he was, and she immediately asked him if Bare had been involved. Vines said, "Yes it's true, they held a gun on me and made me push Gamboa into the mine shaft." Simmons started screaming, crying, and cussing at Vines and then ran into the living room. Chapman went with Vines to the garage, and he identified it as being the place that he came to on December 23, 1981, with Gamboa, Miller, and Hattaway. Vines walked to a point in front of the blue and white trailer where Bare lived in December 27, 1976. There Vines indicated the area where he and Hattaway took Gamboa from the trunk at gunpoint and cut the tape from his wrists, allowing Gamboa to urinate. Vines stated that a handcuff was placed on one of Gamboa's wrists and that he was led up into the woods and handcuffed to a tree. Chapman accompanied Vines to a wooded area above the shop and there Vines pointed out the tree that Gamboa had been handcuffed to. Chapman used a flashlight and observed a piece of fiberglass tape near the tree. He pointed out the tape to Vines, and Vines remarked that it appeared to be the tape that was around the wrists of Gamboa. Chapman and Vines left the area of the tree without disturbing the leaves, tape, or a limb, and returned to join Waddell. Waddell waited for daylight to photograph the tree, its surroundings, and the remnants of tape. Chapman accompanied Vines to the Bare garage and Vines identified an old Hudson automobile that he had seen in the shop on December 23 and 24. Also Vines showed them the air filter that he had previously referred to in his statement along with other items that were there on December 23 and 24, 1981. Chapman found the telephone that had been referred to by Vines on January 5, 1982, along with the other items he had referred to including the maroon Hudson with suicide door and a "Fuzz Buster" on the dash.

On the morning of January 9, 1982, Chapman was present when photographs were made of the tree, tape, and garage and observed Waddell as he removed the tape from its location and placed it in a plastic bag.

On January 9, 1982, Chapman initiated an urgent trace of the three firearms found on January 8, 1982, at the Bare premises.[11]

At about 11:00 P.M. on January 8, 1982, the sheriff and his officers took Paul Bare from his residence to the Ashe County Jail for booking. SBI agents Ernest Bueker and Ross Robinson stayed at his residence and continued the search and continued to interview Patricia Simmons.[12]

At 12:05 A.M. on January 9, 1982, Tommy Chapman and Sheriff Waddell went to Eldreth's Motel to pick up Joseph E. Vines. When Vines got into the car, Sheriff Waddell had one of the blue reinforced garbage bags lying in the front seat, and Joseph Vines said, "That is the same kind of bag that Paul Bare put the marijuana into that we took back to Boone after Gamboa was thrown into the mine."

At approximately 12:20 A.M. on January 9, 1982, Tommy Chapman, Joseph Vines, and Waddell arrived at the Paul Bare residence where Patricia Simmons, Ernest Bueker, and Ross Robinson had remained. Vines told Simmons that it was good to see her again, and Simmons said, "Do I know you?" Vines responded, "I was in the back seat with Red and Gary."

She said, "I remember you, you stuck your head over from the back seat." Simmons called Vines a "son-of-a-bitch" and began crying.[13]

Chapman and Waddell asked Vines to show them the location of the garbage truck that marijuana had been removed from on December 23, 1981, and he did. The old garbage truck contained two new twenty-gallon garbage cans as Vines had described earlier, and these two new trash cans contained marijuana residue. Waddell then asked Vines to show him the tree that Lonnie Marshall Gamboa had been handcuffed to. About 30 feet inside the woods from the old garbage truck, Vines pointed out the tree where Gamboa had been handcuffed on December 23. It was a dead locust tree approximately 12 inches in diameter, and the bark had been recently scuffed off all the way around the tree about waist high. A wrinkled-up piece of fiberglass tape lay on the ground about 3 feet from the tree. Sheriff Waddell retained this as evidence. SBI Agent Bueker also photographed the area of the tree and the garbage truck at 7:30 A.M. on January 9, 1982.[14]

About a half hour later, Patricia Simmons was arrested at the Paul Bare residence for felonious possession of marijuana. Then the search was terminated. The residence was secured by Patricia Simmons before she was taken to the Ashe County Jail.[15]

Paul Wilson Bare was advised of his rights at 9:57 A.M. on January 9, and he made a statement at the Ashe County Sheriff's Office in the presence of

Sheriff Waddell and SBI Agent Ernest Bueker.[16]

Paul Bare was charged with kidnapping Gamboa and with possession of marijuana. Miller and Hattaway, also charged with kidnapping, had fled and were being sought. Miller had forfeited the ten thousand dollar bond he was put under when he was picked up and charged with kidnapping Forester and Callahan in Asheville in early December 1981.[17]

Bare's lawyers immediately requested a hearing for bond to be set. The hearing was held in Wilkes County

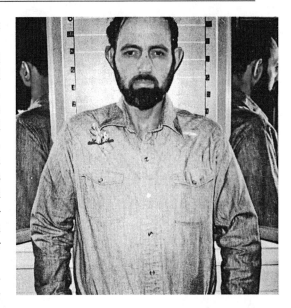

Paul Bare

Superior Court because the Ashe County Superior Court was not in session. Judge Julius Rousseau denied bond on the kidnapping and marijuana charges. Bare remained in the Ashe County jail. A District Court judge in Ashe County also refused to set bail. Bare's attorneys, John Siskind and Edward Marger, stated that they would ask a Superior Court judge to set bond. Several days later a Superior Court judge set bond at $100,000, and Paul Bare was released with orders not to go near the mine or speak with any of the witnesses. The pre-trial hearing was set for March 22, 1982, at the Ashe County Courthouse.[18]

6

Investigation at the Mine

The investigation at the Ore Knob Mine turned up nothing except that it seemed improbable that anyone could enter the shaft to search for the bodies because of soft dirt on the sides. Officers were unsure of what the next step would be.

Newspapers and radio stations were picking up daily on the story by January 12, and television news was showing the story almost nightly. Such a violent crime in the peaceful mountain setting had shocked the local people. Also by January 12, the federal Mining, Safety and Health Administration (MSHA) had moved equipment into the mining area.[1] A mining inspector by the name of Ed Juso from Raleigh was in charge of the search. A camera was fastened to a cable and let down into the hole by a crane. The temperature had dropped to ten degrees and five inches of snow lay on the ground. The mining inspector was very confident of his video camera, but the search was badly hampered by the weather, the shifting dirt, and the fact that everything from car parts to dead animals had been dumped into the shaft. On January 15, 1982, the search was called off. The camera had been able to view only about ten percent of the area because of obstructions. Detective Robinson had seen two images that could have been bodies, but the picture was not clear enough to be certain.[2]

On January 21, against the advice of the MSHA, it was publicized that the mine would be entered on Monday, January 25. Sheriff Waddell had a list of potential volunteers. On January 22, one was chosen. The name of the volunteer was not released at his request; however, plans proceeded even though MSHA had advised that it was unsafe to enter the shaft.[3] The volunteer was required to sign "A General Release and General Covenant Not to Sue." He appeared before notary Elsie Taylor of Ashe County and signed the document.[4]

On January 25, 1982, the Ore Knob Mine area was open to the bitter cold wind sweeping across the mountains. The small fires built to warm onlookers were of little comfort in the freezing mountain weather. The snow stung the faces of the lawmen, the press, and the on-lookers as the crane oper-

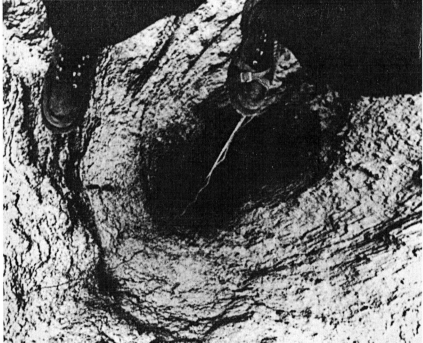

Top: A video camera search is conducted January 12, 1982, but no bodies are found. Only law enforcement and press personnel are there (courtesy Gene Goss). *Bottom:* Gene Goss's feet at the edge of the narrowing shaft (courtesy Gene Goss).

Ross Robinson, Roger Buckner, and Chief Deputy Gene Goss prepare to descend into the mine shaft to search for the bodies on January 25, 1982 (courtesy Gene Goss).

ator prepared to lower the masked man into the huge hole, gaping like an ugly wound on the frozen ground. A wire mesh fence lay back out of the way where it had been pushed. The fence had been constructed at one time in a half-hearted attempt to keep stray animals from falling into the hole. This search, however, wasn't for stray animals, but for two missing men and a woman the police had reason to believe might be in the mine shaft. The self-proclaimed stunt man calling himself "The Nashville Flame" was lowered approximately 200 feet into the shaft to check the area for gases and other hazards that might hinder the recovery of the bodies.[5]

The crowd was silent as the masked man was lowered into the mine. Before the cable had reached bottom, there was a call to be pulled back up. After two unsuccessful attempts, the man called up to say he had spotted a body.

"Are you sure?" asked Waddell.

"Yes, it's there!" replied the "Nashville Flame."

Sheriff Waddell gave instructions to Captain Eugene Goss, a somber looking man with brown hair and eyes, "You help with the body. Roger Buckner will help, too." Captain Goss nodded and prepared to descend into the hole with Buckner and Ross Robinson to retrieve the dead man.

The operation was aided by the Ashe County Sheriff's Department, the Asheville Police Department, the Ashe County Rescue Squad, the Buncombe County Rescue Squad, the North Carolina State Bureau of Investigation (SBI), and Bureau of Alcohol, Tobacco, and Firearms (ATF).[6]

The three men were lowered approximately 230 feet to a point where they could step down on solid ground and anchor to two pilings where passageways led off in two directions. Goss shined a spotlight further offto the right and saw part of a body lying in a semi-fetal position. They unhooked from the crane and hooked onto a life-line. As they worked their way toward the body, they saw another leg sticking out of the debris to the left of the body. Goss held a light, and Officer Buckner made photographs.

After photos were taken, Buckner and Goss moved closer and began to try to retrieve the first body. Both bodies were frozen to the ground and could not be moved. Goss and Buckner dug with pick and shovel around the body on top. It was clothed in a tan colored coat, a blue shirt with red stripes, a pair of denim pants, a tan

This photograph of Eugene Goss was taken in 1982 to be used in his publicity when he ran for sheriff of Ashe County (courtesy Gene Goss).

belt, and a cowboy-type boot on only one foot. Goss also observed that the other body had dark hair and was wearing a thermal top and denim-type pants, and only one shoe.

Finally, they were able to loosen the top body from the ground. Officer Buckner placed a shovel under the hip of the body and Goss slipped both arms around the body to lift it closer to the crane cable. With the increased pressure of the corpse pushing against him, he found himself and the corpse slipping down the steep incline. Buckner reached out, grabbed Goss and helped him to a safer footing. Goss breathed a sigh of relief as he looked at the 50 foot drop with only darkness beyond.

They returned to the point where Robinson had the crane anchor hooked up and were pulled back to the surface along with the first body. There were gasps from the on-lookers when the first body, frozen into a grotesque position, was brought to the top of the hole. The corpse hanging from the cable swayed morbidly in the cold brisk wind, looking like something from the depths of hell.

Around 5:30 P.M., Goss and Officer Buckner descended the shaft again and used the same procedure to remove the other body, believed to be Thomas Forester. They then searched the entire area but found no evidence of any other bodies anywhere in the shaft.[7]

When the second body was brought to the surface and loaded into the second waiting ambulance, the crowd was ready to leave. The cold mountaintop was left alone with its gruesome reminders of man's inhumanity to man that had been brought home with reality to the small mountain community that day.

After the bodies were brought up, Captain Eugene Goss was asked by the press if he thought there were any more bodies in the hole. "We feel sure there isn't anyone else down there," said Goss. "We searched the best we could because we thought Forester's girlfriend might be down there. We didn't find anymore traces of anyone else." Asked why he went into the shaft, Goss replied, "From the beginning, I felt like someone had to go down there because the crime was committed in this county, and it's our job to take care of it."

Goss agreed that Vines' story was hard to believe at first, but after checking with several government agencies that Vines had worked for, there was no doubt left. He believed Vines was telling the truth. "I felt there was one body or maybe three after hearing about Tom Forester and his girlfriend."

Goss described his descent into the mine. "It appeared before you touched down that it was a soft mound of dirt, but once you touched down, it was like a rock that was frozen rock-hard, and it went off in two directions. It was like a huge opening like a base tunnel, and it bottomed out about 50 or 60 feet down on both sides of the mound." Goss said the bodies hit the mound

Gamboa's Body

Body Bag

Top: Lonnie Gamboa's body frozen to the ground in the mine shaft (courtesy Gene Goss). *Bottom:* Lonnie Gamboa's body is hoisted from the mine shaft after being freed from the ground and attached to a crane cable (courtesy Gene Goss).

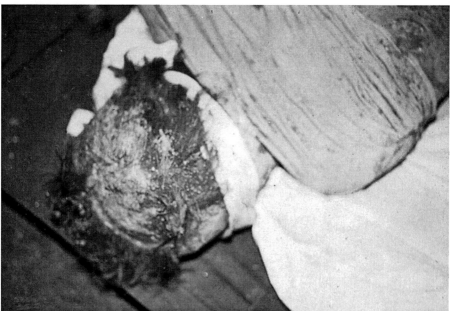

Top: His body on a stretcher, Gamboa's torn shirt reveals large abrasions. Some of his hair is left frozen to the ground below (courtesy Gene Goss). *Bottom:* Gamboa's blindfold had remained in place, verifying Joseph Vines' testimony (courtesy Gene Goss).

Thomas Forester's body had lain beneath Gamboa's. His right ear had been cut off, and he was missing one boot. He, too, is in a grotesque frozen state as he is hoisted from the mine shaft on January 25, 1982 (courtesy Gene Goss).

and rolled down the incline. "There are no more bodies down there. I feel certain we would have found them."

What of the 23 bodies that Vines heard mentioned? Goss said, "What I think is, you are talking about a huge drug ring operating in several states. I think they were referring to several states and several different people. I don't think he meant they were all in this mine." Asked how he felt when he found the evidence, Goss replied, "I think we all had a feeling of relief. It just verified everything right down the line. A lot of people have said, "They were just drug dealers. Why don't you just leave them in there? Why risk your neck for a drug dealer? The simple truth is our responsibility doesn't change — no matter who it is— they still have family and friends who care about them. If it was a member of my family, I certainly would want them out of there." Goss said the owners of the property were making plans to fill in the mine shaft.[8]

The bodies were sent to the state medical examiner's office for identification. Sheriff Waddell received a telephone call on January 27 positively identifying the bodies as those of Gamboa and Forester. The autopsy also confirmed that both men were alive when they were pushed into the mine. Bare had been freed on a property bond put up by his parents and a neighbor. When he heard they had found the bodies, Bare fled to Wilkes County. Later, accompanied by family members, he turned himself in at the Ashe County Sheriff's Department. The whereabouts of Hattaway and Miller were still not known. The charges against Bare, Hattaway, and Miller were changed from kidnapping to murder. Vines had not yet been charged with anything.[9]

The Second Probable Cause Hearing

A second probable cause hearing for Paul Wilson Bare of Laurel Springs, previously charged with kidnapping Gamboa, began at 10:30 A.M. on February 8, 1982, in the Ashe County Courthouse on a new charge of the murder of Lonnie Marshall Gamboa.[10] Alan Ray Hathaway and Gary Hansford Miller were also charged with murder. Both had fled and were being sought by authorities.

Terry Henry of the *Jefferson Times*, in his article printed on January 11, 1982, stated that "the small court house was packed to capacity that morning as Bare's lawyers, Edwin Marger of Atlanta, Georgia, and John Siskind of Jefferson, asked the court to delay the hearing for two weeks. Presiding Judge John T. Kilby denied the motion. In a second pre-hearing motion the attorneys asked the judge to consider information presented by the defense that might impeach the testimony of the state's main witness, Joseph Vines. Judge Kilby didn't rule on the motion but indicated that the defense would be free to cross-examine the witness about any deals made between any law enforcement agencies and Vines for his testimony."

During testimony, Vines admitted that he had pushed Gamboa to his death, saying he was forced to do so while Bare and Miller were pointing guns at him. He explained that he feared for his life. Vines, a paid government informant, said he was cooperating with police fully throughout the investigation.[11]

Testimony showed Forester had been kidnapped two weeks prior to Gamboa, according to the article. Both were thought to have been killed due to owing large sums of money for drugs fronted to them by members of a large-scale drug operation that was under investigation in Florida, Tennessee, Virginia, and North Carolina. Vines explained that he was working undercover trying to get information for the government against Paul Harris, a.k.a.

Sarge, of Asheville, North Carolina. While trying to gain Harris' trust, he had been drawn into the kidnapping and murder of Gamboa by Miller and Hattaway, who also worked for Harris.[12]

Bare's attorney's, in rebuttal, said the defense would maintain that Gamboa was already dead at the time he was put into the mine. The death certificate, filed in Ashe County, listed no specific cause of death for Gamboa, according to testimony in earlier pre-trial hearings. Immediately following the probable cause hearing, Patricia Simmons, identified as Paul Bare's girlfriend, was charged with interfering with a witness after she yelled "murderer" at Vines. In a trial that same day, she was found guilty, sentenced to one day in the county jail, and fined $75.[13]

After all evidence was presented by the state and defense attorneys, Judge John T. Kilby ruled that probable cause was found to bind Paul Bare over to Superior Court on charges of murder in the death of Lonnie Gamboa. Judge Kilby denied bond to Bare after a motion by defense attorneys. Siskind said the defense would pursue a bond for Bare in Superior Court. The $100,000 bond set for the defendant at an earlier hearing was revoked.[14]

Bare's Pre-Trial Hearing

During the pre-trial hearing held for Bare on April 22, 1982, in the Yadkin County Courthouse, Judge Julius Rousseau listened to District Attorney Mike Ashburn and defense attorneys John Siskind and Edwin Marger argue their points for and against trying Paul Wilson Bare for the kidnapping and murder of Gamboa. The defense team made it clear that they would try to prove that ATF Agent Thomas Chapman had been trying for years to find charges to press against Bare. Chapman had been subpoenaed by the defense attorneys to appear at this hearing, but had failed to do so because his office advised against it due to his current involvement in related cases. The purpose of this hearing was for the district attorney and defense attorneys to show what evidence they had accumulated, and to present any new information they had uncovered.

The defense attorneys made a motion to grant bond for Bare. The judge denied bond and set Bare's trial for June 2, 1982, at the Ashe County Courthouse in Jefferson.[15]

7

Callahan in Chicago

The same day the bodies were found there was a call to Illinois police from Betty Darlene Callahan, who was in Chicago. She had managed to escape her captors and had called her mother, who told her about the recovery of the bodies. Callahan then called the local police in Brookfield, Illinois, and the police called the Chicago FBI, headed by special agent Edward D. Hegarty. He sent agents to safeguard the frightened woman. Asheville police went to Chicago to bring Callahan back to North Carolina under protective custody. Police were now convinced that Bare, Hattaway, and Miller were part of an interstate drug ring operating throughout Florida, Virginia, and North Carolina. Before the case would close, there would be many more states added to that list. There were also hints that the Outlaw Motorcycle Club and the Mafia were possibly involved.[1]

With the information from Callahan and what the FBI, SBI, ATF, and other government agencies knew, the case was pieced together dating back to 1978 when the Outlaw club began bringing drugs to North Carolina. Under police protection, Callahan told of a six-week-long nightmare when she was forced to serve as a slave and a prostitute for members of the Outlaw Motorcycle Club in Chicago.

Thomas Stimac, also known as "Westside Tommy," and a Chicago Outlaw named Leroy Gurican were transporting methamphetamine "crack" from Chicago to North Carolina. Alan Hattaway's association with the two men existed as far back as early 1980. In 1980, Hattaway and Gurican were in a bar in Salisbury, North Carolina, when a man was shot and killed in an altercation with them and other Outlaw members. In the summer of 1980, Hattaway resided in Salisbury with a woman named Shelly Tiron. She later testified that Hattaway was a cocaine dealer who made frequent trips to Florida and Tennessee to purchase cocaine for behind-the-scenes financiers.[2]

In the fall of that year, Hattaway and Tiron moved to Laurel Springs, NC, where they lived near Paul Bare. Hattaway had known Bare prior to this move, and, during 1981, the men's relationship was extensive.

During the summer of 1981, Hattaway, Miller, Stimac, and a Marty Curran became close associates of Clayton Boggess and Garth Bluxon. Both Boggess and Bluxon resided in Asheville, and both were dealing cocaine in significant amounts. In the early spring of that year, Boggess had moved to Asheville from Marathon, Florida, where he had been involved in drug distribution. By the summer of 1981, Boggess had reached an agreement with Miller to distribute drugs for him. Boggess traveled with Hattaway to Chicago during this time to transport a kilo of cocaine that had been purchased through Bluxon for Stimac and Curran. During this trip to Chicago, Hattaway told Boggess that he, Stimac, and Curran were going to meet with the Mafia.

In June 1981, Gurican was sentenced to prison. Stimac provided Gurican with money for his legal fees and restitution. He traveled on several occasions to Salisbury to meet with Gurican, using the alias Tom Treiton. In early August 1981, Stimac and Curran made another trip to North Carolina with 1,000 bootlegged Canadian Blues. They met with Tiron and another woman named Lydia Towns and transferred the Canadian Blues. Towns was to smuggle the drugs into prison to Gurican. On August 8, Towns and her young daughter visited Gurican in prison. The daughter placed the bag of Canadian Blues in a trash can, which was then delivered to Gurican.

During that summer of 1981, Hattaway began living with Bluxon and his girlfriend, Sammi. Bluxon, unemployed and dependent on drug dealing for his income, was close friends with Tom Forester and Lonnie Gamboa, as well as other drug dealers in the Asheville area. During the summer, Hattaway introduced Bluxon and Broughton to Paul Bare at his house near the Ore Knob Mine. Broughton overheard Hattaway tell Bluxon that Bare, also known as "Papa Bare" to his friends, was a major drug dealer who could provide him with marijuana to sell.

Stimac visited with Bluxon and Hattaway on at least two occasions during that summer. Records indicate that there were several telephone calls between them. In July, Bluxon asked a friend named Ed Sawyer to pick up certain drug cutting equipment he had left in Asheville and bring it to Atlanta. Sawyer's airline ticket was purchased and waiting for him at the Asheville airport. Bluxon met Sawyer in Atlanta and drove him to the La Quinta Inn, where Stimac and Hattaway were waiting. In Sawyer's presence, Bluxon, Stimac, and Hattaway cut two kilos of pure cocaine, creating a product with a street value of $500,000. The records of the La Quinta Inn for July 18 show that two rooms for four guests were registered under Stimac's alias, Tom Treiton. A false Illinois address was listed.

On Labor Day weekend, Stimac and his "old lady," Toni Somers, drove to Bluxon's residence in Asheville. Stimac made the trip to resolve a dispute between Hattaway and Miller over drugs that he had financed. One night during this visit, Stimac, along with Somers, Broughton, and Bluxon, went to Miller's house. After Stimac and Bluxon talked to Miller, they drove to the Oyster Bar Lounge in Asheville. Tom Forester and a friend named Jay Fagel were also at the lounge that night. Bluxon became involved in an argument with an acquaintance. Forester, standing nearby, did not interfere, but his friend tried to. Fagel was quickly told by a man he didn't know to stay out of it. Later that night, Forester told Fagel that the unknown man he had confronted was Stimac, alias Westside Tommy. Shortly after this Labor Day visit by Stimac, bootleg Canadian Blue Valium surfaced on the Asheville drug market. Among those receiving large quantities for distribution were Bluxon, Forester, and Gamboa.[3]

At the same time Stimac was visiting Asheville, Hattaway had over $40,000 in his possession that he claimed was money relating to his collection activities for the Chicago Outlaws. Following Stimac's Labor Day visit and prior to November 7, 1981, Hattaway and Miller attempted several buys of cocaine in Florida.

In September, Bluxon, Sawyer, and a woman companion traveled to Florida to purchase cocaine. Bluxon failed to buy all of the cocaine for which Stimac had given him money. Several calls were made to Bluxon by Stimac regarding the $20,000 he had given Bluxon for the cocaine. There was also talk between Hattaway and Miller about killing Bluxon, whom they suspected of giving information to the police. In the presence of Betty Callahan, Miller asked Forester to go to Florida to purchase cocaine, stating that Bluxon had botched a deal for Hattaway's people in Chicago. Also in Callahan's presence, Hattaway told Forester if he needed any money to finance drug transactions, he (Hattaway) could get the money from "Westside," the head of the Chicago Outlaws.[4]

On November 7, 1981, Mrs. Taylor, the clerk at the EconoLodge Motel in Asheville, North Carolina, called the sheriff's department communicator saying she had a white male at the desk stating he was looking for Miller and Boggess in Room 142. The man had a gun and told the clerk if the officer didn't get there soon, he was going to Miller's home on Moffitt Branch Road. Officer Rhew arrived and was told by Mrs. Taylor the subject had left in a blue Cadillac. Minutes later Linda Miller of Moffitt Branch Road called dispatch and said there was a shootout at her home and someone was shooting into her occupied dwelling. Officer Rhew arrived and found a blue Cadillac in the driveway, then circled the residence and found James Ronald Anthony, Jr., armed with a 9mm 197 Smith and Wesson handgun, serial number A-685955. Anthony was taken into custody after a short fight in the yard behind the house.

Donald R. Cole, criminal investigator, went into the Gary Miller home to find Miller, his wife Linda, Paula Jo Anthony, white female, and a two year old child, and two bullet holes in the back door. He also saw three shotgun blasts inside to outside through the wooden front door. When Cole was taken upstairs by Gary Miller, he saw bullet holes and broken windows in both south upstairs bedrooms. Cole also located a Remington model 742 30-06 caliber with a 2×7 power Redfield scope and expanded casings in the bedroom to the right of the stairs at a broken window. Also, 12-gauge shells and Remington model 1100 M-532179-V, a stolen firearm from North Kannapolis Police Department. He advised Gary Miller that he was in possession of a stolen firearm. Miller told Cole to follow him into his bedroom.

When they entered the back bedroom to the left of the stairs, Miller informed the officer this was his bedroom and that he was afraid for his wife and child due to the involvement with Anthony, Gamboa, and Boggess. He said there was an immediate threat to deputies and others in the house of being shot by Lonnie Gamboa and Clayton Boggess. The police had already taken Anthony into custody. Miller's next statement to the officer was about the death and murders of the Durham family in Boone. He then told officers to take the other nickel 9 mm Smith and Wesson, serial number A-606544, that he had placed on the kitchen cabinet as additional protection for him and his family until they got out of the house or the people outside were arrested. He also told the officer (and the motel verified the names Boggess and Gamboa) the people were in rooms 142 and 144.

The officer sent units to the motel.[5] While they were at the motel, Clayton Boggess was located on Moffitt Road in front of the Miller home. He had an automatic pistol clip in his pocket and was carrying a large amount of cash. Officer Hembree and other officers located the people in the motel, and an immediate search for weapons was done. They found more weapons and more cocaine, marijuana, and hashish. Lonnie Gamboa's Ford van was impounded. James Anthony's Toyota was searched after a search warrant was obtained. On November 8, 1981, Gamboa's van was searched, and more weapons were found, including a 6mm model 700 Remington with Weaver scope serial number 6700437. The NCIC (National Crime Information Center) showed it to be stolen from Cape Girardeau, Missouri.

The officers returned to Miller's residence with a search warrant, which Miller signed. They located more cocaine, a large amount of cash, and another handgun. Some hours later Gary Miller told Officers Cole and Herb Deweese there was more cocaine in the residence, and he took the narcotics officers back to the house and turned more cocaine over to them.[6]

The officers then interviewed Karen Kirk Young about another weapon that information showed her to have. Young voluntarily turned over the weapon and signed a search warrant. Then she took Officer Cole Hollifield and Officer Smith back to her residence, where she turned over a large quantity of drugs, including 22 pounds of unwrapped hashish in Lebanon gauze and approximately 40 pounds of marijuana. When they returned to the courthouse, she was jailed in lieu of $5,000 secured bond.[7]

On Sunday, November 8, 1981, Officers Call, Rickman, Hembree, and Bill Rhew executed a search warrant for the James Ronald Anthony trailer. They seized 13 weapons and ½ ounce bags of marijuana. While they were at the trailer, Anthony's sister, Paula Jo Anthony, arrived and informed the officers of more guns and items left at her trailer by Clayton Boggess when he was staying with her. After getting written permission from the sister, the officers searched and found an assortment of drug-cutting equipment and paraphernalia, a .22-caliber Colt Huntsman 6" barrel blue steel (serial number 51010885) handgun (the weapon was reported as stolen from Miami, Florida, and a second .22-caliber handgun (a Ruger Mark, serial number 16-23137), reported stolen from Waynesville, North Carolina. Detectives learned that the weapon had been stolen during a first-degree burglary and involved in an armed robbery in Henderson County, North Carolina. In that case, three men had been arrested and confessed to the crimes and said the weapon was supposed to have been thrown into a river.

Further searching of the combined property of the Anthonys showed extensive target practicing, and Paula Jo Anthony showed them three bullet holes in the bedroom wall of her trailer and stated that Clayton Boggess had shot at her home. The officer located two spent .30-caliber casings on her bed. This was evidence of the .30-caliber carbine that Gary Miller talked about.

Agent David Bossard and ATF Agent Tommy Chapman made a final list of all the weapons seized. Chapman traced the weapons for additional locations, and he identified a total of 59 weapons confiscated during searches from the residence of Gary Miller, the Cadillac of James Anthony, the motel room at EconoLodge, the Ford van of Lonnie Gamboa, and the residence of Paula Jo Anthony, the sister of James Anthony, who lived next door. Agents Call and Deweese interviewed Gary Miller at his request, and he continued talking about the incident. Miller told about the people involved in the Boone murders in detail and the existence of a .38-caliber revolver that had been buried and dug up by James Anthony and implied the possible connection of this weapon to the double homicide on Haywood Road in Skyland, NC.[8]

After the shootout on November 7, 1981, at the home of Gary Miller, and the police had stopped the gun battle, Miller was arrested. Large amounts of drugs, money, and firearms were confiscated from the house. In a motel adjacent to Miller's house, Lonnie Gamboa was arrested. Following the shootout, Hattaway disappeared from the Asheville area until approximately

December 12, 1981. On that day, Toni Somers rented a room for someone at the Chalet Motel in Lyons, Illinois; the car tag registered was that of Alan Hattaway. However, on December 12, Hattaway and Miller were seen in Asheville in Sarge's Lounge. Paul Harris had arranged for them to use a van belonging to a plumber named Danny Roberts. Hattaway and Miller left the bar accompanied by Roberts and drove to the home of Forester's friend, Jay Fagel. On the way, Miller complained that Forester had taken a suitcase containing six pounds of cocaine that he and Hattaway were looking for.[9]

Earlier that afternoon, John Charles Fagel, also known as Jay, received a phone call at his home from Tom Forester stating that his bike had broken down at the big supermarket on Lexington Avenue. He asked Jay to help him get it started. Jay said he would be there as soon as he could.

Fagel and his nine-year-old son left to meet Fagel's girlfriend at Bojangles for dinner. Approximately two hours after Forester's call, Fagel arrived at the market. Forester had left word that he had already gone home. Fagel then drove to the In Town Motel followed by his girlfriend in her car. Parked in front of Forester's room was an older model black pickup. Several people were standing around outside. Forester was drinking too much and told Fagel, "Some good ol' boys from Sandy Mush helped me get the motorcycle to my room." Fagel opened the door to Room 15 and quickly shielded the boy's eyes. Inside the room, Forester's girlfriend, Betty Callahan, was walking around nude and talking with two men.[10]

"Jay, I'm leaving. I don't have to take this from Tom." Fagel's girlfriend headed for the car, glaring at Forester. She turned to Jay and said, "If you want to see me, I'll be home."

"What did you say to her, Tom?" Fagel could see that Forester was drunk. Tom replied, "Nothing ... not that much, anyway." Knowing that he could not talk to Forester while he was drunk, Fagel and his son left. They arrived home about 7:30 P.M. Forester called shortly thereafter. He asked Jay if they got home okay, saying, "I know that old Chevy don't run too good." Assuring him that they were fine, Fagel hung up the phone. After making sure his son was in bed, Fagel fell asleep himself, but was awakened at 8:40 P.M. by a knock on the door. Fagel opened the door to find Hattaway, Miller, and a short, dark-haired man standing there.

"Where's Tom," demanded Hattaway. Fagel stalled, knowing that he had come after his motorcycle.

"My house was broken into, and the motorcycle was stolen," Fagel explained. The bike, a black Harley Davidson belonging to Hattaway, had been stored at the Fagel residence for the past month.

"I don't believe a word of that," Hattaway informed him as Miller checked the room where the motorcycle had been kept. Returning to Fagel, Miller stuck the cold tip of a .38-caliber pistol in his ear. The sound of the gun being cocked sent chills down Fagel's spine.

"Now tell us where Tom and the cycle are."

Fagel knew they weren't bluffing. "Tom has the bike. He is staying at the In Town Motel."

"All right. Get in the van outside. You're going with us." Miller motioned with the gun.

"I have my son here," Fagel protested as he backed up. "He can't be left alone. We have no part in the theft, and I don't want him exposed to this."

"Wake him up. He'll go, too. Then we know there won't be any calls made to warn Tom. Since he knows who you and your son are, if anything goes wrong, we have you two." Hattaway kept his hand on his pistol in a ready manner while Fagel and his son got ready and climbed into the van parked outside, accompanied by Miller, Hattaway, and the unknown, dark-haired man driving the van. The dark-haired man got out at the Captain's Lounge in Asheville. Hattaway drove the van to the In Town Motel, where the two men got out and headed for the door just as Betty Callahan was approaching the same door.[11]

Callahan, walking from Shoney's where she had purchased breakfast, was startled to see three men and a boy standing at the door of Room 15. She recognized the men as she came closer. They were Alan Hattaway, Gary Miller, Jay Fagel, and Fagel's son. As she approached the motel door, Hattaway spoke first, "You got your key?"

"No. He may not be here," answered Callahan. Forester, hearing voices, cracked the door just as Hattaway gave it a jarring kick. The door flew open sending Forester staggering back. Callahan was shoved in roughly, ahead of the others and ordered to sit down directly behind the door, which was then closed.

Inside the room, a black motorcycle sat dominating the space. Hattaway went directly to the bike, examined the place where a mural had been removed, and looked intently at the damages where the bike had been wrecked. "This is the bike my dead brother painted." Red's voice had a strange undertone.

"Tom removed the mural so the bike wouldn't be recognized." Fagel glanced at Forester as he spoke.

Taking a cue, Forester asked, "What's going on?" Raising his gun, Miller struck Forester in the ear. The blood trickled from the cut ear down Forester's face and neck onto the insulated undershirt and cotton briefs he was wearing.

"I haven't been this mad in a long time!" Red's voice still had the strange sound as he looked at Forester. "Where's my money?" Forester made a gesture with his empty hands, indicating he didn't have the money.

"How'd the bike get smashed?" Hattaway continued.

"I wrecked it," Forester answered, speaking for the first time since being hit by Miller.

"I ought to take you to the Clubhouse," Red growled.

Miller was eyeing Callahan. "Are you still using the needle?"

"No, I'm on methadone," she replied.

"That's worse!" Miller walked over, grabbed the telephone and jerked it out of the wall. Throwing the phone on the floor, Miller looked under the bed, searching for a gun, but found nothing.

"You owe me $2,300 for drugs. I want it!" ordered Hattaway.

"Come on, strip off. Let's see if you have any drugs on you." Forester stripped down and watched as they searched his clothing and tossed them back to him. Callahan was next. As she was stripping her clothes off, Fagel, who had earlier walked outside to be with his son, stuck his head back in the door, "Police cruiser coming up."

Miller went out the door and walked directly to the cruiser. "We're just friends visiting. We will be leaving shortly." Apparently satisfied, the cruiser pulled off.

"Hurry up, there's a cruiser outside," Miller was rushing Callahan. "Tom, you and Jay put the motorcycle in the van. Come on, let's move!" While the motorcycle was being loaded, the search of Callahan was completed. When she went outside, the cruiser was gone, and Forester and Fagel were sitting in the van. Miller was telling Red the police had received a call because of a disturbance.[12]

The van pulled onto Tunnel Road by the mall on Highway 74 and turned left on Swannanoa River Road. As Miller drove, he kept an eye out for the cruiser while Hattaway kept a gun on the others. They stopped at the Park Drive-in where Miller had once worked. He spoke briefly to the woman at the ticket office. He paid no admission and drove on through, pulling into one of the spaces. Miller then got out and left.

Hattaway ordered Fagel and his son to sit in the front seat. The silence was thick for about an hour. Forester asked, "What about Lonnie?" Hattaway answered sharply, "Jay doesn't know anything about that. We'll talk later." Changing his mind, Hattaway added, "You stick your arm out to help someone, and they cut it off!"[13]

After another lengthy wait, a black Cordoba with Miller at the wheel pulled up alongside the van. Forester and Callahan were placed in the car — Forester in the rear seat and Callahan in the front with Miller. Miller, looking at Fagel, said, "You keep quiet or else! Is that fair enough?" Fagel had gotten out of the van with his son but was ordered to return to it for a short time. A small foreign car drove up with two men inside. The dark-haired man had been at Fagel's house with Miller and Hattaway. He couldn't make out the second occupant. "You and your son will be driven home in the van, and you will drive a small foreign car parked near your car to Sarge's Lounge tomorrow. Leave it there with the keys in it."

Arriving at his house, Fagel was followed inside by the man still holding a gun on him. Once inside, the man demanded his 9 mm handgun. Fagel handed him the gun, and the man held both guns on him while exiting. Fagel and his son left immediately after the man drove off, going to his girlfriend's house because he was afraid to stay at home. The next day, he drove the foreign car to Sarge's Lounge on Highway 81 and left it with the key in the ignition. A friend picked him up and took him back home. The next day, he drove Forester's Chevy to Quincy's Steakhouse on Hendersonville Road and left it because he realized the vehicle carried a tag from a van formerly owned by Forester and was improperly registered. After this, Fagel, fearing for his and his son's lives, kept quiet.[14]

The Cordoba left the drive-in in Asheville about 10 P.M. on December 12, 1981, on a trip that would soon become a nightmare for the two captives.

"What are you going to do to us?" asked Forester.

"Betty here can go up north and work off part of your drug debt at our Outlaw house in Chicago," snapped Hattaway, still angry over the motorcycle. "You can either rob a bank or work on a boat stealing marijuana from others."

Forester then asked, "What about Lonnie?"

"What about him? We know he's talking too much and telling things. We are going to see him next," replied Hattaway.

"We are on our way to Chicago now, so just relax. It's a long ride," Miller said, glancing at Callahan.

"I think we should go to the other place," interrupted Hattaway. Miller nodded in reply and headed the car east.[15]

8

Forester's Murder

After a four-hour drive, they pulled up at a brick house in Laurel Springs, North Carolina. It was 2:00 A.M. on Sunday, December 13, 1981. Miller parked to the left of the house. Callahan noticed a car sitting there that looked familiar — a white 1978 Thunderbird with a blue dash and pin stripes on the side. She had driven the car when it had belonged to Forester. A wrecker sat to the right, and the drive led through the middle of a junkyard.

Miller and Hattaway got out of the car to talk to a large man who had come out of the house. After a few minutes, Hattaway and Miller returned to the car and drove up the driveway to a garage. To the left sat an old trailer. After a short wait, the same man came from the house, his features hidden by his fur-trimmed parka. Miller and Hattaway got out of the car and went into the garage with him. They came back with some rags. After they took Forester out of the car, they blindfolded him and proceeded to do the same to Callahan. They all walked back down the driveway and got into a truck where they were jammed together. Callahan couldn't remember seeing a truck, but it felt and sounded like one. Hattaway and Miller were discussing the prospects of the two bound people. Hattaway made the decision. "We'll take them to the housing project. Take Tom in first, and see if they can make some arrangements for him to pay the money. Then we will take Betty in after we finish with Tom."[1]

After a few miles, Callahan felt the truck turn on a rough, steep road. Everyone got out of the truck except Miller and Callahan. "They're taking Tom to see if some arrangements can be made for him to steal some pot; if not, they will kill him." Miller paused a moment, then continued, "Do you want to take your chances with Tom or would you rather go to Chicago and work with the Outlaws as a prostitute? If you take your chances with Tom, and Tom lives, then you live ... but, if nothing can be worked out, and Tom dies, you die too. When I ask, nod your head which one you choose." Callahan, feeling that Forester didn't have much chance of living, nodded yes when asked about Chicago.[2]

Unknown to Callahan, Forester was not taken to a housing project, but to an old abandoned mine shaft. His left ear would be cut off before he was thrown into the 250-foot hole alive. A life-long resident of the Ore Knob Mine area was watching TV at 2:30 that morning and later recalled hearing screaming sounds which lasted about five minutes. The noise was so unusual that the resident woke another family member who also heard the screaming. Neither contacted authorities.[3]

After what seemed like a long wait, Hattaway and the other man returned without Forester. Callahan kept quiet and asked no questions. Leaving the dirt road, they drove back to the brick house. There, Callahan's blindfold and gag were taken off, and, for the first time, she could see the other man's face, but not clearly. He was about 35 or 40 years old, had a full, dark brown beard and moustache, piercing eyes beneath thick eyebrows, and a balding head. The big man ordered, "Take her to Chicago and get her a job. Make sure she keeps her mouth shut. If she does okay, in a year or two, she can come back here." As the Cordoba pulled out for Chicago that cold December morning, the bleak, gray dawn seemed to have an extra chill.[4]

The Trip

The trip to Chicago began around 5:00 A.M. Sunday, December 13, 1981. After driving all day, they arrived in Chicago around 9:00 o'clock that evening.

During the trip, Miller molested Callahan, and both Hattaway and Miller were using cocaine and Canadian Blue Valium. Both men were armed at all times. Before arriving in Chicago, Hattaway told Callahan he was taking her to the Outlaws in Chicago and mentioned Stimac and Curran by name. "You will do what you are told. You will become an Outlaw 'old lady.'" Hattaway's tone of voice convinced Callahan that he was telling her the truth, and he added, "I might even keep you as my 'old lady.' Then you would work as a prostitute for me, and I would get all the money! Or I might sell you to Stimac." He was enjoying tormenting Callahan. Hattaway also told her that his people in Chicago would not tolerate any foul-ups— that the people were not just the Outlaws but also included "the mob." "These people will put you in a Dempsy Dumpster if you don't do as you are told," he assured her.

When they arrived in Chicago, they registered at Sullivan's Motel. Hattaway phoned Stimac. Stimac's old lady, Toni Somers, secured a lease on an apartment in Glendale Heights, Illinois, that same day, December 13, 1981. She gave false identification and place of employment, as well as a false reason for leasing the apartment where Callahan was kept December 29 and 30.

At the motel, Hattaway and Miller left Callahan alone for an hour after disabling the phone. Miller warned her, "It goes without saying. You do not leave this room." Hattaway added, "If you do leave, it doesn't matter where you go. We will find you. We've got people all over the United States." She had been told during the trip that if she did not follow their instructions, her mother and sister living in Asheville would be killed. Phone records showed that several calls were made on December 13, 1981, between Stimac's Hinsdale house and the Outlaw probate house known as "the Flats."

On Monday night, December 14, Curran came to Sullivan's Motel where Callahan had been kept all day. Curran was armed with a .357 Magnum. Hattaway ordered her to perform sex acts with Curran. After holding her for two nights at Sullivan's Motel, Hattaway and Miller changed motels, taking Callahan with them. They checked into the Chalet Motel in Lyons, where Callahan was held captive on Tuesday night, December 15. While at this motel, they were visited by Stimac. Hattaway told Stimac, "Callahan will prostitute for you." Hattaway looked at her and said, "Take your clothes off and show him what you look like." After inspecting Callahan, Stimac told her to go into the bathroom and shut the door so that he and Hattaway could talk.

On Wednesday, December 16, Stimac came back to the Chalet Motel with Burroughs, another Outlaw. Both men were carrying firearms. Hattaway gave Stimac $100 and told Callahan to go with him. Stimac took her to the car and introduced her to Burroughs. Stimac then asked her, "What type of sex acts do you engage in?" Instead of taking her to his Hinsdale house that night, Stimac sent her to the La Grange Motel, where she spent the night with Burroughs. Telephone records also showed several phone calls between Stimac's Hinsdale house and the Flats prior to transporting Callahan to the La Grange Motel.

During the evening of December 16, Burroughs told Callahan that she would work as a prostitute either for him or Stimac. They would collect all of the money, and, in return, they would protect her. During that evening, Burroughs taught her how to knife fight. He gave her Canadian Blue Valium and ordered her to engage in sexual activities. He also told her that although he was from Canada, he was going to remain in the U.S. because he had been caught bringing pot from Canada. He also told her that he had been shot recently. (Records showed this to be true.)

The following day Callahan was taken to Stimac's house in Hinsdale, Illinois, where she met Toni Somers for the first time. Somers was introduced as Stimac's "old lady." During the evening, Somers told Callahan that she would work as a prostitute out of the Club Algiers in Lyons, Illinois. Somers explained what the financial arrangements were with the club. Before Somers left for work that night, she showed Callahan the Hinsdale house. There was one room referred to as the "Office," and she warned Callahan not to enter that room. During the tour of the house, Somers pointed out an oil painting of a dead biker named "Burrito"—John Klimes—an "Outlaw" who had been blown up by a bomb that had been planted in his car.

After Somers left, Curran, who resided in Stimac's house, ordered Callahan into the bedroom. At Stimac's direction, she engaged in sexual activities, after which he gave her cocaine. She did not spend the night at the Hinsdale house. She was taken by Curran to the Flats near Michigan City, Indiana. Before she was taken from the Hinsdale house, Stimac told her that he, Curran, and Burroughs would make arrangements to get her on the circuit. He also told her that prostitution was controlled by the Mob, but that he had the necessary connection to place her on the circuits. Stimac also told her she would turn her money over to them and that they would provide protection for her. She could not prostitute until she had an identification, which they would provide for her. Furthermore, she was not to go by the name of Betty Callahan anymore or tell anyone she was from Asheville, NC. Her new name was Julie Alvarado, and to cover her Southern accent, she was to say she was from Knoxville, Tennessee. Curran handed her a Wisconsin driver's license and a social security card with that name. The cards had been stolen from the real Julie Alvarado a year before at a bar frequented by the Outlaws in Milwaukee, Wisconsin. Again, she was told that she was not to use the phone at any time. At the end of this discussion with Curran, she was driven to the Flats, where she was kept for five days. She went nowhere and spoke with no one other than the Outlaws who were there. Curran also told her not to tell anyone who she was or where she was from. Callahan asked Curran if she could call her mother and tell her that she was okay. Her request was denied. While they were at the Flats, Curran called Stimac each day. On December 23, Curran took her back to the Hinsdale house.[5]

Miller and Hattaway left Chicago on December 17 and arrived back in Asheville on December 18. That evening Danny Roberts met them at Sarge's Lounge. In the back room of the bar, Roberts gave Hattaway Forester's gun that Hattaway had asked him to pick up from Jay Fagel. Roberts commented that he liked the gun, and Hattaway replied, "You can have it when I'm through using it."

After Gamboa's murder, Vines learned that he had been accepted as a member of the "family" and was now a hit man for the Outlaws, expected to deal drugs and collect money for them. On the night Gamboa was murdered, Hattaway told Vines that he was going to Chicago the next day. Although Vines did not know the names of the Chicago people, he had seen Stimac at Sarge's Lounge late in the summer of 1981.[6]

During the Christmas holidays, Callahan was held by the Outlaw members— Stimac, Curran, and Burroughs— at the Hinsdale home. On occasion, she was taken to the Sybaris Inn Motel, where she was directed to engage in sexual activities with Stimac and Somers. Photographs of these activities were seized in the March search of the Hinsdale house, where she was confronted by Stimac, Burroughs, and Curran, all armed. Stimac was dressed in a black jacket and held an AR-15 automatic rifle. The other two had shotguns. Somers took Callahan to the Glendale Heights apartment that had been leased on December 13. Somers told her that someone had threatened to kill Stimac. Callahan stayed at that apartment until December 30, when Curran picked her up and took her back and forth between the Hinsdale house and the Flats from December 31 to January 1. On January 3, Curran took Callahan to a new location at Stimac's Plainfield Road house in Indian Head Park, Illinois— called "The Ponderosa."

On Monday night, Gary Miller, accompanied by Vines, was arrested by the Asheville police. On that same day, Stimac came to the Ponderosa to talk to Curran. In the presence of Callahan, Stimac told Burroughs and Curran that Miller had been arrested. Stimac told Curran to take Callahan to a phone booth to make a call to the Asheville police which could not be traced. Stimac ordered her to tell the Asheville police that she had not been kidnapped, but that she and her boyfriend had had a fight and broken up. He also told her she had better sound convincing. On Thursday, January 7, Callahan reached Detective Will Annarino of the Asheville Police Department. He taped the conversation. Curran stood near her at the Oasis pay phone and shared the ear receiver, instructing her how to respond to Annarino's questions. Annarino told her he wanted to see her Saturday and that the Asheville police would make arrangements to bring her home if she was truly free to come home. Annarino asked her if Forester was dead. The phone went dead.[7]

By January 6, Vines' information regarding the Gamboa murder had led officials to the Ore Knob Mine shaft. By January 7, there was a 24-hour police guard around the shaft. By January 8, the news media was publicizing the recovery events that were unfolding at the mine.[8] On January 10, Callahan was taken to the Flats again by Curran, and she remained there until January 17, when Curran took her back to the Ponderosa.[9]

On January 10, Hattaway checked into a motel in Panama Beach, Florida, under the alias of Dan Pruitt. Stimac had Hattaway's Panama Beach phone number in his office safe. On January 12, Miller fled Asheville, forfeiting the bond he had posted, and failed to appear in court that day. On January 10, Toni Somers left Chicago, returning to her mother's house in Iowa. She had telephoned her mother and told her that she was contemplating suicide. After she arrived home, Somers told her mother she might be arrested if she returned to Chicago. She also confided in her 15-year-old sister that she was afraid that something might happen to her similar to what had happened to "Burrito" because, as a biker's old lady, she knew too much.

From January 15 through January 18 controversy surrounding the Ore Knob Mine shaft and whether to enter it was in all of the newspapers. On January 18, the press announced that a man had volunteered to enter the mine as soon as all the legal waivers had been signed. On that date, telephone records in Chicago show four phone calls between Garth Bluxon and the Hinsdale house, including a 19-minute call to a pay phone near Stimac's house. On January 19, there was another call between Bluxon and Stimac's house. On January 21, it was publicized that the shaft would be entered on Monday, January 25. On that date there was an 11-minute call between Stimac's house and the Flats. The next day Callahan was taken from the Plainfield Road house to the Skyline Motel in Lyons, where she was kept until January 25, 1982.

On Monday, January 25, at approximately 3:30 P.M. Chicago time, the body of Lonnie Marshall Gamboa was retrieved from the 250 foot deep mine shaft. Two hours later, Forester's body was brought to the surface. At approximately 11:00 A.M. that same day, Callahan was taken by Curran to Nick's Bar in Lyons. Before going to the bar, Curran drove around for two hours. At about 1:00 P.M., they entered the bar. Stimac and Burroughs found them there. While there, they made several calls from a pay phone. At about 5:00 P.M., Curran took her to the Brookfield Motel. He gave her $15 and told her she could leave the room to go to the restaurant next door for food. He told her he would be gone to Milwaukee on business that night.

After Curran left, Callahan called her mother in North Carolina. Her mother told her about the recovery of the bodies from the mine shaft. After talking to her mother, Callahan called the FBI.[10]

The Pieces of the Puzzle

The kidnapping and transporting of Betty Callahan to Chicago where she was forced into prostitution and held prisoner by members of the Chicago Outlaw Motorcycle Club occurred after the murder of Tom Forester. Two weeks later, Lonnie Gamboa was murdered at the same place. Joseph Vines had revealed this murder to Agent Tommy Chapman and Sheriff Waddell, which led to the search of the mine shaft.

On January 25, 1982, both events were revealed. The bodies of Forester and Gamboa were recovered, and Betty Callahan escaped her captors and phoned her mother.[11]

On May 27, 1982, a federal grand jury in Chicago, Illinois, indicted Hathaway, Miller, and four other men on charges of kidnapping Callahan and transporting her to Chicago for purposes of prostitution. Although Bare was not indicted, he was named as a co-defendant in papers filed in the Chicago case. Federal officials said that arrest warrants had been drawn for Bare.

Thomas Stimac, identified as vice-president of the Outlaw Motorcycle Club, and Toni Somers, both from Chicago suburbs of Hinsdale, Illinois, were held with bonds set at $1,000,000 for each. Marty Curran, also of Hinsdale, was held under a $500,000 bond. Robert George Burroughs, named as the president of the Outlaw Motorcycle Club of the Montreal, Canada, chapter, was being sought in the case. At a hearing May 10, 1982, federal prosecutors testified the motorcycle club was planning to take over several prostitution rings in Chicago. Events in the case were traced back to a gang shootout near Asheville, NC, on November 7, 1981, involving Gamboa, Hattaway, and Miller. The drugs and weapons seized in the shootout led to an investigation of drug operations in Florida, Tennessee, Virginia, and North Carolina.[12]

A complaint filed in the U.S. District Court for southern Illinois outlines the kidnapping which occurred more than a month after the shootout. It was based primarily on Callahan's account. The complaint alleged that Miller and Hattaway kidnapped Forester and Callahan from Asheville's In Town Motel and took them to Bare's residence in Laurel Springs on December 12, 1981.[13]

Forester, according to investigators, a small-time drug dealer for the Outlaws, owed Miller and Hattaway $1,500 for drug buys at a daily interest of $800. Early on December 13, 1981, Bare, Hattaway, and Miller took Forester and Callahan to the abandoned Ore Knob Copper Mine near Bare's residence. Miller told Callahan she could go with Forester and take her chances at living or dying, or go to Chicago with them and work as a prostitute. Callahan chose to go to Chicago. Callahan was then taken to Michigan City, Indiana, by Curran. She was held there until December 24, 1981. The complaint says that on that day, according to investigators in North Carolina, Gamboa was pushed into the Ore Knob Mine. Forester was next seen when his body was taken from the mine January 25, 1982.[14]

According to documents filed in that case, Gamboa met Joseph Vines (the state's principle witness in the Gamboa murder), Hattaway, and Miller on December 23 at Sarge's Bar in Asheville, North Carolina. Vines was to talk to Miller about the shootout November 7, 1981, near Asheville. However, Gamboa also owed money to Hattaway and Miller. Vines testified at the hearing in Paul Bare's case that he was a federal informant trying to investigate the Outlaws' drug operation. From December 25, 1981, to January 25, 1982, Callahan was held at various places in Illinois and Indiana, according to the federal complaint.[15]

On January 5, 1982, Miller was arrested and charged with kidnapping Forester and Callahan. He was released on a 10,000 dollar bond. Vines was with Miller when he was arrested.[16]

By January 6, 1982, the mine was blocked off and guarded by Ashe County authorities. Bare was charged January 8 with kidnapping Gamboa. Vines denied any part in the kidnapping of Forester and Callahan, but a source they did not identify suggested that Forester's body might also be in the mine shaft.

There were rumors that the case might be tied to other investigations. The U.S. Attorney for the Western District of North Carolina stated that his office had been involved in other matters incidental to the investigation.[17]

9

The Murder Trial Begins

The weather was warm and sunny, and spring was arriving in the small town of Jefferson in the northwest mountains of North Carolina when the murder trial of Paul Wilson Bare began on June 2. The old-fashioned courthouse was packed, and a crowd was waiting outside for the trial to start. Paul Bare's neighbors were among the group that parted as the lawyers arrived.[1] John Siskind was well known locally, but the other lawyer, the renowned Edwin Marger from Atlanta, had been hired by the Bare family. He made quite a splash with his linen suit, red suspenders, and white hat when he flew in to the Ashe County Airport on his private plane. He had defended Frank Bennet, brother-in-law of Jean Claude "Baby Doc" Duvalier, dictator of Haiti, and several other big names known to be involved in the drug scene.[2]

According to Captain Gene Goss, Marger had asked if "they" had any telephones in the area. People were highly insulted by Marger's condescending demeanor.[3]

Inside the courthouse, the crowd grew quiet as Judge Donald L. Smith was seated and the trial began. The prosecution presented the list of exhibits.

Thomas Chapman, ATF agent, was the first witness called to the stand at Bare's trial. District Attorney Michael Ashburn asked him to state his name and occupation. Chapman identified himself as a special agent with the Alcohol, Tobacco, and Firearms Division of the U.S. Treasury Department.

When the D. A. then asked Mr. Chapman how long he had known Mr. Vines. Chapman said, "I have known Mr. Vines since May 26, 1981, when he came to the ATF office in Asheville to pick up a reward check that had been mailed to him there. I had a short conversation with Vines and told him if he was back in Asheville to get in touch."

Next the district attorney asked Chapman when he heard from Vines again. Chapman hesitated, then replied, "I received a call from Vines early on the morning of January 5, 1982." The district attorney followed by asking Chapman if he became involved in a homicide case in Ashe County due to this conversation. Chapman replied, "Yes, I did."

Exhibits for Paul Wilson Bare Trial for the Kidnapping and Murder of Lonnie Marshall Gamboa

List of Prosecution's Exhibits

1. Chapman's Diagram of Ashe County
2. Bueker's Diagram of Bare's Residence
3. 3" × 3" Polaroid Photos of Lonnie Gambia
4. Lonnie Gamboa's 357 Magnum
5. Lonnie Gamboa's clothing
6. Pants
7. 1 Boot
8. Shirt
9. Blindfold
10. Box of Plastic Trash Bags
11. Wallet
12. 24 8" × 10" Color Photos
13. Audio-taped Conversation between Vines and Bare
25. Plastic Bag — Tape from Gamboa's Hands
26. Color Photos of Mine Shaft Scene
27. Black and White Aerial Photos
38. 8" × 10" Color Photos
39. 357 Magnum Pistol
42. 6 Shells
49. Slide Photo of Cut Hair
61. Deputy Goss' Drawing of Mine Shaft

List of Defendant's Exhibits

1. Vines' Statement Prepared by Chapman
2. Death Certificate of Lonnie Gamboa
3. Polaroid Photos of 3 Children
4. Envelope mailed from Asheville Surgical Associates, P.A. to Joe Koert
5. Tree Limb approximately 6 feet long
6. Videotape of Mine Shaft
7. Pathology Report on Lonnie Gamboa Autopsy
8. Walking Stick with Dagger Handle
9. Straight Razor
10. Chick
11. Rolling Papers — Numerous Packs
12. Letter from V.A. Hospital — Dr. Louge "To Whom It May Concern"
13. Sketches of Bare Property
14. "Close-up" Sketches of Trailor and Exhibit 13
15. Sketches of Bare Property
17. Transcript of Buncombe County Trial
18. FBI Memo
19. 8" × 10" Color Slides of Blue Trailer Entrance and Exit on Bare Property
27. 8" × 10" Color Photos

When the district attorney asked Chapman if he had visited various sites in Ashe County, Chapman replied that he had visited the Ore Knob Mine several times. He also stated that he had visited the Paul W. Bare residence.

Ashburn asked Chapman to point out Paul Bare in the courtroom. He asked Chapman how long he had known Paul Bare. Chapman replied that he first became acquainted with Paul Bare in 1967 or 1968 when he was conducting an ATF investigation.

Ashburn then asked Chapman what other sites he had visited. Chapman cited Hawkins' store and all the area around the mine, including the Peak Creek Road from its beginning on Highway 88 to its end on the Blue Ridge Parkway. He also mentioned the area of the Parkway and the Highway 18 intersection near Myers Motel.

Ashburn then asked Chapman, "Did you in course of the investigation see at any time any houses with motorcycles at them?"

Chapman replied, "Yes sir. On the Peak Creek Road — a house that was first pointed out to me by Mr. Vines. I was familiar with the house four or five years ago. It was referred to as the house where the motorcycle people lived. There was a reference made by Mr. Vines that this was the house pointed out to him by Alan Ray Hattaway as being the house where his wife or old lady resided with some motorcycle people."

Ashburn then asked, "Have you as a result of your investigation prepared a diagram of the sites and the road system?"

Chapman replied, "Yes, I have. Chapman pointed to a stack of papers on the table in front of the district attorney.

Judge Smith asked, "Do you need the board now?"

Ashburn replied, "Yes sir." The judge directed Sheriff Waddell to bring the board in and set it up. He was directed to place it for the convenience of the jury.

Marger, attorney for the defense, rose hastily and asked, "Your Honor, why is the board being set up now?" Judge Smith explained that the evidence was not being accepted at this time, but just being marked as evidence.

The judge then turned to Chapman and asked him to identify and explain the map on the board. Chapman pointed out the road along the Parkway, Hiram Bare's house, and the home of Paul Bare.

"Who is Hiram Bare?" asked the judge. Chapman identified him as Paul Bare's father. Chapman also pointed out the Hawkins' Store and the mine shaft from which the bodies were retrieved.

The district attorney then asked to present the map as evidence. Marger objected. The objection was denied by the judge.

Chapman was asked to approach the blackboard to illustrate his testimony on the diagram and explain what it represented. As Chapman pointed out the routes and homes, Ashburn asked him if there were any restaurants on the diagram. Chapman pointed to the Stop and Shop, and identified it as a complex that contained several types of businesses in it, including a small restaurant.

The district attorney then asked Chapman if the diagram also contained a mine area. Chapman pointed to the mine shafts represented on the diagram. He pointed to one shaft near a gate and identified it as the one from which the bodies of Lonnie Gamboa and Thomas Forester were removed.

The district attorney continued by asking the approximate distance between Bare's house and the mine. Chapman estimated the distance to be about four miles, using the highway map. Marger objected to this line of questioning, and the judge allowed (sustained) the objection. Marger continued to object and wanted the entire statement struck from the record about the distance that was taken from the state highway map, saying this was hearsay evidence. The judge denied this motion because it was not made at the proper time.

The district attorney rephrased and asked what the distance was between the mine and Bare's house. Chapman estimated it to be about three and three-quarter miles. Marger, again, objected, and the judge overruled.

The district attorney asked Chapman what the distance was between Bare's house and the house with the motorcycles. Marger objected, and the judge sustained. Chapman answered anyway, indicating that it was about a mile. The judge sustained again, and Marger moved to strike it from the record, which the judge allowed.

Turning to Chapman, the D.A. said, "I will point out an object on your diagram you have drawn and ask you what it is." Ashburn pointed.

Chapman replied, "That's a white house, that's a white house, that's a motorcycle house, where the motorcycle...." Marger objected, and the judge overruled.

"The house where I observed the motorcycles on the porch and several different cars," continued Chapman. When Ashburn asked him what the distance between that house and Bare's house was, Chapman told him it was approximately one mile.

The district attorney concluded, "That's all the questions at this time. He may be called back later."[4]

Marger's Cross-Examination of Chapman

The judge asked Marger if he wished to cross-examine Chapman, he nodded and asked permission to proceed. Marger began his cross-examination by asking, "You say you first met Vines in May 1981?"

"No sir," answered Chapman. "I met him somewhere around '79 or '80. I was transferred to Asheville, North Carolina, in August '79. We met after that." Marger asked him if he knew Vines by any other names, and Chapman replied that he had also known him as Mr. Vines, Satan, and Kojak."

Marger repeated, "Satan and Kojak?" to which Chapman replied that he had made an error and only learned after the investigation began that Vines also used the name of Kojak.

Marger asked, "Why, if you know, did he use the name Kojak?"

Chapman replied, "He didn't have any hair on his head."

"Shaven off?" questioned Marger.

"He didn't have any hair. I don't know how he got it off," replied Chapman.

"In any event, he didn't look then as he looks now?" asked Marger. Chapman agreed that he did not.

When questioned why Vines was called Satan, Chapman replied, "I don't know." Marger persisted by asking if that name was given to him or selected by him.

"I don't know," Chapman replied again.

Marger continued, "During the period after July of 1981, you visited with Vines several times at the house of a Mr. West, did you not?" Chapman stated that he was there on two occasions.

Marger continued by asking Chapman if Kojak was working for him during that time. Chapman stated that he was not.

Marger asked, "Was he working for any other agency that you know of in the U.S. government?"

"No sir. Can I get the dates?" responded Chapman, and Marger replied that the dates were from July 1, 1981, to the present.

Marger turned to the judge and asked, "May I approach the bench while he is thinking?" The judge asked Chapman if he was ready to answer the question, and Chapman responded immediately that the date he remembered contacting Vines at the residence of Mr. West was June 15, 1981, because he had made a note of that date.

The judge restated Marger's question. "Since that date, has he [Vines] been employed with any government agency that you are aware of or have any knowledge of?" Chapman replied that Vines had not been employed by the government at that time.

Marger asked, "During that time have you, as an agent of the U.S. government, paid Vines any money?"

"Yes," Chapman stated.

Marger inquired, "And that is approximately three thousand, six hundred, five dollars and ninety-six cents, sir?" Chapman stated that the amount was correct.

Marger tried again, "He wasn't working for you at the time you paid him the monies?" Again, Chapman stated that Mr. Vines had never worked for him.

"But the government paid that [amount], plus whatever the county and city paid him?" inquired Marger.

Chapman then replied that the federal government had paid for immediate relocation for Vines because of his testimony in this case and other cases [that] made it necessary to move him to an area where the bad guys couldn't find him.

Marger stated, "I see, so he's the good guy."

The D.A. objected and the judge overruled, adding, "Your witness made the characterization."

"Then Vines is a good guy, is he not?" continued Marger.

"Yes, sir," replied Chapman.

Marger then changed directions by stating, "Let's leave Vines for a moment and go to Mr. Bare. How long have you known Mr. Bare?" Chapman said he had known Bare since '67 or '68.

Then Marger asked, "And what's the relationship that you had with Mr. Bare?"

"Up until his arrest, it had always been fairly good. It was real good to start with, but deteriorated as we progressed," responded Chapman.

"Why did it deteriorate?" asked Marger.

"Because he told me lies," responded Chapman.

"Tells a lot of stories," rephrased Marger.

"Yes sir. He ought to be writing comic books," replied Chapman. Marger's rejoinder was, "And you were reading the comic books he was writing, weren't you, Mr. Chapman?"

The D.A. objected. The judge sustained.

"Now I am going to have to instruct the witness. If you will just answer the questions and stop the characterization, it would help us to a great extent," said the Judge Smith. Chapman agreed to do so.

Marger continued, "Mr. Chapman, he told you a lot of stories that you followed through on, did you not, from '67 right on up to now?"

Chapman corrected him, "No sir. There was a point about 1972 when I had no relationship with Mr. Bare."

Marger continued, "You wanted Bare to be an informant, didn't you?" Chapman corrected him, stating that Bare had volunteered to be an informant.

Marger continued the line of questioning by asking if Bare ever informed on anyone, and Chapman said Bare told them a lot of things about people, but they never turned out to be correct.

Marger rephrased, "He told you about places you could find crimes that were being committed?" Chapman responded that Bare had.

Marger asked, "But you never found the crimes being committed as he indicated they were?" Chapman agreed.

"Would it be true to say, Mr. Chapman, that Mr. Bare, from the period of '67 through '72 at least or probably later, led you on a lot of wild goose chases?" Chapman responded that this was true.

Marger continued, "He told you at one time, for example, about this imaginary still in the mountains and you trekked over miles...."

District Attorney Ashburn objected, and the judge overruled.

Marger continued, "You trekked over miles of mountains and took other personnel and went to this still. When you got there, there was nothing but a hole in the mountain. Is that true?" Chapman said that they didn't find anything described by Mr. Bare.

Marger asked Chapman, "Did you put a lot of time in on it?" Chapman replied that they did put a lot of time into the search.

Marger then asked Chapman if he continued going to Mr. Bare's premises during this time. Chapman replied that he had never gone to Mr. Bare's premises until Bare moved to Ashe County sometime after 1972.

"You just said that you never went near him after '72, did you not?" inquired Marger. Chapman stated that he went to Bare's premises in 1976 when they executed a warrant and seized some property.

"I see, so in '76 you issued a warrant against Mr. Bare," mused Marger. Chapman replied, "No sir, I did not."

Marger then asked if he was present when the warrant was served, and Chapman responded that he was present. When Chapman was asked if Bare was arrested as a result of the search, he said that Bare had not been arrested. When asked if he had spent any time at Bare's house, he explained that he had spent the night.

Marger then asked if he had told Bare that he was going to arrest him. Chapman explained to Marger that they told Bare the information they had found during the search had been referred to the U.S. District Attorney for the appropriate dispensation. When Marger again asked Chapman how many hours were spent at Bare's premises that night, Chapman explained that they had seized some dynamite and had to wait for a qualified person to come to the scene and destroy it because they were not qualified to remove it from its location.

"Mr. Chapman, that's not all you were doing there is it — waiting for someone to remove the dynamite?" asked Marger.

Chapman replied, "Once we found the dynamite we could have gone in a couple of hours, but for that...." (He was interrupted by Marger.)

Marger stated, "During the period of time spent there, you saw things peculiar in your eyes, were they not?" Chapman replied affirmatively. He explained that Mr. Bare was saving a lady who was diabetic from probably going into a coma.

Marger asked, "Did you see that?" The D.A. objected, and the court (judge) overruled.

Marger continued, "Did you see that?" Chapman replied that Mr. Bare had explained that the woman was a diabetic.

"Now, other than the fact that all these years of being interested in Mr. Bare, and nothing ever came of it, would it be true to say, sir, that you have always felt that Mr. Bare is a bad guy?"

Chapman replied, "Not always, but after his conviction of shooting a man's face off in Wilkesboro, then he became a felon. He is also a possessor of firearms. I am sworn to enforce the federal firearms law. We did what the taxpayers paid us to do. We pursued Mr. Bare and did prepare a case in 1976 with reference to his possession of firearms, being a convicted felon, and also his possession of explosives."

Marger asked, "Now that was when Bare shot Mr. Johnson, was it not?"
Chapman replied, "Gilbert Johnson."

Marger continued, "He did it because Mr. Johnson had run off with his wife, is that correct?" Chapman replied that he did not know because he was not present.

Marger continued, "Did that at high noon?"

Chapman responded, "I don't know, sir."

Marger persisted, "Did it in the open?" Again Chapman responded that he did not know.

Marger pressed Chapman with another statement, "But, at that time, you decided he must be a bad guy because of the fact he shot a man that ran off with his wife."

Again Chapman stated, "No sir. Once he was convicted and then out of prison, we received information about his actions which related to violations of the law that I am sworn to uphold."

Marger asked, "Did any of the things you investigated lead to a conviction of Bare?" Chapman said that they had not.

Marger continued, "Now that period of time, Mr. Chapman, when you say you really had nothing more to do with Mr. Bare after 1972, you must have meant you had nothing to do with him after '76. Is that what you're telling the jury?"

Chapman answered, "No sir. After '72, I had no relationship as an officer-informant with Mr. Bare."

"So he hadn't panned out as an informant, and you hadn't gotten a conviction as far as anything you had done with Mr. Bare," commented Marger.

The D.A. objected.

"I'll strike it," said Marger.

"All right," replied the judge.

The cross-examination continued. "Now, when is the first time Mr. Satan Jo-Jo Vines told you about Paul Bare?"

"About 10:15 A.M. on January 5, 1982," Chapman replied.

Marger continued, "Had you spoken to him on the phone prior to that time?"

Chapman answered, "Yes sir, I received a telephone call at my residence early on the morning of January 5, requesting that I meet him and have a conversation with him. He told me he had something he didn't want to discuss on the phone, and, subsequently, we set up a meeting for that morning."

Marger then asked, "Now were you accompanied to that meeting by any other officer — state, federal or local?" Chapman replied that Officer Stan Keel of the FBI Asheville office and Officer Bob Kiser of the SBI accompanied him to meet Vines.

"Now where was this meeting?" Marger continued.

Chapman replied, "We first met with Vines as he walked along the road in Asheville. Then we went to a parking lot that is adjacent to, and a part of, the Blue Ridge Parkway system. In this parking lot, we met and discussed the events that led to this trial."

Marger continued, "Now, that was the first time Mr., let's say Kojak, met with you. Was that the first time, sir, January 5, 1982?"

Chapman then said, "I'm confused here."

Marger said, "So let's start again. I understood that your testimony was, that the first time that Kojak met with you in regard to the murder of Lonnie Gamboa was on the fifth day of January, 1982."

Chapman then answered, "Yes, sir that's correct."

Marger continued, "The murder or murders supposedly occurred on that date, sir?"

"On December 13 or 14, or December 23 or 24," replied Chapman.

"Oh, you have two murders that you're talking about, sir. Is this case involving another murder?" asked Marger.

Chapman replied, "No sir, it was the two dead people in the mine shaft." Marger continued, "When did you find the two dead people in the mine shaft?"

Chapman replied, "January 25, 1982, when the bodies were recovered."

"But on January 5, Mr. Kojak met with you and told you that somebody or people had been murdered. How many people did he tell you had been murdered?" questioned Marger. "He told me..." began Chapman. The district attorney objected.

"Objection sustained at this time," said Judge Smith.

Marger rephrased, "Did he tell you that...."

"Objection as to what he told you," said the district attorney. The court sustained. Marger tried again, "Well, Officer, based on what he told you, did you take any action?"

"Yes sir, I did," replied Chapman.

Marger continued, "Because of his testimony, did you pursue a course of conduct that resulted from whatever he told you?"

Chapman replied, "I don't understand what you mean by 'conduct.'" Marger rephrased, "Did you do anything because of what he told you?" Chapman answered, "Yes sir, I got in touch with Sheriff Waddell."

Marger then stated, "I'd like to request the court's advice as to whether I may go to the testimony that caused him to pursue a certain conduct."

Judge Smith replied, "I'll just have to rule or object as we proceed. I don't know what will be objected to and what won't."

"Had Mr. Vines ever told you before January 5, sir, anything about this particular matter?" asked Marger.

Chapman answered, "No, sir, he had not."

Marger continued, "Is there any federal officer that has advised you at this time that he, Vines—Kojak, went to him and told him about this situation?"

The district attorney objected.

"You mean prior to January 5?" asked the judge.

"Yes, Your Honor," answered Marger. Chapman shook his head no.

"His answer is 'No,'" said Smith.

Marger continued, "So that the first time to your knowledge that Kojak discussed this murder, which I believe took place on December 23, 1981, was some thirteen days later, is that correct, sir?"

Chapman paused, "I'm counting the day. Yes, sir, I was out of pocket from December 23 to the day before New Year's. I went to Georgia to visit my parents."

Marger changed tactics. "Do you usually investigate murder cases or bodies thrown into mines?"

Chapman replied, "No sir, I do not."

Marger continued, "What does the ATF have to do with cases of murders by being thrown into mines?"

Chapman responded, "The involvement is that Mr. Vines came to ATF and told us as an agency. We referred the information and pursuant to request for assistance from Sheriff Waddell, we have helped in this case."

"But from the 23rd day of December, to your knowledge, Kojak was not able to tell any other law enforcement officers other than yourself, of the brutal murder of Lonnie Gamboa, is that correct?" snapped Marger.

Chapman replied, "No, it's not."

Marger next asked, "Now did anything happen on January 4, the date Mr. Kojak-Vines came to you, that you think has any bearing on the fact he came to you on January 5?" The district attorney objected and the court overruled.

"I'm not aware of anything," answered Chapman.

"You're not aware Mr. Miller...."

"Objection," said the district attorney, "he said he wasn't aware of anything."

"I have a right to impeach this witness!" said Marger. The judge overruled.

Marger began again, "I'd like to refresh your memory, Mr. Chapman, if you have forgotten, but...."

The district attorney objected, and the court again overruled.

Marger began again, "But, on January 4, the very day, eight o'clock in the evening before Kojak came to you the next morning, Mr. Gary Miller, who is also accused in this case, but a fugitive, was arrested in Asheville, was he not?"

Chapman answered, "I wasn't there, but I understand that's correct."

"But you don't put any connection between the Mr. Miller, one of the participants supposedly in this case with Kojak, who was arrested the night before Mr. Kojak came forward to you thirteen days after the murder to tell you about something which he felt he was doing for whatever reason he was doing it?" Marger emphasized.

The district attorney objected. The court sustained because of the form of the question. Marger rephrased the question by asking Chapman if he knew that Miller was arrested on the day before Vines contacted him. Chapman stated that he had heard that, but, since he was under oath and he had not seen any court documents pertaining to Miller's arrest, he could not positively say he was aware of it.

When Marger asked Chapman to confirm that this particular case had taken more time since January 5 than any other case he was working on during this period, the district attorney objected, and the court sustained. Marger then rephrased to ask if Chapman had spent a great deal of time on this case. Chapman replied yes, but that it was not the case he had spent the most time on. He then asked Chapman if he made notes on the initial meeting with Kojak on January 5. When Chapman said he had not taken notes on the meeting, Marger asked him if this was his normal method of investigation — to take no notes with regard to something of this nature. The district attorney objected, and the court sustained. Marger continued by asking if anyone else took notes, and Chapman said that he did not know of any notes that were taken during the meeting.

When Marger asked Chapman what Vines told him during the meeting, the district attorney objected, and the court sustained. Marger then asked Chapman if he took any action based on what Vines told him.

Chapman replied, "Yes, I did. The information was first referred to the Detectives Division of the Asheville Police Department. It was about thirty minutes later that the information was referred to Sheriff Thomas Morrisey of the Buncombe County Sheriff's Department in Asheville, NC. About 7:30 to 8:00 A.M. on that date, I called Sheriff Richard Waddell of Ashe County, NC, and told him I had to meet him on the following day with reference to the mine shaft."

Marger asked Chapman if Kojak had described in detail all the things that happened on December 23 when he met with him on January 5. Chapman said that it was not in as much detail as he did in a later statement. Marger then asked if he had described Paul Bare's residence.

Chapman replied, "Yes sir, he described completely the Paul Bare residence, mobile home, house, and junk yard."

When Marger asked the same question in a slightly different way, Chapman reiterated, "I knew that the junk yard, residence, and house that he referred to as being the residence, junk yard, and mobile home of Papa Bare was in fact Paul Wilson Bare's."

Marger continued, "Did you ever hear Paul Bare called Papa Bare before this case?" Chapman stated that he had not heard that before.

Marger persisted, "You immediately knew, upon hearing the description of the property discussed with Mr. Vines, that this must be the Paul Bare residence, didn't you?"

Chapman replied, "No sir, I did not."

Marger pushed, "He didn't tell you it was Paul Bare's residence?" Chapman stated, "No, sir, he did not."

When Marger asked, "He hadn't met Mr. Paul Bare?" Chapman replied, "He told me he met a person known to him as Papa Bare, and he also described two vehicles, one of which I saw parked outside this courtroom on July of 1981 when the Higgins trial was being tried here. He described this as being a car that was operated by Papa Bare's girlfriend. I asked him to stop outside and see if he could find a car near our location that was the same color. He stepped outside of the car owned by the State of NC and said the car was the same color as the car we were seated in."

Marger continued, "Are you indicating to this jury my client also committed this other murder you're talking about or had anything to do with it?"

The D.A. objected, and the court sustained.

Marger apologized, "I'm sorry, your Honor, I thought he mentioned a murder."

"He mentioned a trial, as I understood it," said Judge Smith.

Marger proceeded, "Now, Mr. Chapman, would it be true to say that on January 5 that your interest was not only from the point of view of just another police officer, but that you finally had Mr. Bare?"

Chapman replied, "No sir."

Continuing the cross-examination, Marger said, "Now I believe you have already testified that at no time during this entire period has Mr. Bare been employed by you or to your knowledge any other state, federal, city or county agency."

Chapman questioned, "I understood you to say Mr. Bare."

Marger corrected himself, "I'm sorry, I meant Mr. Kojak — Mr. Vines." Chapman nodded affirmatively. Marger asked if this covered the time from June 1 of '81 until this time.

Chapman corrected Marger saying, "No sir, since he, at a point somewhere in May, to my knowledge, was in Asheville, NC. At some time during this period of time since February '81, he has been in the temporary Witness Protection Program detail, and I am the supervisor of that detail."

Marger restated, "So from February of '81, he's been under the Federal Witness Protection Program?"

Chapman corrected Marger, "No sir, under the temporary Federal Witness Protection Program."

Marger questioned, "February 1981?," Chapman replied, "No sir, February 1982. I think I made an error there."

Marger summarized, "Let me check again to make sure we haven't missed any dates. From June 1981 until you took him under your wing, do you know of any employment he has had for anybody?" Chapman said that Vines had worked for the FBI at one time, beginning June, 15, 1981.

Marger asked "Start from June '81, then sir, from that date forward did he work for the FBI?"

Chapman replied, "I don't know. I was told he did perform some work for them by Agent Turner and by Mr. Vines himself."

Marger again stated, "After June 15, 1981?"

Chapman replied, "Yes sir."

When Marger asked about July 1981 and if Vines was employed by the FBI or other agencies, Chapman stated that he was not employed by the ATF, and that he did not know about the other agencies.

The judge called a recess and asked everyone to return in 20 minutes.

When court reconvened, Chapman was shown a statement taken from Vines in Waddell's office relating to Vines' employment during the period of July '81 through January '82 and his means of living. Chapman confirmed it as the statement taken while he was at Waddell's office.

Marger stated, "You have informed the court that another report was made by you to your supervisor, and you have provided the original of that report to be copied, is that correct?" Chapman verified that it was correct. Marger asked him when the report was dated, and Chapman said, "I don't know. It would be about a month later."

Marger then stated, "So Vines was not employed from November 7, 1981, to January 5, 1982," and Chapman replied, "Correct." Marger followed with another question, "So at the time Kojak pushed Gamboa into the mine, he was certainly not an employee of the government."

The district attorney objected, and the court sustained, adding, "It's repetition."

"No more questions," said Marger.

Under re-examination, the district attorney brought out the fact that $3605.96 was paid Vines from February '82 through June '82.

The judge had a few questions also. He asked Chapman, "In your testimony, you have referred to being out of pocket between December 23 and some later date," said the Court.

"Yes, sir, that's correct," stated Chapman.

He asked Chapman to explain "out of pocket"? Chapman replied, "Well, I went to Georgia without telling anyone where I was going except the people in the office that would have regular knowledge that we went home for the holidays."

The judge asked, "Well, 'out of pocket,' does that mean out of the office or what?"

Chapman replied, "Yes, sir, that's correct. I wasn't referring any official duties."

The judge asked for the specific dates, and Chapman answered, "December 23 through December 31, 1981."

Marger, during cross-examination, called Agent Ernest Bueker, SBI Agent, who showed diagrams of the Bare and mine premises which were, according to Bueker, clear to scale. He explained in detail all the things shown on the diagram. Marger stated that he had no more questions for Bueker, but that he might recall the witness.

Judge Smith called a recess.[5]

10

Sharon Gamboa's Testimony

Security was tight at the old courthouse. Some of the people didn't leave their seats for fear of not getting back into the courthouse. The scenery outside was entirely different from that inside the old courthouse. Everyone was anxious to get back to the trial, and the few remaining seats filled quickly.[1]

After the recess, Sharon Gamboa was the next witness called by District Attorney Michael Ashburn. She and Gamboa had been married six years and had two infant children. She was given a photo and identified it as her husband, Lonnie Gamboa, from a picture made March 1981.

"Do you know individuals named Alan Hattaway and Gary Miller?" asked the district attorney.

She replied, "I knew a Mr. Hattaway." Ashburn then asked her to describe Hattaway.

She answered, "Large — six-two, large frame, red hair, red beard." Ashburn then asked her when she last saw this man, and she replied, "May '81." Ashburn asked her how many times she had seen Hattaway.

She replied, "Not for several months after I first met him. I'd say offhand, about two months."

Ashburn then asked her, "Do you know an individual named Kojak or Satan or Joseph Vines?"

"Yes sir. I knew him by Kojak."

Ashburn continued, "Did you know him by that name on December 23, 1981?" She stated that she did.

Ashburn asked her where she first saw him, and she replied, "At my home."

Ashburn then asked her what he looked like. She described Kojak as "Large, bald, had a large coat on."

Ashburn asked her when that was, and she replied, "December 21, 1981." Ashburn continued the questioning, "Who was present besides you and your children?"

She replied, "He was with someone, Alan Hattaway, I knew as Red."

The district attorney then asked, "Where was your husband?"

She answered, "He was there."

He continued, "What transpired there?"

She answered, "They ate dinner with us."

The district attorney asked her if she knew Gary Miller, and she replied, "Yes sir." Ashburn then asked how long she had known Miller, and she stated that she had known him since February 1, 1981.

Sharon Gamboa testified as to what time they arrived and what time they left. She also testified that Lonnie Gamboa left with them, came back, and left again.

"Came back at what time?" asked Ashburn.

She replied, "About eleven o'clock, they came back about eleven o'clock."

Ashburn asked her, "Was that the first time you saw Vines?"

She replied, "Yes. They came back the next morning. They were going to Georgia to get some things."

When Ashburn asked her who went, she replied, "My husband, Kojak, and Red left about nine o'clock. They came back and dropped Lonnie off about five o'clock that evening."

Ashburn continued, "Did you see Red or Vines after that date — December 22?"

She replied, "Vines came back the next morning about ten o'clock."

When asked to describe that morning, Sharon said, "My husband left out the front door. Somebody was waiting outside. After he left, I looked out the window, and Kojak was in the car with him, in an old blue car."

When questioned further, she said, "Lonnie had left the house about nine o'clock that morning to get a transcript of a trial." She also identified her husband's gun and clothing.

When asked to describe what she did after the phone call from her husband asking her to deliver the marijuana, Sharon Gamboa said, "I got in my car and went to West Asheville, met a boy at McDonald's, followed him back to his car, and he put two white bags in the back of my car."

Ashburn then asked, "Where did you go?"

In a low voice she replied, "I went to the Country Food Store in West Asheville where I was to go in the store while someone took out what...." Ashburn instructed her, "Would you use the microphone?

She continued, "Then I went to the Country Food Store to meet a brown Granada where they took the two white bags out of my car."

"What were your instructions as to what to do upon your arrival?"

"To go into the store, take my time about coming out, and leave the car unlocked."

"Did you see anyone when you arrived at the Country Food Store?"

"I just looked at the people in the car. I didn't notice anyone else."

"What is this Country Food Store near?"

"The Holiday Inn–West," she replied.

"Do you know what was in the bags?" inquired the district attorney.

"No sir," she answered.

"Did Lonnie tell you what was in the bags on the telephone?" asked Ashburn.

"No," she replied.

"Did he tell you what the purpose was in picking them up?" asked the district attorney.

Sharon said, "No. He said everything would be over with. After I left the store and went back to my car, the bags were gone. I got into my car and went home."

"Did you receive any further conversation from your husband after that?" inquired Ashburn.

"No," she answered.

"Did you make any type of report to the police department?" queried Ashburn, and she replied that she had not called the police.

"Did you anytime after contact the Asheville Police Department?" inquired the district attorney.

"No," she answered.

"Did you later talk to an officer named Ross Robinson?" asked Ashburn.

"Yes. I got in touch with him through my attorney," she replied. "Did you talk to him and relate what had occurred?" asked Ashburn.

"Yes," answered Sharon Gamboa.

Ashburn asked her if she knew when this was, and she replied, "Not offhand."

Ashburn tried again. "Do you recall approximately how many days after the 23rd?"

She replied, "About a week and a half. I had called my attorney the following day when my husband was missing."

"Did you receive a call from Mr. Vines after that?" asked Ashburn.

"The 29th, he called to ask for Papa Bare," she replied.

"What did you respond?" asked Ashburn.

She replied, "I recognized his voice and asked him where Lonnie was. He told me he had dropped him off at a river-front bar, and a girl in a blue Honda picked him up."

"Any other conversation?" queried Ashburn.

She related, "Just that I was going to have an investigation."

"That's all for now. You may examine her. I wish to reserve the right to recall this witness," closed Ashburn.[2]

Marger cross-examined.

"Sharon, you and I have met before, have we not?" asked Marger.

"Yes sir," said Sharon.

"Where was the first time?"

"Where? Denver, Colorado. We met again in Atlanta," volunteered Sharon.

"During that time you related to me many of the things you have related to the jury at this time," stated Marger. She replied that she had.

Marger continued, "When you received the call from Kojak on the 29th, you knew your husband had left your house with him on the 23rd, did you not?"

"Yes," she replied.

Marger then asked, "Had you ever heard before of a Papa Bare?"

"No," replied Sharon.

Marger continued, "Ever heard of Paul Bare?"

"No," she replied.

"You had met Vines before you testified?" stated Marger.

"The 21st,"stated Sharon.

"And you had met Hattaway?" asked Marger.

"Yes," she stated.

"And you met Miller before, had you not?" continued Marger.

"Yes," she stated.

"When you testified that Lonnie told you everything would be over with, what did you believe he meant?" asked Marger.

"Everything would be all right, that he would get back in touch with me," she answered.

"Actually, he was having some problems with some of these people, was he not?" asked Marger.

"Yes sir," she stated.

The district attorney objected and the court sustained.

"As to Mr. Hattaway?" restated Marger.

"I'm not sure," she said.

"As to Mr. Miller?" queried Marger.

"Yes," she stated.

"As a matter of fact, one of the problems he was having was a shootout on November 7 in which both your husband and Mr. Miller and others were involved, is that correct?" asked Marger.

"Yes," Sharon replied.

"Mr. Miller was claiming that your husband owed him a large sum of money," stated Marger.

"Yes," she stated.

"As a matter of fact, about the 21st, the day you first met Mr. Vines, your husband agreed to pay some things of value to get out of the trouble he was in with Mr. Miller, is that not correct?" asked Marger.

"Yes sir," she stated.

"And one of the reasons that Mr. Vines went to Atlanta with your husband was to extract a skull and crossbones and a turquoise ring from your husband, who had it in safe-keeping with someone else, is that not correct?" asked Marger.

"Yes, that's correct," stated Sharon.

"And you knew Mr. Vines went to Atlanta with them for that purpose?" asked Marger.

"Yes," she stated.

"Now your husband agreed to pay them other things of value?" asked Marger.

The district attorney objected.

"To Mr. Miller, others things of value the 23rd, was he not?" continued Marger.

"Yes," stated Sharon.

"As a matter of fact, he agreed to give them the title to the property he owned," asked Marger.

"Yes sir," she stated.

"He agreed to give them his van, is that correct?" asked Marger.

"I understood it was his Jeep," replied Sharon Gamboa.

"Now, when he went to see Mr. Smith that morning, he went there for the purpose of having Mr. Smith prepare some deeds, did he not?" asked Marger.

"Yes," stated Sharon.

"But he never signed those deeds, did he?" asked Marger.

"No." stated Sharon Gamboa.

"He decided he wasn't going to give that property to them, did he not?" asked Marger.

"Yes," stated Sharon.

"Did you ever hear your husband speaking on the phone to Vines on the morning of the 23rd or any other time?" asked Marger.

"No sir," she stated.

"Now, Sharon, did your husband usually carry a big gun like that?" asked Marger.

"Just on a few occasions," she replied.

"Is it true, Sharon, that at this point in time your husband had decided he wasn't going to stand another bit of the blackmail he was having from Mr. Miller?" stated Marger.

"Objection!" stated the district attorney.

"Was your husband being blackmailed by Mr. Miller?" asked Marger.

"I believe so," stated Sharon Gamboa.

"Did you know when your husband left the house that he did not intend to be blackmailed any more by Mr. Miller?" asked Marger.

"I really don't know," she replied.

"Have you, at any time, heard of Mr. Bare except for the call on the 29th?" queried Marger.

"No sir," she stated.

District Attorney Ashburn objected to the witness telling what she believed. The judge sustained.

"At the time he called you..." began Marger.

"Objection!" said Ashburn.

"Sustained," said the court.

"Did Mr. Vines call you on the 29th?" asked Marger.

"Yes," stated Sharon.

"Did he in fact tell you that your husband had gone off with another girl?" asked Marger.

"Yes," replied Sharon Gamboa.

"Did he tell you that he had pushed your husband into a mine shaft?" asked Marger.

"No," stated Sharon.

"But on the 29th, your last word to Mr. Vines was that you were going to have the disappearance investigated," asked Marger.

"That's correct," stated Sharon.

"Do you know of any reason, Mrs. Gamboa, why Paul Bare would want to kill your husband?" asked Marger.

"I don't know Mr. Bare. I couldn't answer that," stated Sharon.

"Thank you," said Marger.

"Re-cross?" the court asked the district attorney.

"No, sir," answered the district attorney, shuffling the papers in his hand.

"You may step down," the judge told Sharon Gamboa.[3]

The court was dismissed for the weekend.

11

Vines' Testimony

After the weekend recess, the crowded courtroom had a few new faces, but the seats were still full, and the walls were lined with onlookers. Before Vines was called to testify, there were several agents from the FBI, SBI, DEA, sheriff's departments, and other government agencies from Florida, North Carolina, and other states who testified that Vines was a reliable informant, and that they trusted him because he had always been truthful about the cases that he had worked on with them. They also stated that his testimony in court was accurate and useful.[1]

The next witness called to the stand was 32-year-old Joseph Vines. He was born in Baltimore, Maryland, where he lived the first eight years of his life. He testified he never knew his father. His mother had seventeen children and rescued six more off the street. Then they had moved to West Virginia.[2]

When District Attorney Ashburn asked where he moved to next, he told him that they had moved to Florida, which was where he had spent most of his life when he wasn't traveling. When the district attorney asked him what he meant by "traveling," Vines explained that he started traveling in his early years of working as an undercover informant. He stated that he began this work in Florida ten years ago and had worked in different states and areas. He said his first assignment came from Richard Barton, Martin County Sheriff's Department, but nothing came of the information he had turned in.

The district attorney asked, "What caused you to go into this type of work?" Marger objected, but was overruled.

Vines answered, "Before that, I had been in Atlanta, Georgia, and I watched a small boy 12 years old throw his guts up from an overdose of junk." Marger again objected and moved to strike Vines' answer, but was overruled.

When the district attorney asked if there were any other reasons that had led him to becoming an informant, he replied, "Yes sir. I had a good friend of mine, and a guy gave her what she thought was mescaline, but turned out to be STP instead." Marger objected, and the objection was sustained. Vines was instructed to describe only what he had seen himself. Vines

93

continued by saying his friend had gone to see someone and had not been seen for two weeks. She was found walking the streets and ended up in a mental institution.

Marger objected and the court sustained.

Ashburn then asked Vines what other types of work he had done at that time in Florida. Vines replied that he had worked on a flower farm, and did other general work, and that he remained in Martin County where his mother was living at the time.

When asked about the next time he did any undercover work, Vines replied that it was in West Palm Beach about ten years ago where he worked for Paul Sheridan and Jimmy Greer of the Palm Beach Sheriff's Department. Marger asked for reconfirmation of the names and Vines stated them again. When asked what kind of work was done for them, Vines stated that he had set up "buys." When asked to explain to the jury what this meant, he stated that this consisted of setting up drug buys so agents could come in and make an arrest. He said that he set up approximately four to five buys a night for three weeks to a month. When asked, he said was not doing any other type of work at that time, but remained there about one month.

When asked where he went from there, he said Mr. Sheridan referred him to what used to be the Bureau of Narcotics and Dangerous Drugs, known today as the DEA or Drug Enforcement Agency. When asked, Vines said the DEA was a federal agency. After being referred to the DEA, Vines contacted Wayne Henderson and Bob Holliday. Vines stated that he did undercover drug business wherever they sent him for two to three years, and that he did no other work during this time.

Vines was asked if he did any type of intelligence gathering, but Marger objected, stating it was a leading question. The court instructed Ashburn not to lead his own witness, and the trial continued. Ashburn asked if Vines did anything else for the DEA. Vines testified that he picked up information on different motorcycle clubs and different activities, and on people who were "wanted."

The district attorney asked Vines if he had adopted any nicknames at any time; he stated that he had. The first name he used for a while was "Satan."

During Vines' explanations, the judge left the room to take a call. When he returned, the proceedings continued.

When the district attorney asked Vines when he adopted that particular nickname, Vines explained that it was more or less to try and make things easy for him to pave the way with other people. When the district attorney asked Vines what types of people (doctors, lawyers, hippies, bikers) he was referring to, Vines replied, "All different classes." Vines confirmed that he had used many different aliases in his time, and when specifically asked about Asheville, he stated that he was using the nickname "Jo-Jo." He had been using this one approximately one year. He also said he did not give a last name.

When Ashburn asked Vines if he had altered his appearance at any time through the years, he stated that he had many times. When asked how he had done this, he replied, "Sometimes I have had my hair below my back, at my shoulders, had my head shaved, a full beard, a goatee, a mustache, had hair dyed, frizzed...."

Ashburn then asked whether he had gone by any other name in Asheville, and Vines replied, "Yes sir, I acquired a nickname from Sarge, nickname of "Kojak."

Ashburn then asked, "Who is Sarge?"

Vines replied, "I think his name is Paul Harris. He is the owner of a bar, Sarge's Lounge."

Ashburn continued by asking where Vines next worked after his employment by the DEA in West Palm Beach. Vines said he went to Tampa, Florida, but he did not remember the exact year or month.

After working for the DEA, Vines went to Tampa, Florida, but he did not remember the year or month he went there. When he arrived in Tampa, he went to work for the U. S. Customs Agency on a smuggling gang. The operation was smuggling cocaine into the country on banana boats. Vines related that he could not get useful information on the smuggling operation. At that time, he connected with an outlaw motorcycle member and bought some LSD from the man for the DEA. He had been referred to Mr. Lowell Miller with the DEA.

When Ashburn asked him where he went next, Vines said that he returned to Stuart, Florida, where his mother was living, and he did undercover work for Glen Lockwood from the Martin County Sheriff's Department.

Ashburn asked, "What type of work did you do for him [Lockwood]?"

Vines replied, "Buying drugs myself while being wired."

Ashburn continued, "When you say 'wired,' would you explain to the jury what that means?"

Vines replied, "That means I had a bug placed on my ... a little transmitter placed on my body. I'd go make a buy, and they'd be able to hear everything going on. Then I would bring the drugs back out to the agents."

When Ashburn asked Vines how many cases he had completed there, Vines could not recall the exact number, but said he had cleaned up and worked on some burglary cases for Lockwood.

Vines recalled that the first time he worked for Officer Lockwood lasted approximately one to two months. During that time, he worked on flower farms and did odd jobs on the side.

Vines testified that he went to Fayetteville, North Carolina, next. He did not recall exactly when this move occurred, but he estimated it to be before 1978 or 1979. There, he worked for the sheriff's department doing the same type of work — undercover drug buys and taking agents with him to make the buys. He stayed in Fayetteville about a month and a half.

From there, Vines traveled to Cleveland, Ohio, where he worked for Ken Shockley of the ATF (federal bureau of Alcohol, Tobacco, and Firearms). Vines continued his testimony. He said that he was working for the ATF buying black powder, such as M-80 firecrackers, and this led the ATF to the discovery of plastic explosives.

Marger objected and the court overruled.

Vines continued his testimony, "I couldn't give you make-up, all I know is explosives."

Vines remained in Cleveland around two months and then went to a "regular job" in Columbus, Ohio, as a sub-contractor for a painting company for three to five months.

Ashburn asked Vines where he went next, and Vines replied, "To Lenoir, North Carolina.

There he began doing undercover buys again and working undercover on burglary investigations that took him into two or three states. He traveled mostly in North Carolina and Tennessee.

The district attorney then asked Vines, "Do you recall who you worked for at Broyhill Furniture?"

Vines replied, "Yes sir, Charlie Powell."

Ashburn asked him who else he worked for, and Vines replied, "Well, I coordinated through Charlie, everything went through Mr. Powell, and he's also a member of the sheriff's department."

Ashburn continued, "Did you hold any other job while you were there?"

Vines replied, "Yes sir, I did some intelligence work for them inside their factories, held a job at the Broyhill Furniture Factory at the time."

His job was to report on what was being done incorrectly in the company and what could be done better to save money. He was also to set up drug buys and to check for people stealing furniture or buying stolen furniture. Vines worked for Mr. Powell from April 1978 to February 1979.

Vines was then sent by Broyhill to Charlotte to check out a furniture rental company. The rental company had reported a lot of furniture missing. His contact there was Charlie Powell. Vines worked about two weeks and was transferred to Atlanta, Georgia, to another furniture company. Vines explained that they had reported furniture and a lot of other things missing. He was asked to check out the top management and all of the workers to see what was wrong — why there was so much breakage and what was happening to the furniture.

Vines asked if he could back up for a second because there was something said earlier that he wanted to explain. The first time he started working at Lenoir, he also did work for the FBI. Bill Redding was also involved in that. Vines said that he met Officer Redding in 1979 or 1980. His assignment involved taking Agent Redding to Tennessee to a house where some men had been dealing drugs and weapons. No one was there, but they ended up buying a stolen boat and trailer. Vines said he did no other work for Redding at that time. Vines explained he did some work for Redding at a later date in Charlotte. He went to Charlotte and gathered some information for him on the Hells Angels and a girl they had kidnapped. This occurred in February or March of 1980.

Vines returned to his previous testimony. After explaining about going to Atlanta for Broyhill, Vines said he went back to Rutherford County, North Carolina. There, he worked for Broyhill on the security force. His job was to check security and find out about any kind of stolen furniture or anything that might be wrong within the management. He remained there two or three months.

From Rutherford County, Vines returned to Stuart, Florida, to do some work for Mr. Lockwood on a burglary. Vines clarified he went to Florida in November or March of 1981, but he was unsure of the exact time and date. He started out looking into an operation where kids were stealing weapons and guns and trading them for drugs. At the time they entered into the situation, they were trying to trade machine guns for drugs. He was there three to four months until March 1981.

At that time, he began working in Tampa for Jim Myers, Florida Division of Law Enforcement. Vines gathered information on motorcycle clubs, the "Outlaws," and he set up drug buys and helped break up a marijuana smuggling ring. He also worked for a Mr. Dowdy there. This was approximately March of 1981 to July of 1981.

At this point, Ashburn asked Vines, "When did you arrive in Asheville?"

Vines replied, "I believe in July of 1981."

Ashburn continued, "And where did you go when you arrived in Asheville?"

Vines' responded, "First place I went was to Sarge's Lounge."

"And why did you go to Sarge's Lounge?" asked the district attorney.

"Because I had been told that was the hot spot where everyone hung out," answered Vines.

Ashburn asked Vines what "hot spot" meant, and Vines replied, "Lots of people hung around there who did drugs, sold them and things of that nature."

The district attorney asked Vines if he contacted any law enforcement officers, to which Vines responded, "Yes, sir, I did. I got in touch with Tommy Chapman, at ATF."

"When did you contact Officer Chapman?" queried Ashburn.

"When I was working in Lenoir, I had a check that was sent to me from the ATF in Ohio. I went there [Chapman's office] and picked up the check. That was the first time I had met Mr. Chapman," answered Vines. "I told him I was working for Broyhill and was in the middle of an investigation, and he told me any time I was in the area to give him a call."

The district attorney continued, "Did you contact any other officer?"

"Yes, sir, I also got in touch with Bill Redding of the FBI," responded Vines.

Ashburn then asked, "Do you recall about when you contacted Agent Redding?"

"I believe it was after I had been here a while," responded Vines.

"Were you given any assignment by Agent Redding?" continued the district attorney.

Vines replied, "Yes, sir, he wanted information on motorcycle clubs and also had asked me to infiltrate an area where there were some young suspects that were 'wanted' and that I had known before when I was working in Lenoir."

Ashburn then asked, "Did you meet other officers?"

"Yes, sir, Mr. Chapman at one time brought over a Mr. [Thomas] Frye from the SBI," replied Vines.

"State Bureau of Investigation?" asked Ashburn.

"Yes sir," responded Vines.

"As a result, did you have a conversation with him?" asked Ashburn.

Vines responded, "Yes sir, at that time Mr. Chapman told me I couldn't work for him because I had some checks that I hadn't known about that were bad, and Mr. Chapman said he couldn't use me until this was cleared up. Mr. Frye, at that time, told me of a Mr. Miller, Gary Miller — told me he was a cocaine connection and that he worked at the drive-in which is situated right next to Sarge's Lounge."

When Ashburn asked if Vines had talked with any other officers, Vines stated that he thought he had talked with another SBI agent, but that he could not recall his name.

"When did you go to work for Sarge?" Ashburn asked.

"Can't remember the exact date — took me a few weeks to gain Sarge's confidence — sometime in December, around the 1st," answered Vines.

"What kind of work did you do?" asked the district attorney.

"Bouncer — keeping trouble down at the club," replied Vines.

"When did you meet Gary Miller and Alan Hattaway?" asked Ashburn.

"Around the middle of December. I had seen Gary around but I had never met him formally," answered Vines.

"How did you meet these two people?" asked the district attorney.

"I was introduced to them by Sarge of Sarge's Bar and was told I was going to be doing some work with them so [that] I could become a part of their 'family,'" stated Vines.

"What occurred after that?" queried Ashburn.

Vines began, "After that, the next day on the 21st, I was instructed by Mr. Miller and Mr. Hattaway to ... first of all, we went down to the Pizza Hut in a shopping mall on U.S. 70, and we rode through the parking lot to make sure there weren't any police officers sitting around in the parking lot. I was then told to drive, or instructed to drive Mr. Hattaway's car to the Pizza Hut and park at the back door and to go in and wait for an Italian-looking guy whose name was supposed to be Mr. Gamboa."

"And what did you do after receiving those instructions?" continued the district attorney.

"Well, I went there and was to wait until Gamboa came in, and Mr. Hattaway and Mr. Miller were watching in the parking lot for him to come in. I sat there until 5:30, and Mr. Gamboa had not shown up. Then Mr. Hattaway came in and about five minutes after Mr. Hattaway came in, Mr. Gamboa came in," replied Vines.

"Would you state whether or not you had ever seen Mr. Gamboa prior to that date," instructed the district attorney.

"No sir, I had never seen him before," answered Vines.

"What occurred?" asked Mr. Ashburn.

Vines responded, "Mr. Gamboa and myself and Mr. Hattaway were sitting at a table. They were having some discussion about some rings that Mr. Hattaway had given Mr. Gamboa to be sized down. Also they were talking about some money that Mr. Gamboa was supposed to have owed Red [Hattaway]. At that time, Mr. Gamboa said he only owed him $30,000. Mr. Hattaway said he owed $120,000, and he wanted to know what happened to the $380,000 worth of drugs that had come into town that they hadn't received any money back on."

"What happened then?" asked Ashburn.

Vines related, "He also wanted to know about the rings. One ring was a gold skull and crossbones with diamond chips down each bone, two large diamonds for eyes and a large ruby in the mouth. He wanted to know when we were going to be able to get those from ... and Mr. Gamboa said he gave them to a girl — Kathy — in Atlanta, and she had them, and we could go get them. Also Mr. Hattaway asked him if he had any property to help pay back on the money he owed him, and Mr. Gamboa said he had two acres of land he'd sign over to him, also his title to his van and the title to a trailer."

"Any further discussion of money?" asked the district attorney.

Vines responded, "Yes, he was asked how much he [had] put down. Mr. Hattaway asked Mr. Gamboa how much he paid for his drugs and Gamboa said he put $2,000 down on it and didn't have any money, and he'd try to pay him so much a month."

"What occurred after that?" continued Ashburn.

Vines replied, "After Mr. Gamboa told him that, Mr. Hattaway asked if he knew where any of the drugs were, and Mr. Gamboa said he knew where he could pick up 4,500 Canadian Valiums."

"All right, sir, what happened after that?" questioned the district attorney.

"I think we left about 6:00—5:30 or 6:00—left about 6:00 or 6:30. I would imagine from there we went, I believe we did go to Mr. Gamboa's house and leave Mr. Hattaway's car."

"All right, sir," said Ashburn.

Vines continued, "We then drove to the Candler [NC] area and picked up the Blue valiums at two different places, or went to two different places to pick them up."

"Whose car were you in?" queried Ashburn.

"Mr. Gamboa's four-wheel-drive vehicle."

"Where did you go?" continued Ashburn.

"We went to the Candler area somewhere, I couldn't get there, never been over in that area before, and I didn't know any of the roads over there," said Vines.

"Were drugs picked up?" asked the district attorney.

"Yes, we went to one place, a house over the hill. Mr. Gamboa went in and came back with 500 Blue Valiums, and then we went to another place and at that time I thought Mr. Gamboa picked up another 4,000," stated Vines.

"Where did you go from there?" continued the district attorney.

"Went back to Mr. Gamboa's home," answered Vines.

"Is that the 21st?" asked Ashburn

"Yes sir," answered Vines.

About what time did you arrive at the house?" continued Ashburn.

"Probably about 9:00 P.M.," stated Vines.

"And who was present besides yourself, Mr. Gamboa, and Mr. Hattaway?" asked the district attorney.

"Mrs. Gamboa and a child," replied Vines.

"And what did you do then?" continued the district attorney.

"We had dinner. At that time, Mr. Gamboa made a call to Atlanta, I believe, to a Kathy to tell her we were coming down to pick up the rings," replied Vines.

"Any further conversation?" inquired Ashburn.

"Just the same conversation that had transpired at the Pizza Hut," responded Vines.

"About what time did you leave that night?" inquired the district attorney.

"I believe about 10:00 or 10:30," replied Vines.

"And where did you go?" continued the district attorney.

"From there we went back to Sarge's Lounge, where I was dropped off," stated Vines.

"What happened the next day, the 22nd?" queried Ashburn.

"The 22nd we were supposed to meet with Mr. Gamboa and go to Atlanta, Georgia, to pick up the rings," replied Vines.

"And you say 'we.' Who were you referring to?" asked Ashburn.

"Mr. Gamboa, myself, and Mr. Hattaway," responded Vines.

"And what, if anything, in fact did you do?" asked Ashburn.

"I believe we got over there around 11:00 [A.M.] and did go to Atlanta," replied Vines.

"Do you recall about what time you arrived there?" inquired the district attorney.

"It was around 3:00 or 4:00 in the afternoon," stated Vines.

"And what transpired in Atlanta?" continued Ashburn.

Vines said, "We went to a place, a ham house where they sell hams, and Mr. Gamboa went inside. Mr. Gamboa was driving, by the way. Mr. Gamboa went to the place where they sell hams and brought out this young 18- or 19-year-old girl—kind of chunky, long brown hair—and said it was Kathy. She got in the back seat of the car next to me, and Mr. Gamboa got in the driver's seat. At that time, she handed Mr. Hattaway the rings he was looking for."

"And..." queried Ashburn.

Vines continued, "And at that time, Mr. Hattaway told her not to come back up to Asheville to testify in court. She told him she had to because she had signed a waiver of extradition, and he told her again not to come back up there and testify if they could not extradite her."

"What time did you leave Atlanta?" asked the district attorney.

"Around 4:30 or 5:00—I'm sure it was around 4:30," replied Vines.

"Where did you go?" queried the district attorney.

"Drove straight back to Mr. Gamboa's home in Asheville," answered Vines.

"About what time did you arrive?" asked the district attorney.

"Around 8:30 or 9:00," responded Vines.

"And what did you do upon your arrival?" continued the district attorney.

"Upon our arrival, I think we sat around and talked—left about 10:00 [P.M.]. At that time, we went back to Sarge's Lounge—Mr. Hattaway and I," stated Vines.

"Was there any conversation about property at that time?" queried the district attorney.

Vines answered, "Yes, the morning of the 22nd. Mr. Gamboa had told Mr. Hattaway after we were in the car, that his lawyer was in court all morning, and he couldn't get anything signed over. The next day, or that night, he said he'd have it arranged by the next day for the property to be signed over. I was supposed to call Mr. Gamboa the next morning and give him the name and address of who to put the property and titles into."

"Were any firearms exhibited to you at any time?" asked the district attorney.

"Yes sir, on the 21st, the first night I met Mr. Gamboa." We were there at the house, and Mr. Gamboa showed us a Ruger .44 Magnum and an AR-15," replied Vines.

The district attorney continued, "At this time, I am giving this exhibit to you that I have labeled for ID purposes as State's Exhibit 4. Can you identify this?"

"Yes sir, it looks like the gun Mr. Gamboa showed us," Vines replied.

"Now, did there come a time, or was there a time, when you received a pistol or firearm?" continued Ashburn.

"Yes sir, on the 21st," stated Vines.

"Who did you receive that from?" asked the district attorney.

"Mr. Hattaway, well, Mr. Miller was present when it was given to me," stated Vines.

"And was there any particular reason you were given a firearm?" asked the district attorney.

"At that time, I had just gotten over being cut. A guy pulled a gun on me in a bar and they said, since I was becoming a part of the family, I should have something to carry with me, and I should keep it with me at all times," responded Vines.

"Did you, in fact, keep it with you at all times?" asked Ashburn.

"When they were around, I had it on me. When they were not, I usually kept it locked up in the trunk," answered Vines.

"Will you state whether or not you, at any time, ever fired that firearm?" asked the district attorney.

"No sir, I never fired it," replied Vines.

"All right, sir, after leaving Mr. Gamboa's house on the 22nd, where did you go?" asked the district attorney.

"We went back down to Sarge's Lounge," stated Vines.

"And was there any further conversation about the property?" inquired Ashburn.

Vines replied, "Well, that night Mr. Gamboa told Mr. Hattaway he would have it done by the next day. Also, that night we met Mr. Miller at Sarge's Lounge, and Mr. Hattaway, at that time, told Mr. Miller everything that had transpired during that day."

"Will you state whether or not there was any mention of any particular name that property was to be put in?" inquired the district attorney.

"I don't remember the name — there wasn't that night — the next morning there was," replied Vines.

"What did you do the next day — December 23rd?" the district attorney asked Vines.

Vines responded, "Like I said, Mr. Hattaway had told Mr. Gamboa that night he had to go to Virginia and wouldn't be there. As we were going down to Sarge's that night, he explained to me the reason was that he wanted to make sure he wasn't set up; he said he had warrants [out] on him with the police department in Asheville. Anyway, the next morning — morning of the 23rd — I received a call about 9:00 or 9:30 — I believe that's the time — Mr. Hattaway instructed me to call Mr. Gamboa and give him a name and address in which to put this land and property."

"What was that name?" asked the district attorney.

"I don't remember the name," replied Vines. "I believe it was Hattaway, but I'm not sure."

"And what, in fact, did you do after receiving a name from Hattaway?" queried the district attorney.

Vines responded, "He also asked Mr. Gamboa to provide him with the transcript from the trial that Mr. Gamboa and Mr. Miller were in when they had this shootout, and he also asked me to ask Mr. Gamboa if he had the transcript of the trial and which, when I called back and gave Mr. Gamboa the name and the address, I also asked about the transcript, and he said that he had the transcript, and it cost him $370 to get it from his lawyer."

"What time did you call Mr. Gamboa back, or call him the first time?" asked the district attorney.

"First time, I think it was around 9:00 or 10:00," replied Vines.

"And what did you instruct Mr. Gamboa when you called him back or called him?" asked Ashburn.

Vines said, "I just gave him the name and asked if he had the transcript, and he told me 'Yes,' and I told him I'd give a call back. I hung up and waited. Mr. Hattaway called back in a couple of minutes."

"Did you have any conversation with Mr. Gamboa over the transfer of the property?" inquired the district attorney.

Vines answered, "Yes sir. He said that his lawyer couldn't do it because the courthouse was closed that morning."

"Then, did you receive another call from Hattaway?" asked Ashburn.

Vines responded, "Yes sir. He told me to take my car and go and pick Mr. Gamboa up, that he wanted to read the transcript to see if he knew which one was lying, Mr. Gamboa or Mr. Miller."

"When he told you that, what did you do?" asked Ashburn.

Vines stated, "I went to Mr. Gamboa's residence and, at the time I pulled up in front of his door—called him back and told him I was coming first—and then I went to his residence in my car which was a 1968 blue Dodge. When I first got there, I sat a few minutes and beeped the horn, and Mr. Gamboa didn't come out. I beeped again and started to get out when Mr. Gamboa came to the door and told me he'd be out in a few minutes."

"Will you state whether, at any time, you saw Mrs. Gamboa?" asked the district attorney.

"Yes sir. I thought I saw her in the door just before Mr. Gamboa came out and got into my car," stated Vines.

"What occurred when Mr. Gamboa came out to your car?" asked Ashburn.

Vines said, "He pulled the .44 Ruger Magnum out of the back of his pants and laid it on the front seat. He had a brown manila envelope in his other hand."

"And when he got into the car, where did you go?" inquired the district attorney.

"We went to the River Lounge, which is a bar about a mile or two from Sarge's, and I was ... we were supposed to meet Mr. Hattaway there. We got there, and Mr. Hattaway's car was there, but he wasn't there," responded Vines.

"What happened to the Ruger?" asked the district attorney.

"Mr. Gamboa put it in the back of his pants when we went inside the bar," said Vines.

"What happened next?" continued Ashburn.

Vines continued, "Okay, we went inside the bar, and Mr. Hattaway wasn't there, so Mr. Gamboa and I ordered a beer, and, at that time, the former owner of the River Lounge, Dick, served us a beer, and we paid for it. Mr. Hattaway came in at that time. We went over and sat down at a table, and Mr. Hattaway said he didn't want to read the transcript inside the bar—that we would go for a ride, and he would read it."

"What occurred when you got into the car?" asked the district attorney.

Vines responded, "As we were going out the door, Mr. Hattaway handed me his car keys and told me to drive—said he would sit in the back seat with Mr. Gamboa and go over the transcripts with him. At that time, he told me to drive toward Sarge's."

"What happened to the Ruger?" asked the district attorney.

"Mr. Gamboa stuck it under his left leg—took it out of the back of his pants and stuck it under his left leg," stated Vines.

"Where did you drive to?" asked Ashburn.

"To the parking lot of Sarge's Bar," responded Vines.

"What occurred upon your arrival at Sarge's Bar?" continued Ashburn.

Vines continued, "At that time, Mr. Miller—we pulled up there and stopped the car; at that time, Mr. Miller pulled up from the side of the building with some junk cars sitting up there—pulled up next to us and got out, walked around, and got into the passenger's side in front. At that time, he asked Mr. Gamboa why he was telling lies on him and told him he shouldn't be doing it. At that time, he pulled an automatic, either a 9mm or a .45."

"Who pulled it?" asked Ashburn.

"Mr. Miller, and pointed it at Gamboa. Mr. Hattaway also pulled one out," continued Vines.

"What did Mr. Hattaway, or 'Red,' do with his?" asked the district attorney.

"Pointed it at Mr. Gamboa, and pulled the hammer back—was holding it on him," explained Vines.

"What occurred next?" asked Ashburn.

"Mr. Miller told me to hold Mr. Gamboa's hands together," said Vines.

"What happened to the Ruger under his left leg?" asked the district attorney.

"Mr. Miller reached over and took the Ruger away from him," said Vines.

"And where did he put it?" the district attorney continued.

"Under the front seat, under the driver's side where I was sitting," explained Vines.

"Upon being instructed in that regard, what occurred?" continued the district attorney.

"Mr. Miller got out of the car, went to his car, and got a roll of silver duct tape and a roll of fiberglass-like plastic reinforced tape, the type you wrap boxes with," explained Vines.

"Then what happened?" continued the district attorney.

"At that time, Mr. Miller taped Mr. Gamboa's hands together," responded Vines.

"With what kind of tape?" Ashburn asked again.

"With the fiberglass or fiber-type tape," replied Vines.

"Everyone remain seated," said the judge. I ask you jurors to be back in your seats at 9:00 A.M. on Monday morning. At that time, we will resume this trial. Sheriff, keep everyone else here a few minutes, and then just recess everyone. Remain seated until the sheriff announces court is adjourned for the weekend."[3]

12

Vines' Testimony Continues

While court was recessed for the weekend, *Jefferson Times* reporter Terry Henry received a call threatening to blow the courthouse "all to hell." Monday morning Judge Smith ordered tighter security, requiring all spectators who had entered the courtroom to leave, and anyone re-entering to be searched. When the turmoil settled down, the courtroom remained full of spectators. There was also tighter security outside where a crowd waited, hoping to hear or see some of the proceedings.[1]

Judge Smith pounded his gavel, and the crowd grew silent as he stated, "All right, sir, do you realize you are still under oath?"

"Yes sir," Vines answered, settling into his chair more comfortably.

"The witness is with you, Mr. Ashburn," continued the judge.

"Thank you. Mr. Vines, after Mr. Miller taped Mr. Gamboa's hands together with the fiber-like tape you described, what occurred next?"

Vines began, "At that time we all got out of the car, and Mr. Miller helped Mr. Gamboa out of the car into the trunk of the car."

Ashburn asked, "Was there any comment made as to where they were going?"

Vines responded, "To Virginia to talk to the big man."

"Then what happened when you got back into the back of the car?" inquired the district attorney.

"Mr. Miller told Mr. ... told me and Mr. Hattaway to hold our guns on Mr. Gamboa, and Mr. Miller had his gun out also, and he unlocked the trunk" replied Vines.

"When you say, 'he' ... " prompted Ashburn.

"Mr. Miller. Mr. Miller then unlocked the trunk and helped Mr. Gamboa into the trunk of the car," explained Vines.

"What occurred next?" asked the D.A.

Vines continued, "At that time, Mr. Miller took a ... what appeared to be an automatic weapon in a black leather jacket out of the front seat of Mr. Hattaway's car and put it, laid it in the front seat of his car."

"What color was this car?" asked Ashburn.

"Mr. Hattaway's car was black. Mr. Miller's car was a tannish color, tannish-brown with the sides rubbed down — looked like it was ready to re-paint."

"What happened next?" asked the district attorney.

"At that time, Mr. Hattaway drove. I rode with him in the front seat of the black car with Mr. Gamboa in the trunk, and Mr. Miller followed us."

"Was there any conversation between you and Hattaway as to what was to be done with Mr. Gamboa?" asked the district attorney.

"They were first taking him to talk to the big guy about the drugs that were missing and no money [paid]. They were more or less just trying to scare Mr. Gamboa."

"Who drove — who drove the car?" inquired Ashburn.

"Mr. Hattaway drove the car," replied Vines.

"Where were you seated?" inquired the district attorney.

"I was seated in the passenger side of the black car," answered Vines.

"Where was Mr. Gamboa?"

"Trunk of the black car," replied Vines.

"Where was Miller?"

"In the brown and tan car behind us," replied Vines.

"Where did you go from there?"

Vines replied, "From there, we took 40 — Highway 40 — over toward Morganton to Highway 18 and then followed up until we came to the Parkway. There we turned left on the Blue Ridge Parkway. Then we went the road maybe ten minutes or so and turned right onto an old paved rural road. Then we went down past a white house, and Mr. Hattaway told me he had lived there before with a girlfriend before she went to live with the Hell's Angels and...."

"Did you observe ... excuse me, go ahead," responded Ashburn.

Vines continued, "There were three motorcycles on the porch he [Hattaway] said after he moved. He just let a guy live there, you know, rent-free. After that, we went down, I guess, maybe a mile, and we made a right turn onto a dirt road. Then we followed the dirt road back up until we came to Mr. Bare's house where we turned right to his house and went into the junk yard behind it."

"Where did you drive to after turning into Bare's house?" asked Ashburn.

Vines replied, "We went up the drive there between his house and like a little shed on the right-hand side, drove up to an old blue trailer, looked kind of run-down, and [we] parked in front of that."

"What occurred after you parked in front of this old blue trailer you described?" inquired Ashburn.

"Mr. Hattaway told me to stay in the car. Mr. Miller had pulled up alongside of us. He and Mr. Miller went back to a garage behind the trailer," replied Vines.

"When you say 'he,' you mean Hattaway?" asked the district attorney.

"Mr. Hattaway and Mr. Miller," answered Vines.

"Went to a garage?" asked Ashburn.

"Yes sir."

"Did you observe who was at the garage?" asked the district attorney.

"There were three people standing there besides Hattaway and Mr. Miller."

"Who did you see at that time?" prompted Ashburn.

Vines continued, "At that time Mr. Hattaway came back, I mean, Mr. Miller came back and told me to get out of the car and [he] took the keys out of the ignition. At that time he told me to hold my gun. I was at the left side of the car. Mr. Hattaway was on the right side, and Mr. Miller was directly behind me. He opened the trunk and helped Mr. Gamboa out of the car."

"Prior to your getting out of the car on the occasion you are now describing, did you have any conversation with Mr. Gamboa?" asked Ashburn.

"Yes sir. Mr. Gamboa asked me if he was going to get out of this. At this time, I told him I didn't know."

"Where was Mr. Gamboa?" asked Ashburn.

"In the trunk — also asked if he could go to the bathroom," replied Vines.

"And what did you state?"

Vines replied, "Told him he would have to wait until Mr. Hattaway came back to the car."

"Who opened the trunk?" asked the district attorney.

"Mr. Miller opened the trunk."

"Who all had guns out at that time?" asked the district attorney.

"Myself, Mr. Miller, and Mr. Hattaway."

"The other three individuals you have described upon your arrival, as being there at the garage, where were they at the garage?" asked Ashburn.

"Over like facing the garage, they were on the right-hand side next to a yellow Volkswagen. There was a tractor there," responded Vines.

"While this Mr. Gamboa was taken from the trunk, what were these three doing? These three other people?" inquired the district attorney.

"Two seemed to be standing around watching the other gentleman fix a tractor."

"Did you see Miller and Hattaway approach it after they got out of the car while you were still in it?" asked the district attorney.

"No, sir, I didn't see it at that time."

"Then what happened?" continued the district attorney.

"Then Mr. Miller told me to hold my gun on Mr. Gamboa. He then took the tape loose from his hands, and he put handcuffs around, I think, his left wrist, stated Vines.

"When you refer to 'he,' who?" inquired Ashburn.

"Mr. Miller," replied Vines.

"And what occurred after ... you had some earlier comment about Mr. Gamboa's request to use the bathroom?" prompted Ashburn.

"Yes sir. Mr. Miller let Mr. Gamboa relieve himself right there."

"Do you recall on which hand the handcuff was put by Mr. Miller?" asked Ashburn.

"It was on the left," stated Vines.

"Then what occurred?" asked the district attorney.

"Then Mr. Miller and Mr. Gamboa and myself walked up the hill back up to the trees, I guess, maybe a hundred feet up, maybe about ten or twenty paces back into the trees."

"Yes sir. What happened when you got to this tree?" asked the district attorney.

"At that time, Mr. Miller put Mr. Gamboa — told him to put his arms around it, and handcuffed Mr. Gamboa to the tree."

"Do you know what kind of tree it was?" inquired Ashburn.

"No sir, just a tree," stated Vines.

"After Mr. Gamboa was handcuffed to the tree, what happened?" continued Ashburn.

"We went back down, Mr. Miller and myself went back down to the garage where the other people were," replied Vines.

"Prior to leaving the tree would you state whether anything was taken from the person of Mr. Gamboa?"

"No sir," replied Vines.

"Was it or was it not?" asked Ashburn.

"No, sir, it was not," answered Vines.

"And where did you go back to?" Ashburn asked Vines.

"We went back to the garage," replied Vines.

"What occurred at the garage?" inquired Ashburn.

"I was introduced at that time, I believe, by Mr. Hattaway to a gentleman by the name of Papa Bare," stated Vines.

"Is the individual you are referring to at this time, in the courtroom?" asked Ashburn.

"Yes sir, sitting there with the blue shirt and beard," stated Vines.

"At defense counsel's table?" asked Ashburn.

"Yes sir," stated Vines.

"Where were these other two individuals at that time?" prompted the district attorney.

"They were standing there," replied Vines.

"Standing how far from you when you were introduced to the individual described to you as 'Papa Bare'?" inquired Ashburn.

"Right next to me," stated Vines.

"Then what occurred?" asked Ashburn.

Vines continued, "Then Mr. Miller asked Papa Bare to make some phone calls to some people. Two of the ladies were out of Florida. They wanted to trade cocaine for Quaaludes and also asked him to run down a name which happened to be my real name."

"What name was that?" asked Ashburn.

"Gene Vines."

"During this period of time that you got to Asheville and up to the time you heard Miller tell Bare to check out the names of these two girls and the name 'Vines,' what name had you been under?" asked Ashburn.

"I had been going under 'Jo-Jo,' and when I got hurt during the summer, I used my wife's maiden name, 'Koert,' when I went in the hospital," replied Vines.

"What time during the summer was that?" asked Ashburn.

"I don't remember exactly. It must have been late summer."

"Then what happened after Miller asked Papa Bare to do that?" continued Ashburn.

"He went inside the garage and made a phone call," stated Vines.

"Where was the phone located?" asked the district attorney.

"On the right-hand side of the wall, I'd say probably around three or four, maybe five feet from the entrance," explained Vines.

"How far were you from him at the time?" asked Ashburn.

"I was standing in the doorway," replied Vines.

"About how far from the telephone?" continued Ashburn.

"About three to five feet, I guess," estimated Vines.

"What occurred as you stood there?" asked the district attorney.

"At that time, he made a call and repeated the names over the phone. He hung up the phone, came back out, and told Mr. Miller that the machine was down, so it would be a while before they could give him anything on the names," responded Vines.

"Then what occurred?" inquired the district attorney.

"At that time, Mr. Hattaway walked back to the black car. He came back over with the gun and handed it to Mr. Bare. Mr. Bare asked him if it was the Smith and Wesson, and he said no, it was a .44 Magnum."

"And the transcript you mentioned earlier?" inquired the district attorney.

"They were standing around reading that. Mr. Miller was standing there reading it, and the older gentleman that was there at the time was looking over his shoulder at it."

"Where were these three individuals when the gun was handed to Bare?" asked the district attorney.

"Standing by a flatbed truck right there," responded Vines.

"How far from Bare?" asked Ashburn.

"About the distance from you and I," replied Vines.

"And what were they doing at that time?" inquired the district attorney.

"They were looking over the transcript over his shoulder," stated Vines.

"And when you and Mr. Miller went up the hill to that tree you have described, where were they?" asked the district attorney.

"Standing by the tractor," replied Vines.

"When I refer to 'they,' I am referring to the other two people," stated the district attorney.

"Standing beside the tractor beside Papa Bare," stated Vines.

"What occurred next?" asked Ashburn.

"I believe the older guy and the other guy left. And, at that time, we hadn't eaten that day. So I'm not sure if it was Mr. Miller or Hattaway brought up the subject of us not eating. I believe it was Mr. Hattaway, and we decided to get something, and Mr. Bare said he'd go up and talk to Mr. Gamboa to make sure he didn't holler or anything while we were gone and then him and Mr. Miller went up to where Gamboa was handcuffed to the tree."

"When Bare made the statement about going up to the tree to make sure he didn't yell, where were the other two men?" asked Ashburn.

"I believe they had already left or were on the way out," said Vines.

"About what time was this?" asked Ashburn.

"About 5:00 or 5:30 [P.M.]," replied Vines.

"At about what time did you arrive at Bare's place?" asked Ashburn

"Somewhere around 3:00–3:30 [to] 4:00," replied Vines.

"At any time did you see any women on the premises?" inquired the district attorney.

"Just before we went to eat, Mr. Hattaway and I were lying in the car. At that time an old maroon-colored car drove up, and there were two ladies in it — two young ladies. At that time, Mr. Hattaway told me that one of them was Patty, who was Bare's girlfriend."

"Do you know her last name? What occurred then — or go on," said Ashburn.

"I popped my head up and looked at her and then lay back down. They stopped a couple of minutes and left," replied Vines.

"They who?" asked Ashburn.

"Mrs. ... or Patty and the girl she had with her."

"Where did you go then?" asked Ashburn.

"We went down — well, Mr. Bare walked on down to the house, and we all got in the car — Mr. Miller, Mr. Hattaway, and myself — and drove down to the house to pick up Mr. Bare. He had something to do in the house before he left. At that time, a red Pinto or hatchback car drove up, and there was an older man in his fifties in there. Mr. Bare stood by the door and talked to him for a while, and then he left. Mr. Bare got into our car, and we drove down to a restaurant in what looked like a gas station."

"Which car did you take?" asked the district attorney.

"Mr. Hattaway's black car."

"When you say 'we went,' who was in the car?" asked the district attorney.

"Mr. Hattaway, Mr. Miller, myself, and Mr. Bare."

"Where did you go?" asked the district attorney.

"We went to a little store or restaurant-gas station type thing. Not far from there."

"What direction did you take to get to this place you have just testified to?" asked the district attorney.

"We went back out onto the dirt road; made a left there; followed Mr. Bare's driveway down to the asphalt road; made a right there; and went down, I think, a mile or two to a stop sign; made a left there; and then came up on this place on the right-hand side of the road."

"Do you recall seeing any name of the establishment there?" asked the district attorney.

"No sir."

"What occurred upon your arrival?" asked the district attorney.

"We went in and ordered something to eat. There was a lady in there that I took to be the owner or manager. She was tall — I'd say, in her 30s; blonde hair. Mr. Bare and Mr. Hattaway were joking with her about dyeing her hair again; and there was a heavy-set, real heavy-set waitress that waited on the table which we were at."

"Did you have anything to eat?" inquired the district attorney.

"Yes sir. I got a cheeseburger and, I think, a cup of coffee. I took a couple of bites and had to go to the bathroom to throw up, so I didn't eat anymore."

"How long were you at the restaurant?" asked the district attorney.

"I'd say, probably about a half hour."

"And when you left the restaurant, where did you go?" asked the district attorney.

"We went back to Mr. Bare's place," replied Vines.

"Were there any mailboxes around in the area there at Mr. Bare's driveway?" asked Ashburn.

"Yes sir, there were two small mailboxes and one of them had the name 'Bare.'"

"Any other name on the mailboxes?" asked Ashburn.

"I didn't see anything else," replied Vines.

"About what time was this you arrived back at Bare's place?" asked the district attorney.

"About six o'clock," replied Vines.

"What occurred on your arrival back at Bare's place?" the district attorney continued.

Vines replied, "On the way back there was some talk about who was going to go out, had to check some money and take care of some business. Mr. Hattaway said, at the time, he wasn't feeling good. Since I was sick, he'd stay with me, and Mr. Miller and Mr. Bare would go check the money."

"What time did they leave?" asked the district attorney.

"Soon as we got there," replied Vines.

"Where was Red or Hattaway in the vehicle?" asked the district attorney.

"Mr. Hattaway was lying in the front seat of the black car, and I was lying in the back seat."

"What was the next thing that occurred?" continued the district attorney.

"We laid there until about nine o'clock. We were both sick, and about nine, Mr. Miller came back to the car and told me to come with him. We went up the same way ... to the area where Mr. Gamboa was handcuffed, and at that time, he un-handcuffed Mr. Gamboa. He then kicked back some leaves and told me to pick up a wallet and some keys and a bag with some 'grass' or marijuana and a chunk of hashish in it," related Vines.

"How far was that from the tree?" inquired the district attorney.

"Maybe three or four feet," stated Vines.

"Would you state whether or not, in your opinion, Mr. Gamboa could reach them with his feet?" probed the district attorney.

"No sir, I don't believe he could have," responded Vines.

"And what happened next?" continued the district attorney.

"He un-handcuffed Mr. Gamboa and told me to hold my gun on him, and he held the other handcuff, only handcuffed one hand, then went back down to the garage where they took the other handcuff off of him. At that time, Mr. Bare was there with Mr. Hattaway and had a fire going in this broiler-type stove, and he had a leaf, a paper bag with, I think, milk, brownies, Coca-Cola — stuff like that — in it, and told Mr. Gamboa to take what he wanted."

"Where was this fire that you..." continued Ashburn.

"It was in a stove, a broiler-type stove in the right the corner of the garage," said Vines.

"What else was in the garage?" continued Ashburn.

"There was a car that Mr. Miller had told me earlier belonged to John Dillinger — an old car, kind of square, with a fuzz buster sitting on the dash," stated Vines.

"Do you recall what color it was?" asked the district attorney.

"Maroon — same color as the other car," said Vines.

"Which other car?" asked the district attorney.

Vines responded, "The one Patty was driving earlier. There was also a yellow wrecker, an old car, the body of an old car, kind with a rumble seat, and it had boxes piled all over it, and there was a Honda motorcycle there with a tarp over it, and saws. There was a bench with a bench grinder on it — air conditioner filter on it."

"What color was the air filter?" asked Ashburn.

"Blue," stated Vines.

"What happened next, Mr. Vines?"

"Well, Mr. Gamboa warmed himself up, ate what he wanted, and drank — I think he drank some milk. I am not for sure what he ate or drank; and then Mr. Miller asked Mr. Gamboa where his list was of the people that owed him for drugs. Mr. Gamboa told him it was in his wallet. Mr. Miller had instructed me to pick it up earlier and put it in my pocket before we came down; and, at that time, Mr. Bare told me to take everything out of my pocket and lay it on the floor — which I did — and Mr. Gamboa went into his wallet and got out a piece of paper like notebook paper and handed it to Mr. Miller."

"What happened next?" asked the district attorney.

"Mr. Miller asked Mr. Gamboa if he knew where there were any more drugs, and Mr. Gamboa told him that there was 50 pounds in a Jeep at somebody else's house and that he had the key to the Jeep on his key ring; and then Mr. Miller asked Mr. Gamboa to call his wife and have her to pick it up and deliver it to a ... asked if she could pick it up and deliver it, and, at that time, Mr. Gamboa said, 'Yes,' and Mr. Miller went and made a phone call."

"About what time was this call made?" asked Ashburn.

"Around 9:30 or 10:00," replied Vines.

"After that phone call was made, what occurred next?" asked Ashburn.

"Mr. Miller came back over and gave Mr. Gamboa instructions to call his wife and tell her to deliver the 50 pounds of pot in her vehicle to the Country Food Store next to the Holiday Inn West in the Candler area and to go inside and to the bathroom and wait around five or ten minutes, then come back out, get in her car, and go home. He said that two ladies would be there to pick it up," replied Vines.

"Approximately what time was that phone call made?" asked Ashburn.

"Shortly after the other one — I'd say two or three minutes," answered Vines.

"What happened then?" asked the district attorney.

"Mr. Miller dialed Mr. Gamboa's number to Mr. Gamboa's house. Mr. Gamboa spoke to his wife," stated Vines.

"What did he instruct her to do?" asked Ashburn.

"What Mr. Miller had said, from what I could understand," said Vines.

"Go on," prompted Ashburn.

Vines continued, "At that time, Mr. Miller gave him an hour time limit. At that time, Mr. Bare asked him if he could get rid of some pot, and Mr. Gamboa said he have to look at it first. At that time Mr. Bare went over to the left-hand corner of the garage and came back with a five-gallon white plastic bucket; and when he pulled the top off, it was full of pot. At that time Mr. Gamboa told him it looked pretty good, but he'd have to try it. So, at that time, Mr. Bare went over and got some papers and rolled a joint for Mr. Gamboa."

"When you refer to a 'joint' and 'pot,' would you state to the jury what you are referring to?" instructed Ashburn.

"Yes sir. When I'm talking about a 'joint,' I'm talking about a cigarette paper where the pot is rolled in the form to smoke," stated Vines.

"After the defendant rolled this cigarette for him, what occurred?"

"Mr. Gamboa lit it up and offered it to me, and I told him my throat was too sore, and I didn't want to smoke any of it. After Mr. Gamboa got done smoking it, he told Mr. Miller he could probably get $250 or $260 for a pound," stated Vines.

"Please continue [telling] what occurred," said Ashburn.

Vines responded, "Okay. At that time, Mr. Gamboa asked Mr. Hattaway if he had any Blue Valium. Mr. Hattaway told him, 'Yes,' and he gave him two, which Mr. Gamboa took. Then Mr. Gamboa asked if he could roll another joint of pot that he had with some hash in it; which he did and smoked that. At that time everything seemed all right. They were telling him that as soon as the pot was delivered, they would get a phone call. Mr. Miller called a couple of times to see if it had been picked up yet. When he finally got confirmation on it — that everything would be fine — that the 50 pounds would square him [Gamboa] with the big man, but he would have to wait before he could go anywhere. After that, Mr. Miller, Mr. Hattaway, and Mr. Bare went over in the corner and talked for a few minutes; and then Mr. Bare came back over and told Mr. Gamboa he was going to have to wait at the big man's house — that he couldn't wait there — that he'd have to stay there until the pot was delivered by the two girls. Then he left."

"Who?" asked Ashburn.

"Mr. Bare left and went somewhere — gone maybe five minutes, and he came back. At that time, he had, I think, a white rag or a towel in his hands. He told Mr. Gamboa that he was going to have to blindfold him because the guy didn't want him to know where his house was, and that, even though we were going through the back way through the fence, that he still had to blindfold him. We went outside, and at that time, Mr. Bare put the blindfold on Mr. Gamboa. At that time, Mr. Miller, Mr. Bare, and myself...."

Ashburn interrupted, "Excuse me just a moment at this time. I'm going to hand you what I have marked for identification as State's Exhibit Number 9 and ask if you can identify that."

"It could be the blindfold Mr. Gamboa — was put on Mr. Gamboa. I can't state for sure because I have just seen it out in the dark," responded Vines.

"All right, sir. After the defendant blindfolded Mr. Gamboa, what occurred?" asked Ashburn.

"Mr. Gamboa, Mr. Miller, Mr. Bare, and myself got into a truck. Mr. Bare drove the truck. Mr. Miller sat next to Mr. Bare. Mr. Gamboa sat next to Mr. Miller, and I was on the outside next to the door," stated Vines.

"What kind of truck was it?" inquired Ashburn.

"A light green truck," replied Vines.

"State whether or not there was plenty of room in the truck when you four got in it," continued the district attorney.

"It was kind of tight, and it had a shift on the floor with a rather large, black knob on it," stated Vines.

"All right, what happened next?" asked Ashburn.

Vines continued, "Okay. Then I was told to pull my hat down over my eyes. I had I guess you might call it a Russian hat made out of imitation fur with ear flaps, and I pulled the ear flaps down, and since I didn't have any hair, it could be pulled right down over my eyes. So then we drove...."

"Who drove?" asked the district attorney.

Vines responded, "Mr. Bare. He drove about ten or fifteen minutes before we stopped; and on the way over, Mr. Bare was making comments about he hoped the guy put the dogs up before we got there so we didn't get bit by the dogs. At that time, once we stopped, I was told to get out and help Mr. Gamboa out of the truck. Mr. Miller and Mr. Bare got out on the driver's side of the truck, and Mr. Bare reached under the seat and got a pump shot gun. At that time, I opened my door, had a hard time getting it open because of all the briars that were on that side. I helped Mr. Gamboa out of the truck on the passenger side; at that time, Mr. Bare led us about five or ten minutes up this little hill loaded with pines and seedlings, and I helped Mr. Gamboa, and Mr. Gamboa could hardly walk, and Mr. Miller was behind me; and we roamed around a few minutes, and finally I could see this fence Mr. Bare was heading for. We followed him up there. At that time he took Mr. Gamboa by the arm and helped him through a hole in the fence."

"When you say 'he,' who are you referring to?" inquired Ashburn.

"Mr. Bare," replied Vines.

"What occurred at that time?" continued the district attorney.

"At that time, he motioned with the shotgun for me to go in after Mr. Gamboa, which I did," stated Vines.

"When you stepped through the fence, what did you see?" asked the district attorney.

"A hole," stated Vines.

"Describe the hole that you saw," prompted the district attorney.

"Just a huge hole with a fence around it," stated Vines.

"How far was it from the fence to the edge of the hole?" asked Ashburn.

"Maybe three feet," answered Vines.

"What occurred next?" asked the district attorney.

Vines replied, "At that time, Mr. Miller, who was holding this nine millimeter on me, motioned for me to push Mr. Gamboa into the hole, which I did. I tapped him just enough to make him take a step forward."

"How did Mr. Miller motion with his gun?" asked Ashburn.

"He had the gun in his right hand and motioned with his left hand," stated Vines.

"In the manner you are now describing or exhibiting?" inquired Ashburn.

"Yes sir. At that time when Mr. ..., when I tapped Mr. Gamboa on the shoulder, he took a step forward and went into the hole. There was a root about two or three feet down, and Mr. Gamboa's left ankle caught behind that root and he was just hanging there. At that time, Mr. Bare told me to reach down and help him up. I told him I couldn't reach him because I was scared if I reached down, they were going to push me over," stated Vines.

"Okay. What happened next?" continued Ashburn.

"Mr. Bare brought me a limb, I guess, about six feet long, maybe three or four or five inches around," stated Vines.

"Where were Bare and Miller?" asked the district attorney.

"Outside the fence," stated Vines.

"And how did he bring you what you have just described?" asked Ashburn.

"He handed it to me through a hole in the fence," stated Vines.

"How wide was the hole in the fence?" asked Ashburn.

"Maybe four or five feet up, looked like the fence had just been ripped open," stated Vines.

"What kind of limb was it?" asked the district attorney.

"Pardon?" said Vines.

"What kind of limb was it he handed to you?" asked Ashburn.

"Just a limb about six feet long and four or five inches in diameter," stated Vines.

"And after he handed you the limb, what occurred?" asked the district attorney.

"He told me to give the limb to Mr. Gamboa and pull him up. At that time he told Mr. Gamboa to try to get up. At that time, Mr. Gamboa says, 'I can't! I think I've broke my leg! Mr. Bare screamed at him and told him to try, and Mr. Gamboa reached up and grabbed hold of the limb, and I pulled him out. At that time, Mr. Bare made a motion with his shotgun for me to shove Gamboa again," stated Vines.

"Would you stand up and demonstrate the motion?" directed Ashburn.

"Yes sir. Had the shotgun in his hand and going like this with the gun," stated Vines.

"You may sit back down. How far was he from you when he made that motion in the manner you just demonstrated?" asked Ashburn.

"About half as far as you are to me," stated Vines.

"What happened next?" continued the district attorney.

"I pushed Mr. Gamboa." stated Vines.

"How did you push him?" asked Ashburn.

"I just pushed him, reached out and pushed him, and he went into the hole," stated Vines.

"When did you first realize that what you just described might occur?" asked the district attorney.

"When we were at the fence and I was motioned to go in," stated Vines.

"At what point did you see the hole?" asked Ashburn.

"Just as we got up to it. He had already taken Mr. Gamboa by the arm and had put him through the fence before I saw the hole," stated Vines.

"After you pushed Mr. Gamboa, what occurred?" continued the district attorney.

"I got out to the other side of the fence real quick because I thought I was going in, too, at that time," stated Vines.

"Did you hear any noise?" asked Ashburn.

"It sounded like Mr. Gamboa had hit the sides a couple of times. At that time, Mr. Bare threw the limb I had helped Mr. Gamboa with, threw it through the fence into the hole," stated Vines.

"Do you recall how far across the top the hole was?" asked Ashburn.

"No, it was just big," stated Vines.

"After the limb was pitched into the hole by Bare, what occurred next?" asked Ashburn.

"Then Mr. Bare told me and Mr. Miller to pick up some rocks, couple of rocks apiece and throw them down the hole to make sure Mr. Gamboa wasn't hung up anywhere in the hole, which Mr. Miller and I did. We threw two stones about this size," said Vines.

"Is that about eight inches across?" inquired Ashburn.

"Like river rocks—kind of oblong and round," responded Vines.

"How long, total time, would you estimate you were at the mine?" inquired Ashburn.

"Not more than ten or fifteen minutes from the time we got out of the truck until we got back," replied Vines.

"Where did you go?" asked Ashburn.

"Like I say, we came back on the asphalt road and then turned left and went back past the restaurant where we had eaten earlier — the restaurant and gas station — and then went back to Mr. Bare's house or the garage," stated Vines.

"Why did you push Gamboa into the mine?" asked Ashburn.

"I thought I was going to go," stated Vines.

"When you got back to Bare's house, what happened?" asked the district attorney.

At that time, when we got there, Mr. Hattaway said they'd been talking — Mr. Miller, Mr. Bare, and Hattaway were talking, got Mr. Gamboa's wallet and laid all of his business cards out [that] he had phone numbers on," stated Vines.

"Would you describe the appearance of the wallet?" directed Ashburn.

"Yes. It was tan, like canvas-type flat wallet folded over twice. I think it had dark brown trim on it. I'm not for sure," stated Vines.

"What was the location of the air filter?" continued Ashburn.

"It was laying on top of a work bench that had a grinder on it," stated Vines.

"Who placed the items on the air filter?" asked Ashburn.

Vines responded, "Mr. Bare just dumped them out of the bag on the air filter, and also, at that time, Mr. Hattaway said that Mr. Gamboa had gone in easier than the guy he had to put in two weeks before."

"Then what occurred?" asked the district attorney.

Vines replied, "They checked all the ... looking over the phone numbers and stuff and put those in a plastic bag-type like a sandwich bag, all the cards with the phone numbers in. I think Mr. Bare picked up the Visa and the insurance cards, and I think the college cards and the pictures, and went over to the stove and threw them in, and I assume they would have burned.

"What was retained?" asked the district attorney.

"All that was lying there at the time was the business cards, the keys, Mr.

Gamboa's driver's license and Social Security card, and the money, the pot and the hash," stated Vines.

"Then what occurred?" asked the district attorney.

"At that time after everything was bagged up, Mr. Hattaway told Mr. Miller to give me the money, and they were going to throw the wallet away, and Mr. Bare said he would keep it and, at some time, drop it at the scene of the crime somewhere so it would be found, and they'd think Mr. Gamboa was still running around," stated Vines.

"What happened to the money?" asked Ashburn.

"I took the money and spent it," stated Vines.

"Who gave it to you?" asked the district attorney.

"Mr. Miller gave it to me. Mr. Hattaway told him to," stated Vines.

Ashburn continued, "All right, sir. Where did you go— excuse me— what time was it you had been at the mine?"

"Twelve o'clock," responded Vines.

"That night?" asked Ashburn

"The 23rd," stated Vines.

"Where did you go from the garage?" asked the district attorney.

Vines responded, "At that time, after Mr. Hattaway went out to clean the trunk of the car or something, and Mr. Miller and Mr. Bare said they wanted to show me something, and they walked me up back toward where Mr. Gamboa was tied to the tree before, and took me up the side of the hill, and we must have walked about half an hour or so up one side of the hill and down the other side, we came upon a clearing, and Mr. Bare shined a flashlight on something in the clearing and told me it was a D.C. 10, and that was how they got their drugs in."

"What was your physical condition at that time?" inquired the district attorney.

"For the last two weeks, I had had the flu and running a temperature of 103 [to] 104 degrees," responded Vines.

"Would you state whether or not there were any stops along the way to this object that was told to you to be some kind of airplane?" inquired Ashburn.

"Yes sir. I had to have them stop four or five times because I was so weak I couldn't walk too much. I had to stop and rest," responded Vines.

"Did you have a watch or anything?" asked Ashburn.

"No sir," replied Vines.

"How many times would you say you stopped and rested?" asked the district attorney.

"About four or five times," repeated Vines.

"How long did you stay stopped on these occasions?" asked Ashburn.

"Couple of minutes," repeated Vines.

"Did you get a good look at this object that was pointed out to you and told to you that it was an airplane?" asked the district attorney.

"Not really. I wasn't interested at the time, just wanted to leave, still wasn't sure something wasn't going to happen to me," replied Vines.

"All right. After you left that area you have just described, where did you go?" asked the district attorney.

"Back up the same way we came, and we came down and went to an old garbage truck. And at that time, Mr. Miller and I were standing at the back of the truck, and Mr. Bare went around to the left front side of it and opened the door, and up in the garbage truck there was about five or six garbage cans, and Mr. Bare brought two or three of the cans from the front of the truck to the back of the truck and handed them to us," stated Vines.

"When you refer to 'us' you are referring to..." continued Ashburn.

"Me and Mr. Miller," replied Vines.

"Then what happened?" asked the district attorney.

"We took the garbage cans back to the garage," stated Vines.

"How far was the truck from the garage?" asked Ashburn.

"Maybe a hundred yards. It was just above where Mr. Gamboa was tied to the tree before," stated Vines.

"Then what occurred?" inquired Ashburn.

"Then Mr. Bare came out with like two reinforced blue and white garbage bags. He pulled the top off one of the garbage cans and put the bag over the top. The garbage can was full of pot, and he picked the garbage can up and dumped the pot into the bag, and Mr. Miller put it inside a green garbage bag," stated Vines.

"At this time, I will hand you what I have marked as State Exhibit 10 for identification purposes and ask if you can identify that," stated the district attorney.

"Yes sir. This is the wallet, Mr. Gamboa's wallet," stated Vines.

"At this time, I am going to hand you what I have marked for identification purposes as State Exhibit 11 and ask if you can identify that," continued the district attorney.

"That's the same kind of bag the pot was put into," stated Vines.

"What happened to the pot?" asked the district attorney.

"The pot was then loaded into the back of Mr. Miller's brownish-tan car," stated Vines.

"After that was done, what occurred?" continued Ashburn.

"Mr. Hattaway was outside with Mr. Miller and I. We were fixing to leave, and Mr. Hattaway took the machine gun out of Mr. Miller's car and put it into the front seat of his car. At that time there was a little digital clock on the dash of the car, and it read 2:00 A.M."

"What, if anything, happened to the firearm you had?" asked the district attorney.

"Mr. Hattaway told Mr. Miller to trade guns with me because the gun that I had was 'hot' and that the other one, even though it could be traced back to the Outlaws in Florida, it wouldn't be 'hot,'" stated Vines.

"From the time you received the gun from Hattaway and Miller, until the time you gave it back, had you ever fired the firearm?" asked the district attorney.

"No sir," responded Vines.

"What happened next after you gave the firearm back?" continued the district attorney.

"Mr. Miller gave me another .38. At that time, Mr. Hattaway said he was going to leave. He was supposed to go to Charlotte that night, but told Mr. Miller he wasn't going to because he was too sick, and he'd stop and spend the night at Myers Motel."

"That's Hattaway?" asked the district attorney.

"Yes," stated Vines.

"What occurred next?" continued the district attorney.

"Mr. Hattaway left, and we pulled out behind Mr. Hattaway. Mr. Miller and I were in the brownish car," stated Vines.

"Where did you go?" asked the district attorney.

Vines answered, "We drove to Boone, North Carolina, where we went to a house Mr. Miller said was his house, and he had built it. It was a brick house, and there was, I think, a red and white Pontiac there. I'm not sure of the make, and a Jeep — brown-colored Jeep — and at that time, Mr. Miller got out and went in the house. Looked like there was two ladies in the house. The window blinds were open. I could kinda see through the window. Mr. Miller, after about ten minutes, came back out and told me to get in the Jeep, that we were taking the Jeep back home and leaving the pot there. So we did, and Mr. Miller drove almost into Marion, NC, and said he was tired and asked me to drive the Jeep. At that time, I drove from there to the top of the mountain where the Buncombe County line was; then Mr. Miller took over driving and drove me to the place where I was living at the time. I got out of the Jeep. He handed me a fifty dollar bill and told me to take that money and the money they had given me of Gamboa's and buy Christmas gifts for the wife."

"All right, sir. Did Mr. Miller leave at this time?" asked the district attorney.

"Yes sir. He did," replied Vines.

"Was there anyone else at your home other than your wife?" asked the district attorney.

Vines replied, "Yes, there was a bunch of people there. See, we were living with another lady, and she was in the habit of bringing eight to ten guys home at night, and there'd be a pot party all the time, usually."

"What did you do that day, the 24th, after you got back to Asheville? About what time did you arrive back in Asheville?" asked Ashburn.

"I think about six or six-thirty — somewhere in that area," replied Vines.

"Your Honor, may I approach the bench?" (Defense counsel approaches the bench.)

"All right, sir. What did you do on the 24th?" asked the district attorney.

"On the 24th?" asked Vines.

"That afternoon?" asked Vines.

How long did you sleep that day when you got home?" asked the district attorney.

"Until the afternoon sometime," replied Vines.

"Do you recall what time you got up?" asked the district attorney.

"I think mid-afternoon — two or three," responded Vines.

"All right, sir. What did you do that afternoon?" asked the district attorney.

Vines responded, "When I got up, I went to Sarge's Lounge, and soon as I went in, Sarge walked up to me, called me in the back room. When I went back, Sarge kissed me on both cheeks, shook my hand, and said, 'Welcome to the family.' And then he asked me what I thought about the hole, and I told him it scared me, and he said, 'It scared me the first time I was up there, too.' And he told me Gary had given him the cards we had brought back with us — the cards with the phone numbers and stuff on them — and that he was checking out the phone numbers and the people on the cards."

"Did you attempt to call anyone that day?" asked Ashburn.

"When I first got in, I attempted to call the ATF and FBI office in Asheville," answered Vines.

"Did anyone respond or answer?" asked the district attorney.

"No, I didn't get any answer," responded Vines.

"After this happened at Sarge's, what occurred next?" asked Ashburn.

"I kept trying over the Christmas holidays, kept trying to get in touch with somebody and let them know what was going on," stated Vines.

"What did you do Christmas Day?" asked Ashburn.

"I believe I first stayed at home," replied Vines.

"And who did you contact or attempt to contact after that?" asked Ashburn.

Vines replied, "After Christmas, the first person I got hold of was Mr. Johnny Turner with the FBI in Hickory. Mr. Turner I had met, but I trusted

Mr. Redding more, so I asked for Mr. Redding's home [phone] number that I had lost. At that time, I got in touch with Mr. Redding and explained to him what was going down about the murder and everything and told him I couldn't talk because I didn't know when somebody was going to come in the door."

"Did you tell him any great detail?" asked Ashburn.

Vines replied, "No. I just told him there had been a murder and some other things, and I needed to talk. He said he would get in touch with Stan Keel, FBI agent in Asheville, the following Thursday. I told Mr. Redding that Mr. Miller and Mr. Hattaway stated we were going to leave in three days the morning we came back [from Bare's] — that would be on Thursday. Mr. Redding told me that he was supposed to get in touch with Stan Keel on the following Thursday and would drive over to Asheville himself, even though he was retired. I didn't know that at the time."

"You are referring to Agent Redding?" inquired Ashburn.

"Yes, sir, and he said he was going to drive over, and he had set an appointment for me to get with Mr. Keel and him the following Thursday," replied Vines.

"Did you at any time meet with Keel, or were you contacted by the FBI?" asked Ashburn.

Vines replied, "Not at that time, no sir; shortly after that a couple of SBI agents came into the bar looking for me. Sarge got all excited about it and wanted me to go into hiding."

"Do you know which officers they were?" asked the district attorney.

"Not for sure, they came in and asked my wife about me. Asked for me by name, as a matter of fact, around New Year's, I believe," replied Vines.

"When that happened, were you given any instructions?" inquired Ashburn.

"I was told by Sarge to go into hiding and stay there three or four days before I came back," replied Vines.

"What happened after that?" asked the district attorney.

"After that, I went to a lady friend's house of mine and stayed for two or three days. On the day of the 4th, I came back into town to the River Lounge with a group of people. I was surrounded by people the whole time. I was at this other lady's house and got a call from Miller telling me he was going to come down to the River Lounge, for me to be outside. He didn't want to come inside. He was going to talk to me about something," stated Vines.

"What was the mechanical condition of your car?" continued Ashburn.

"It wasn't running at that time, hadn't been running for a week and a half," replied Vines.

"After you received that phone call, what happened?" continued the DA.

"Mr. Miller came down to the River Lounge," responded Vines.

"How did you get down to the River Lounge?" asked Ashburn.

"I had come down with some other people that came from the apartment where I was staying with the lady friend," replied Vines.

All right, that was on the 4th?" asked the district attorney.

"Yes sir, and Mr. Miller came down and picked me up. At that time, we started back up to Sarge's. He told me he was coming back up to see Papa Bare to do a contract on a guy we had talked about before we left," stated Vines.

"Would you describe that, talking about that before you left," continued the district attorney.

"Yes sir. The gentleman in the red Pinto, or little red car that I had seen earlier at Mr. Bare's house before we went to eat dinner — was something concerned with him. They called the guy 'Took' — a nickname for him. He was supposed to be a good friend of Mr. Bare's. At that time Mr. Took had somebody that was supposed to be in the Dixie Mafia," answered Vines.

"Who was this information relayed to you by?" asked the district attorney.

Vines explained, "Mr. Bare and the guy had somebody.... They had been running 'shine' or doing something, and the guy had a truck that was supposed to have been his and some other money or something. Anyway, something happened to the deal. It went sour and the guy was bleeding, this guy, Took.

"Do you recall where this individual you referred to, this guy lived?" asked the district attorney.

"You mean the person that was supposed to be killed?" asked Vines.

"Yes sir," said the district attorney.

"He was supposed to live in this city. No, I mean, wait a minute. He was supposed to be in the next city over," Vines replied.

"In Wilkes?" asked the district attorney.

Vines responded, "In Wilkesboro, right. He was supposed to have property on the Wilkesboro line, or the county line over near the Parkway. Mr. Bare said because it was so close to the Parkway that he and I would be the ones that were going to do it. He'd have the guy come out on the pretense that we were going to buy some land on the Parkway because it was for sale. At that time, we were supposed to use a small caliber gun. Mr. Bare said to use that for the reason we were near the Parkway, and it wouldn't make so much noise. I was supposed to shoot the guy, and Mr. Bare and I were supposed to leave. This was supposed to be done by the 11th of January."

"All right, sir, going back to where you have previously been in your testimony, you were told by Miller that you and Miller were going back to Papa Bare's that night," asked the district attorney.

Vines continued, "Yes sir, we were going back up and take care of the contract. All of a sudden, all these cop cars pulled Mr. Miller's car over. Then Mr. Miller threw a gun, a .32 revolver, and the reason I know exactly is because it was Sarge's gun, and I had seen it many times before. He took Sarge's gun out of his pocket and threw it up in the window. He handed me a small bag of pot and a gram of cocaine. He told me to put them under the seat where they couldn't find it. I just laid it on the floor where they could find it."

"What happened next?" asked Ashburn.

Vines continued, "They pulled us over. I had left my gun locked up in the trunk of the car because I hadn't expected to get in touch with Miller. I left it locked up in the trunk of the car, but I still had a shoulder holster on."

"Why did you have that on?" asked Ashburn.

"I had bought the shoulder holster two weeks before. I was tired of carrying a gun in the back of my pants when I was around them," stated Vines.

"Did you have a gun at that time?" asked the district attorney.

"It was locked in the trunk of a car. I didn't have one on me," answered Vines.

"Then what happened?" continued the district attorney.

"Then the officer got us out, threw us up against — you know — searched us, and frisked us. One officer asked me where the gun was. I told him I didn't have one. They went through my pockets and found a bunch of shells for the gun. At that time, I asked them why they were doing it. They said Mr. Miller was under arrest for kidnapping some guy and a chick."

"Do you recall the guy's name?" asked Ashburn.

"I don't know what the name is. I think it was Mr. Forester and his girlfriend," stated Vines.

"Then what happened? Were you arrested?" asked Ashburn. Vines replied, "I was put in a separate car, and I then told the guy I had been doing some undercover work, and that I was trying to work on Sarge, which I was at the time. In the past, I had seen Sarge a couple of times with machine guns for sale. He also wanted me to drive 'hot' cars, which I never had time to do because I was messing around with the motorcycle club."

"Had you reported that information to anyone, about seeing Sarge?" asked Ashburn.

"Yes sir, Mr. Chapman and Mr. Redding, on different occasions, about it," stated Vines

"Well, what happened to you?" asked Ashburn.

Vines responded, "At that time I told the officer to get in touch with Tommy Chapman because they didn't know Mr. Redding. So I told him to get in touch with Tommy Chapman, and he would explain it to him. Then they took me to Sarge's Bar. There is a little park on one side, and they let me out on the road right there and left me. I got on the phone, trying to cover myself, and called Sarge's son. Sarge's son came down, well, he didn't come down. First of all, he said, 'Wait until I get back in touch with you.' About two or three minutes later, Sarge called. At the time, Sarge was in the VA Hospital, but Sarge called me and told me that Miller's wife would be down with his son, and for me to tell them what had happened, and to do whatever they wanted me to. Mr. Miller's wife, whom I had never met before, and Sarge's son came down to the Lounge. I explained to them what happened. Then she asked me to go down, told me the car was parked at an Exxon station on Highway 70, and they had left it unlocked. She wanted me to go down and get the cocaine and pot out of the car."

"Approach the bench," said the Judge Smith. "I want everyone to remain seated. Sheriff, I am going to let the jury go for the day. I will ask that they be back in their seats at 9:30 A.M. tomorrow. Remember the instructions I have given you concerning the possibility you might be influenced by anything other than you see or hear in this courtroom. The jurors may go. Sheriff, hold everyone else here in the courtroom except the attorneys, of course, until five minutes to five. Then recess court. All right, gentlemen, let me see you a moment."

Recess

On Thursday, June 3, 1982, the Court opened at 9:30 A.M. "Before you bring the jury in," began the judge, "put into the record that yesterday the court furnished both the state and the defense a copy of an issue and recommended as to the punishment form and the instruction on that phase, that being the second phase of this trial, if we should ever reach that. That which I have previously used, and indicated to them that these wouldn't be following verification — would have to be changed as to the evidence. This was the general outline of what I would use in phase two, if it becomes necessary. Is that correct?"

"Yes sir," answered Ashburn.

"Yes," said Marger. "One matter. I had asked, and I thought the court had suggested to the prosecution that we be given all statements prior to the time the witness is put on the stand."

"I said that would save us time," replied the judge.

"This is one missing thought. Mr. Ashburn may not know anything about it, Judge."

"Step over here, and talk to me about it," said Ashburn. (Counsels conferred.)

"Let me have the jury," said the judge. (Jury entered the courtroom.)

"All right, call your witness back around." The buzz of voices diminished as Vines took the stand and Ashburn prepared to question him again.

"Mr. Vines, prior to January 5, was there any time you called Mrs. Gamboa?"

"Yes sir," responded Vines.

"When was that?" asked Ashburn.

"I don't remember the date," stated Vines.

"And what were the circumstances under which you called her?" queried the district attorney.

Vines replied, "There was a note given to my wife at the bar which had a phone number on it. It was given to my wife by Gary Miller, and..."

Marger objected, "That's hearsay."

"Well, I'm going to sustain your objection," said the Judge Smith. "I don't know if it's hearsay, but it's not responsive."

"As a result of the information you received, what happened next?" asked Ashburn.

Vines replied, "I called the number and asked for Papa Bare, but it was Mrs. Gamboa."

"What did you say to Mrs. Gamboa?" asked the district attorney.

"I was kind of shocked at the time. I didn't think it was her that I was supposed to talk to. I gave a statement from Miller about picking her husband up and taking him to the River Lounge where he met a young lady in a blue Honda with Georgia tags and left."

Ashburn then asked, "What happened on January 5th with reference to contacting Mr. Chapman?"

Vines explained, "I didn't have Agent Chapman's home phone number. I called information and found out the number was listed in the phone book, which I thought was unusual." I called Mr. Chapman about 2:00 A.M. and told him I had to get with him and Mr. Kiser of the SBI."

"Then what happened?" asked Ashburn.

Vines related, "I believe Mr. Chapman called Mr. Kiser, and Mr. Kiser called me back. I'm not sure. Anyway, a meeting was set up for 10:00 A.M. that morning."

"And where did you meet?" asked Ashburn.

Vines explained, "I left the place where I was staying and started walking down the road. They picked me up."

"Why did you walk?" asked Ashburn.

Vines stated, "My car was out of commission."

"As you were walking down the road, state whether or not you were picked up," continued the district attorney.

"Yes," replied Vines.

"By who?" inquired the district attorney.

"By Mr. Kiser, Agent Chapman, and Stan Keel of the FBI," stated Vines.

"Where did you go?" asked Ashburn.

Vines stated, "We drove from there to the Blue Ridge Parkway, up to the parking lot where we usually met."

"What transpired at this parking lot?" asked the district attorney.

"I first asked Mr. Keel why he hadn't contacted me and explained to him that Bill was supposed to have called and set up a meeting. He said Bill never called him. Then I explained to him the whole thing in detail and what was going on," stated Vines.

"How long did this conversation take?" asked the district attorney.

"I'm not sure—twenty minutes, maybe thirty," stated Vines.

"Where did you go from there?" asked Ashburn.

"To the FBI office in Asheville," responded Vines.

"After the FBI office, where did you go?" asked the district attorney.

"I was told by Mr. Chapman and the others to go someplace near a phone where I could talk freely. From there I went to a lady friend's house where I stayed until about 4:00 P.M. At that time, I had somebody push my car down to a local gas station. I was in the station. They got it fixed about 6:00 or 6:30 P.M.," stated Vines.

"Did you go back where you had been?" asked the district attorney.

"Yes, I went back to the lady friend's house," stated Vines.

"Did you receive a call from anyone there?" asked the district attorney.

"Yes sir. Between 8:00 and 9:00 P.M., Mr. Chapman called me," stated Vines.

"As a result of that phone call, what did you do?" asked the district attorney.

"Mr. Chapman told me to get my wife and be ready to leave that area," stated Vines.

"What did you do?" asked the district attorney.

"I picked my wife up at Sarge's bar at 1:00 A.M. when she got off. The next morning we left—the next afternoon we left," replied Vines.

"Would be January what?" asked Ashburn.

"Sir?" asked Vines.

"Where did you go?" asked the district attorney.

"We drove from there. I told Mr. Chapman I'd call him on the road. I drove to Virginia—Bluefield, Virginia. At that time, I called Mr. Chapman at his house, but I couldn't get him. He later called me back at a motel where I was calling from," stated Vines.

"When you called, did you leave a message with anyone?" asked the district attorney.

"Yes sir, his wife," replied Vines.

"What time did he call you back?" asked the district attorney.

"Shortly after I called him," stated Vines.

"What happened then?" asked Ashburn.

"I took my wife to her parents' house, or to her sister's house where her parents were staying. I dropped her off. Then Mr. Chapman called me again," stated Vines.

"What date would this be?" asked the district attorney.

"The 7th. It was about noon when Mr. Chapman called and told me to go to Marion, Virginia, which I drove to. I met with him and Sheriff Waddell," stated Vines.

"And where did you drive to from there?" asked Ashburn.

Vines replied, "They arranged for me to leave my car at the sheriff's department in Marion. I could ride back with Sheriff Waddell and Mr. Chapman to Ashe County and Jefferson."

"State whether or not you related the events that occurred to the sheriff at that time," directed the district attorney.

"Yes, I related everything to him on the way over," stated Vines.

"While driving to Ashe County from Marion, state what occurred," asked Ashburn.

"Sheriff Waddell, after I told him the story, asked me questions. Then we came here and..." related Vines.

"Before arriving here, was there sometime you approached the Parkway?" asked the district attorney.

"Yes sir. Mr. Waddell got over on Highway 18. He didn't come directly to the sheriff's department. We came on the entrance way to the Parkway, and I said, 'That's where we are supposed to turn,'" stated Vines.

"What did you do from that point?" asked Ashburn.

"I led them from there to the house where the motorcycles were and to Mr. Bare's house and where the restaurant was and the gas station. I directed him almost to the hole, to the mine shaft. After we got to the mine shaft, as soon as we got out of the car and went up the hill, I told him that's where we had been," stated Vines.

"Did you detail what transpired at the mine, show him the location?" asked Ashburn.

"Yes sir, I showed him the root Mr. Gamboa got hung up on," stated Vines.

"Where did you go from there?" inquired the district attorney.

"We went back to the sheriff's office, I believe," stated Vines.

"At the sheriff's office, would you state whether or not you gave a detailed statement which was transcribed later?" asked the district attorney.

"Yes sir, I did. I gave a statement and was advised of my rights," stated Vines.

"Did you read over the statement?" asked the district attorney.

"Yes sir. The next day," replied Vines.

"Make any corrections?" asked the district attorney.

"Yes, we had to make several corrections in it," stated Vines.

"What kind of corrections were they?" asked the district attorney.

"Different parts, different areas, different dates, things that had been said when we took the statement down. Officer Chapman and Officer Bueker were there at the time, as were Sheriff Waddell and a secretary. As we were going down, everybody was asking questions, so the sheriff's secretary kind of got it jumbled up," stated Vines.

"All right, sir, what occurred after that January 8th?"asked the district attorney.

"At that time, we came over to this area to your office," stated Vines.

"After talking to me, did you return to the sheriff's office?" asked Ashburn.

"Yes sir, we did," responded Vines.

"Was there a time on January 8th when you called Papa Bare?" asked Ashburn.

"Yes sir, there was," replied Vines.

"About what time was that?" asked Ashburn.

"I believe around 6:00 or 7:00, somewhere in that area," stated Vines.

"Was that A.M. or P.M.?" asked the district attorney.

"P.M." responded Vines.

"Would you state whether or not this call was tape-recorded?" asked the district attorney.

"Yes sir. It was made from the sheriff's department. Sheriff Waddell was present, and I believe Mr. Bueker was present, along with Mr. Chapman and Mr. Goss," stated Vines.

"After the telephone conversation, well, excuse me, at this time I am going to hand what's been marked for identification as State's Exhibit #12, and ask you to look at it to see if you can identify it," stated Ashburn.

"Yes sir, that's the tape taken off the machine. The time is on it, and my initials and the Sheriff's. I know I initialed it," stated Vines.

"All right. The state is prepared to play it at this time," stated the district attorney.

"Sheriff, take the jury out," said the judge. (The jury was taken out of the courtroom.)

"Have you gentlemen listened to it?" asked the judge.

"Yes, we have a transcription of it," replied Marger.

"You have a transcription, but have you heard it? I was wondering about the quality of the tape. Do you know what the quality of the tape is?" asked the judge.

"I can hear it very clearly, both parties," said Ashburn.

"Put it on and let it run about 15 seconds so I can tell what the quality is." About 15 seconds of the tape was played. The tape was allowed into evidence. Vines and Bare could be heard talking. Vines told Bare he needed some money. Bare said he didn't have any money and asked Vines to call him back the next morning.

Marger objected, but the judge allowed the tape to be admitted.[2]

On Thursday, June 3, the cross-examination of Vines began. Defense lawyers attempted to discredit Vines' character. They said that ATF Agent Chapman had been responsible for Vines' well-being. Captain Eugene Goss of the Ashe County Sheriff's Department had been assigned to guard Vines while the trial was on-going.

Defense Attorney Edwin Marger and co-counsel John Siskind made it clear that they would contend that Vines was blaming Bare to protect himself. On cross-examination, Marger asked Vines, "Does lying under oath bother you?"

"Yes sir. I don't lie intentionally under oath," stated Vines.

Marger brought up the four to five months Vines spent in a mental institution. In addition, he asked Vines about his dismissal from the army for a mental condition. Vines admitted that he had spent several months in a mental institution for treatment of a nervous condition when he was 17.

"I was also discharged from the army due to my mental condition after I found out my wife was pregnant," stated Vines.[3]

Marger contended that Gamboa was killed before being pushed into the mine; however, Dr. Page Hudson, chief medical examiner of North Carolina, stated that, based on tests done on Gamboa, in his opinion, Gamboa was alive when he was pushed into the mine and had taken one or more breaths after the fall. Tests had confirmed this.

"Could a limb, say, like this," holding up a limb that he had brought into the courthouse, "have been used to kill him?" asked Marger.[4]

"It could have caused the trauma to the head," stated Dr. Hudson. "It would have had to be an awfully hard blow. In my opinion, he died from the fall."[5]

Marger contended that Vines, whom he continually called "Good old Satan," had clubbed Gamboa with the limb, killing him before he pushed him into the mine. Marger said, "We have here a study of a man who has made his living as a perpetual Judas Iscariot betraying those around him."[6] Marger contended that Vines began dealing drugs and became involved in other illegal activities after he stopped receiving money for "informing."

Vines admitted to some drug deals and smoking marijuana. "You have to do some of those things to get them to trust you. You have to gain their confidence to get information," Vines stated.[7]

Marger concluded by suggesting that Gamboa's murder may have been an initiation for Vines' membership into a gang that dealt in drugs and also suggested that Gamboa might have been killed because he owed the leaders of the gang dealing drugs. The defense team contended that their client, Paul Bare, knew none of the others charged in the crime.

"I have no more questions for this witness," Marger told the judge.

The judge asked, "Does the state wish to ask further questions of this witness?"

"Not at this time, your honor, but we may wish to recall this witness later."[8]

"Is the defense ready to call its witnesses?" asked Judge Smith.

"Yes, your honor."

Family members and several neighbors testified that Paul was a good son, father, and neighbor. There were also 34 character witnesses called.[9] Paul Bare was called to the witness stand to testify on his own behalf. He stated that he had nothing to do with Gamboa's murder and knew neither Gamboa nor Vines. Bare admitted knowing Alan Hattaway because he lived in a trailer on Bare's property and that he had seen Hattaway, Vines, and Miller, whom he barely knew, at the trailer on December 23, but he never saw Gamboa.

Bare told the jury he wasn't guilty and asked the jury not to give him the death penalty. District Attorney Ashburn asked that Bare's remarks be stricken from the record, and the court allowed.

Two defense witnesses, Gary Miller and Alan Hattaway, did not testify because they had been on the run from the law since Bare's arrest. The defense rested its case.[10]

The judge asked, "Does the state wish to cross-examine the witness?"

"Yes, your honor." Ashburn paused a moment before approaching the stand.

"Mr. Bare, have you heard the taped conversation that was recorded when you talked to Mr. Vines?" The tape had been introduced earlier in the trial. On the tape Bare and Vines had talked for about three minutes. Bare appeared to know Vines on the tape. Vines asked Bare for money. Bare said he didn't have any, but for Vines to call him back the next morning.

Bare replied to Ashburn, "I didn't know who I was talking to, and he hung up before I could find out who it was." However, Bare did have time to ask the caller where he was.

"No more questions, your honor. The state rests its case."

The judge called a short recess before final arguments were presented and instructions were given to the jury.

On Wednesday afternoon, June 9, 1982, the seven men and five women on the jury deliberated for four hours without reaching a verdict. They were instructed to return Thursday morning to resume deliberation. On Thursday, June 10, after meeting for 42 minutes, they returned a verdict of guilty of first degree murder and kidnapping of Lonnie Gamboa.[11] It was announced that the sentencing phase of the trial would begin Monday, June 14, when the jury would decide whether Paul Bare would live or die for the murder conviction. Bare, dressed in a dark blue suit and brown boots sat expressionless. The Bare family was stunned.

The following week, the jury sentenced Paul Bare to life imprisonment. If all appeals failed, Bare would be eligible for parole in 20 years. The trial had lasted two weeks, and the most surprised person of all was the big-time lawyer Edwin Marger, who was so sure he had won his case. He shook his head in disbelief. "This is the first case that I have been retained for that I have lost in 30 years." Marger, the 54-year-old, New York–born, Miami-raised, and Atlanta-based lawyer, could not believe his record of 30 successive "wins" had been broken by a jury of housewives and farmers in the small mountain town of Jefferson, North Carolina.[12] Edwin Marger, his investigator, Wallace Shandley, and his paralegal, Didi Nelson, left in Marger's private plane with the taste of defeat in their mouths.

After the trial ended, Paul Bare was transported to the N.C. Department of Corrections in Raleigh, North Carolina. His lawyers filed an appeal which was later denied.

13

Fugitives Captured

While the Bare trial in Ashe County was being held, the hunt for Alan Hattaway and Gary Miller, both charged with murder and kidnapping, continued. Several phone calls concerning rumors as to their whereabouts came into the sheriff's office, but despite several near misses, this information had not yet netted the two fugitives.[1]

On June 10, 1982, Buncombe County authorities received information that Miller and Hattaway were at a house in the rural Fairview section. Eight officers arrived at the home about 5:45 A.M. As they neared the house, they heard dogs barking and guns firing. A woman came out on the porch and started screaming when she saw the officers; she was taken into custody when she attempted to run.

The officers' orders to come out of the house were met with gunfire. A few minutes later, William Hays, the homeowner, surrendered and was ordered by deputies to lie on the ground. Suddenly, someone from inside the house opened fire on Hays as he lay on the ground, hitting him in the lower right leg. Deputies Hembree and Jones, carrying a shotgun and a rifle, charged the house. They were shooting high as they went in when Hembree's shotgun malfunctioned. Both of the deputies were wounded, after which Allen Sorrell, also a Buncombe County resident, surrendered. Miller and Hattaway were nowhere to be found.[2]

Deputy Jones and Hays were treated for wounds and released. Deputy Hembree was in serious but stable condition after surgery on wounds received in the shootout. Hays was placed in Buncombe County jail after treatment at the hospital. Sorrell and Hays were charged with assault on an officer with a firearm and assault with a deadly weapon inflicting serious injury. The woman on the porch, Kathy Lunsford Hays, Hays' wife, was charged with assault on a law enforcement officer with intent to kill.[3]

Also, while the Paul Bare trial was in progress, Ashe County Sheriff Richard Waddell received word from Caldwell County Sheriff Bliff Benfield that a man thought to be Miller was living in a trailer park at the Castleberry

Campground in Caldwell County. Miller's trailer was placed under surveillance for three days. His appearance had changed drastically since he went into hiding; he had gained 30 to 40 pounds, shaved off a thick walrus mustache and had removed his false teeth.

At 4:00 P.M. on June 10, 1982, the same day of the Fairview incident and also the last day of the Bare trial, more than 20 officers from federal, state and local agencies surrounded Miller's trailer on the Catawba River, ten miles south of Lenoir. Miller, returning from a fishing trip, entered his trailer unaware that officers were clearing the area of civilians and surrounding the trailer. An officer knocked on the door, and when Miller opened it, he was grabbed and pulled from the trailer, shoved to the ground and searched. The authorities couldn't positively identify him until he put his false teeth in.[4]

"I'm Richard Waddell, sheriff of Ashe County," Waddell informed Miller, "and you're under arrest for murder."

Three pistols and $800 were taken from the trailer. Miller was taken to the Caldwell County Jail, where he was allowed to call his attorney before being whisked away under heavy security to Ashe County, where he was locked up. Agent Robert Pence and Sheriff Waddell credited the Caldwell County Sheriff's Department with the arrest. "I'm pleased the man is apprehended," Sheriff Benfield agreed, "without anyone being hurt."[5]

FBI Agent Robert Pence, in charge of the Charlotte, NC, office, said Alan Ray Hattaway contacted the police through an attorney the morning of

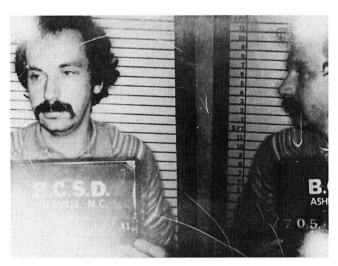

June 10, 1982. Most of the day was spent arranging for a secure place and time for his arrest. Hattaway surrendered to FBI agents in Newport, Tennessee, at 6:30 P.M., shortly after the arrest of Miller. He told the FBI when he surrendered that the Outlaw Motorcycle Club as well as the police were after him, and he feared for his life. Hattaway was held

An earlier mugshot of Gary Miller from his arrest in Asheville in November 1982 following the Moffitt Branch Shootout (courtesy Gene Goss).

in the Knox County Jail in Tennessee until he was sent to Chicago to stand trial on federal kidnapping and forced prostitution charges. Miller, who was being held in the Ashe County Jail without bond, was also sent to Chicago and charged with the same counts. After the Chicago trial, both men would be returned to North Carolina to face the charges against them for the kidnapping and murder of Lonnie Gamboa and Tom Forester.[6]

14

The Chicago Trial

It was October 1982. Joe Vines, who was still in protective custody, and Tommy Chapman went to Chicago for the Alan Hattaway and Gary Miller trials for the kidnapping and forced prostitution of Betty Darlene Callahan. Chicago was a major change from the mountains of Asheville. Vines felt at home in the heavy traffic and hordes of people. He was glad to be out of the cursed mountains that had meant bad luck for him.[1]

Judge Marvin E. Aspen presided at the Chicago trial of the following defendants:

Thomas Stimac — aka West Side Tommy
Robert George Burroughs — aka Snoopy
Alan Ray Hattaway — aka Red, Ron Miller
Marty Curran — aka Scarface
Gary Miller

All were on trial in the United States District Court of the Northern District of Illinois, Eastern Division, during October-November 1982. The trial brought out the close alliance the defendants had with the criminal Outlaw Motorcycle Club and other organizations such as the Hell's Angels. There were local, regional, and national chapters of the Outlaw Motorcycle Clubs in the U.S. and Canada. The Outlaw Clubs in Chicago and North Carolina derived much of their income from drug distribution and prostitution. Prior to his arrest, Stimac was a member of the national ruling board of the Outlaws. Prior to assuming national power and control, Stimac was president of the Chicago Chapter of the Outlaws.[2]

Evidence seized during the search of Stimac's Hinsdale house reflected that Stimac had substantial contacts throughout the United States and Canada with known members of motorcycle gangs, including the Hell's Angels and the Banditos of Texas. Robert George Burroughs, known as "Snoopy," was the main overseer of the Canadian Chapter of the Outlaws. He had been a frequent visitor to Chicago and was known in North Carolina, where he attended a national Outlaw meeting with defendant Marty Curran. The meeting was held at the Charlotte, NC, clubhouse in early June 1979. Later, on July 4, 1979, five members of the Charlotte Outlaws were shot and killed while sleeping in the clubhouse.[3]

Defendant Marty Curran, also known as Scarface, was an active member of the Chicago Chapter of the Outlaws. At the time of his arrest, Curran was also responsible for overseeing the operations of the Northern Indiana Probationary Chapter House. The "Probate House," also known as the Flats, was located on a farm outside Michigan City, Indiana. It became an active meeting place for members of the Outlaws.[4]

Gary Miller was not a member of the Outlaws Club. His involvement, however, arose from his being a supplier of cocaine and marijuana. He was a business associate of defendant Hattaway and Paul Wilson Bare. Alan Hattaway, also known as "Red" and Ron Miller, admitted to activities for the Outlaws— drug-running, money collecting on drug debts, and committing murders for the Outlaws, the Hell's Angels, and others. Hattaway wore a $20,000 diamond and gold ring which signified his status as a hit man for the Outlaws.[5]

In the summer of 1980, Hattaway resided in Salisbury, NC, with his girlfriend. In the fall of 1980, they moved to Laurel Springs in Ashe County where they lived near Paul Bare. Hattaway and Bare knew each other beforehand.[6]

The network of associates grew. In the summer of 1981, Hattaway, Miller, Stimac, and Curran became associated with Clayton Boggess and Garth Bluxon, who resided in Asheville. Bluxon was also friends with two other men, Thomas Forester and Lonnie Gamboa, who were also drug dealers in Asheville.[7]

In the summer of 1981, Hattaway introduced Bluxon to Paul Wilson Bare, telling Bluxon that Paul was also known as Papa Bare to his friends. Bare lived about five miles from the Ore Knob Mine, where the bodies were later found.[8]

Stimac's phone number was found in Forester's wallet when the body was searched after being brought up from the mine shaft. Gamboa's telephone number was entered several times in Stimac's various address books. Moreover, Gamboa and Forester both knew Paul Bare, who had participated in the murders of both men.

Stimac knew Paul Bare, and his telephone number was entered several times in Stimac's address directories. Paul Bare's card was found locked in Stimac's office safe on March 23, 1982, during the search by federal authorities of the Hinsdale house.[9]

On December 21, 1981, Gamboa, Hattaway, Miller, and Vines met. Vines was a paid government informant who, at the time, was working undercover at Sarge's bar. On December 23, 1981, Vines was asked to pick up Gamboa and meet Miller and Hattaway at a local bar. Vines had been told that they were only going to scare Gamboa. Instead, they drove to Paul Bare's house in the Laurel Springs area of Ashe County, NC.

When the murders came to light in January 1982, Callahan was still being held in Chicago and had been unable to call anyone. When Stimac heard that Miller had been arrested and charged with kidnapping Callahan, he ordered Curran to take her to a phone where she could call the Asheville police and tell them that she had not been kidnapped, that she had left willingly. Stimac told her she better sound convincing. On Thursday, January 7, 1982, she was able to reach Detective Will Annarino of the Asheville Police Department, who taped the conversation. Curran shared the earpiece of the phone with her, instructing her as to her replies to Annarino's questions. Annarino told her that he wanted to see her on Saturday and that the Asheville Police would make arrangements to bring her home if she was truly free to come home. Annarino asked her if Forester was dead. The phone went dead at this point.[10]

On February 29, 1982, Burroughs and Curran were arrested in Illinois by the Indian Head Park police, who charged them with unlawful use of weapons. At that time, Curran was still carrying the Colt .357 Magnum revolver, and Burroughs was carrying a .22 Magnum revolver in his boot holster loaded with nine rounds of ammunition. Both guns had been used in the abduction of Callahan.[11]

On March 23, 1982, government agents with a federal search warrant entered the Hinsdale house. Burroughs was present at the time. Agent Steven Henderson told Burroughs he would see him at his deportation hearing scheduled for April 15, 1982. Burroughs responded that he wouldn't bet on it.

On April 15, 1982 Burroughs failed to attend the deportation hearing. Stimac had posted a $5,000 cash bond for Burroughs in that procedure. Burroughs had fled to Canada, where he was arrested in July 1982. At the time he left the United States, the unlawful use of weapons charge was still pending.

While Stimac's Hinsdale house was being searched on March 23, Stimac drove toward his house but spotted the law enforcement officers and sped away, contrary to the request of the officers to stop. He fled and was pursued by two ATF officers who stopped his car. Stimac reached toward his glove compartment. Before he could open it, the agents issued several warnings. After securing Stimac, the agents discovered a fully-loaded clip for the pistol lying on the car floor.[12]

On March 23, Stimac was served with a grand jury subpoena for an appearance on April 8, 1982. The government advised him at that time that they were seeking to serve Toni Somers with a subpoena to appear before the same grand jury. Somers was Stimac's "old lady." On March 28, Stimac purchased a one-way airline ticket for Mrs. R. Nelson which was used by Somers on March 29, when she flew from Des Moines to Chicago. The ticket purchased by Stimac was refundable only to Stimac.

On April 1, Somers appeared in Lake County State Court seeking dissolution of her ten-year marriage to David Nelson. Somers had filed for divorce in 1980. On February 4, 1982, her divorce action was dismissed for want of prosecution. On April 1, the divorce order was negated. Somers attempted to expunge the February 4 order.

The court granted Somers' petition for divorce based on her false claim she had resided 90 days in Lake County prior to the proceeding. Also taken into account was the fact that there were no children involved.

On the same day, Stimac and Somers applied for a marriage license in DuPage County. They were married by a judge the next day. In April 1982, they returned to Iowa to get Somers' pearl-handled gun she had carried while guarding Callahan because she had been unable to carry it on her plane trip to Chicago.[13]

Several items had been seized during the raid at the Hinsdale house that implicated Stimac, Burroughs, and Curran in the charges against them. Among the items were notes to Stimac from Burroughs regarding the promotion of prostitution activities and their chances of taking over the Dream Girl Fashions business. The connections between the Outlaw Motorcycle Club and several clubs in the Chicago area were proven by notes taken from the investigations of the government agents.[14]

On her trip to Chicago, Somers was told that the Outlaws had connections to the Mob. Clayton Boggess was told that Stimac, Curran, and Hattaway had met with members of the Mafia. The Chicago Outlaws Club's connections with organized crime families dated back to 1977. A highly reputable government informant advised that Stimac and Curran had connections with those families. Stimac was the person in the Outlaws Club who had access to the Mafia even for the other Outlaw clubs in the United States.[15]

Also found during the search of the Hinsdale house were disguise kits, various cosmetics, ski caps with nylon stockings sewn in, and other items to conceal a person's identity. The items could have been used during home burglaries or by hit men. The "to do" notes included a methodical plan to start a company called Westside Security that would install home burglary systems. The notes also included specific instructions for manufacturing pipe bombs.

The agents seized several weapons during the search of the Hinsdale house including one semi-automatic military-type rifle, two shotguns, a rifle, hand guns, and buck knives. Also seized were brass knuckles and handcuffs.

Additional evidence indicated the violent world the criminals inhabited and created.[16]

The court records from Chicago showed additional facts. In 1981, Debra Elmhorst lived with Stimac in the Hinsdale house. She had worked for Stimac in the past and is shown in photographs taken from Stimac's house. On the night of August 6, 1981, Maureen Jurjovec, who also resided with Stimac and worked at the Club Algiers and Club Taray, took Debra Elmhorst to the Thatcher Forest Preserve in Cook County. Jurjovec and Elmhorst were accompanied by two bikers— Jocko Rey and Stop Gozdecki. In the presence of Jurjovec and Gozdecki, Jocko Rey shot and killed Debra Elmhorst.[17]

Brought out at the time of the trial was the evidence seized in the search of the Hinsdale house — notes made by Stimac regarding Jocko Rey's visit to his house in which he told of fearing for his own life. On May 1, 1982, Rey was found dead of gunshots to the head in an automobile located in a parking lot in Elk Grove Township. He left a suicide note saying, "The thing I have on my mind is John Klime's death that they are trying to blame on me. I didn't do it. I didn't even know where John lived. So, if I go to prison, I will be killed by the Outlaws because they think I killed him. If I don't go to prison, I'll be hunted by them and by Debbie's family for her death. It is useless to kid myself any longer."

John "Burrito" Klimes had been killed on October 8, 1981, by an explosive device placed under the front seat of his Blazer. The explosion occurred at the intersection of First Avenue and the Santa Fe railroad tracks in Chicago. He had attempted to withdraw from the Outlaws, but Stimac did not allow this. On one occasion before his death, Stimac had severely beaten him at the Chicago Clubhouse. This beating arose from a dispute over a drug business. Based on information given to the government by witnesses, Klimes was killed by a bomb made by the Outlaws. After his death, Stimac took over the drug business.[18]

Kimberly Kalas, a 17-year-old dancer at the Club Algiers, was found murdered on July 27, 1982, in Black Partridge Forest Preserve located five miles southwest of Stimac's Hinsdale house. The cause of death was strangulation and knife wounds inflicted. Prior to her death, Kalas told a government witness that she had made arrangements to meet Stimac and that he would take her home. Kalas was not sexually abused, and there was no evidence of a struggle before she died. Before she died, she was slowly strangled, and superficial knife wounds, common to the method used to obtain information from victims, were inflicted. Based on information given by a government witness, Kalas was going to be a witness in this case against Stimac.[19]

In August 1982, Betty Callahan was the target of an attempted hit by Gary Miller. She was placed in the witness protection program. Miller approached Clifford Haller, an inmate at the Metropolitan Correctional Center, for help in finding a hit man to murder Callahan and Joe Vines, also a federal protection witness in this case. Miller told Haller that he knew where Callahan was located and that there would be no problem doing the job once the contract killer was hired. On August 18, 1982, Haller contacted the U.S. Attorney's Office regarding the contract on Callahan. Haller was interviewed by ATF Agents Richard Paul and John Malone.[20]

By August 26, 1982, arrangements had been made for an ATF agent from Cleveland, Ohio, to pose as a contract killer. An undercover telephone number was obtained where Miller could contact the prospective hit man. Haller gave Miller the number. On September 3, 1982, Haller advised the agents that Miller had tried unsuccessfully to contact the hit man. Miller told Haller that his sister-in-law worked for the telephone company and had checked the address for the phone number and traced it to the federal government. Miller said he had his wife call the number to see who it was. Southern Bell Telephone Company of North Carolina advised ATF that in fact a telephone call had been made from the home of Miller's father to the Cleveland, Ohio, undercover number on September 1, 1982. In addition, the ATF was advised that a relative of Gary Miller's was an office employee of Southern Bell in August and September.[21]

Records showed that Stimac owned the house at 11415 Plainfield Road, Indian Head Park, Illinois, and had possessory interest in the house on 91st Street in Hinsdale, Illinois. The evidence reflected that Stimac had been dealing drugs since 1977 and had not been employed during that time. Consistent with his drug dealing, the last U.S. income taxes filed by Stimac was for 1976.[22]

The government submitted that all of the defendants were participants in criminal associations and all posed substantial risks to "a free and lawful society." The government urged that all of the defendants be imprisoned for a substantial period of time.

On November 3, 1982, following a three-week jury trial at which the government elicited evidence from more than 55 witnesses, Judge Marvin E. Aspen submitted the following charges to the jury:

Defendants Stimac, Curran, Miller, and Hattaway have been found guilty of one of the gravest crimes punishable under federal law, namely the unlawful abduction and holding of a person. All of the defendants have been found guilty of the serious crime of conspiring to transport a woman for purposes of prostitution. The judge handed down the following sentences:

1. Stimac, due to the seriousness of the felonies, should be sentenced to no less than 30 years because of the conspiracy and the power he had, including a life or death sentence over Ms. Callahan.

2. Hattaway and Miller both received life sentences for their roles in the events.

3. Curran received no less than 20 years imprisonment.

4. Burroughs received a sentence of 5 years imprisonment.

The prosecution successfully demonstrated the dangers of each of the defendants to society because of their participation in criminal associations. Chief prosecutor for these cases was U.S. District Attorney Dan K. Webb. He was assisted by Assistant U.S. Attorney Richard L. Miller, Jr., and Assistant U.S. Attorney William R. Coulson.[23]

Both Hattaway and Miller received lengthy prison terms. Both were awaiting transport back to Asheville, North Carolina, to stand trial for the kidnapping and murders of Tom Forester and Lonnie Gamboa.[24]

At the conclusion of the trial, ATF Agent Thomas Chapman returned to Asheville, North Carolina. Joseph Vines was relocated in the Federal Witness Protection Program.[25]

15
Vines' Trial

After the Chicago trial for Hattaway, Miller, and three members of the Outlaw Motorcycle Club was over, Joe Vines and his wife were relocated to Washington State under the witness protection program, where they remained for a few months. Vines was restless and edgy using the name of Eric Orso. He decided to fly to Hawaii. Vines had used many aliases, but he did not like this one because it was associated with all the trouble this last case had brought him. The only thing he was happy about was the fact that he had helped put some big-time crooks and murderers behind bars.

The flight was pleasant enough, and he hoped that a few months in Hawaii would help him relax and forget the past year. He didn't like hiding out and waiting for someone to let him know when Hattaway and Miller would be tried in Asheville, NC, for the kidnapping and murder of Tom Forester and Lonnie Gamboa. He would be called to testify against them.

The weather was always nice in Hawaii, but Vines found out that he was wrong about being able to relax there. The confining size of the island made him tense and frightened, especially when he learned that the $50,000 contract placed on him by the Hell's Angels Motorcycle Club was still in effect. There was no place to hide on the small island. Vines caught a plane back to Florida, where he had lived and worked as an informant for a good part of his life. He felt relieved to get back to familiar surroundings.

Vines and his wife were expecting a baby, and the little girl was born in Florida. Vines was working as a waiter and bouncer in a bar. When he needed a driver's license, he contacted a former government agent for whom he had previously worked. The agent helped him get the driver's license in his own name — Joseph Vines.

In the meantime, Vines and his wife had separated, and he was wrestling with how to spend the rest of his life. He had found a job as a construction worker and was living in a trailer in Lake Worth, Florida. He was trying to decide if he wanted to continue working as a government informant. Vines had not been charged in the kidnapping and murder of Lonnie Gamboa in

Ashe County, but he was still edgy about the $50,000 price placed on his head by the Hell's Angels Motorcycle Club.[1]

Gary Miller and Alan Hattaway were charged with the same crimes of kidnapping and murder, but during the Ashe County trial of Bare, they were on the run.[2] Miller was captured in a trailer park in Lenoir, NC, on June 10, 1982, the same day that Bare's trial ended. Hattaway turned himself in to FBI agents in Tennessee on the same day. Hattaway told authorities in Tennessee that he feared for his life because of the Chicago Outlaw Motorcycle Club and the Asheville police. His arrest had been arranged by his lawyer.[3]

Both Miller and Hattaway were then sent to Chicago to face kidnapping and forced prostitution charges in the case of Betty Darlene Callahan. The case was over two years old when they were returned to North Carolina from prison to face charges in the 1981 deaths of Forester and Gamboa.[4]

Vines knew he was supposed to testify against Miller and Hattaway in Asheville. He was living in Florida at that time and said he was not contacted to appear at the trial. Vines had told the authorities he would be there if they would let him know about the date of the trial.[5]

Vines had told the authorities in Ashe County that he was working on infiltrating the Outlaw Motorcycle Gang when Miller and Hattaway involved him in picking up Gamboa and taking him to Laurel Springs to the home of Paul Bare. Later when the shaft was entered and two bodies were found, Vines had no connection to the body of Tom Forester, but District Attorney Ronald Brown said his testimony was critical in the trial of Miller and Hattaway for the Gamboa murder.[6]

Hattaway and Miller were allowed to plead guilty in a plea bargain because District Attorney Ronald Brown of Buncombe County said he couldn't seek the death penalty without Vines' testimony. The plea bargain was reached in closed hearings on pre-trial motions. Both pled guilty to two counts of second degree murder in the deaths of Forester and Gamboa, and three counts of first degree kidnapping that included the abduction of Callahan.[7]

Joseph (Jo-Jo) Vines was indicted February 14, 1984, on kidnapping and murder charges in the death of Lonnie Marshall Gamboa of Asheville.[8] Vines had no idea that he was being sought by the Asheville police or that a grand jury had indicted him and declared him a federal fugitive for unlawful flight to avoid prosecution in the kidnapping and murder of Lonnie Gamboa.[9] Vines had been indicted under the names of Jo-Jo Vines, Eugene Vines, and Eric Orso, the name Vines was given under the Federal Witness Protection Program. District Attorney Brown said he would request that the FBI issue a warrant for unlawful flight against Vines because he had not reported to federal authorities as he was required to do.[10]

Vines was located by authorities at the Lake Worth, Florida, trailer park on March 14, 1984. He was shocked when the charges against him were read aloud. He thought that case was behind him. Vines declined to waive extradition to North Carolina. Buncombe County District Attorney Ronald Brown said it would be 60 to 90 days before they would know if he could be brought back to Buncombe County. Vines really did not want to go back to Asheville.[11]

Brown filed extradition papers, and Vines was taken to Asheville on May 14, 1984. Vines told the authorities and anyone who would listen that he had been promised by District Attorney Mike Ashburn of Wilkes County that he would not be charged because of his involvement in the Ashe County trial of Paul Bare. At the Bare trial and during the pre-trial hearing, Vines did testify that there was no deal made with District Attorney Michael Ashburn that would keep him from being charged with Gamboa's death; however, Vines told the court that the district attorney specifically stated to him, "You know I haven't made any deals with you, but you won't be charged." Vines also said that Ashburn told him to say at the Bare trial that he had not been promised anything by Ashburn.[12]

Vines felt sure he would not be held responsible for the charges. He knew that his testimony in Ashe County in 1982 had resulted in Paul Wilson Bare's receiving a life sentence in prison.

At this time, attorneys for Paul Bare said they would petition for a new trial based on the belief that Vines had lied when he stated that he had not testified in exchange for immunity. The attorneys also said they had new evidence that pointed to Bare's innocence.[13]

The Asheville mountains were ablaze with colors varying from subtle pinks to bright oranges and reds, and the highways were crowded with tourists as the trial began on October 15, 1984. Joe Vines paid little attention to the people or the mountains because he knew Superior Court had convened on the fifth floor of the Old Courthouse in Asheville, and jury selection was under way for his trial. He felt betrayed by the people who had assured him he would not be tried for the kidnapping and murder of Lonnie Gamboa in December 1981.[14]

Security was tight during jury selection in the Buncombe County Courthouse. Everyone was searched before being allowed to enter the courtroom. Judge Robert Lewis said no one would be allowed to take the names of jurors or to broadcast them.[15]

Vines knew from watching the news that evening that three jurors had been chosen — two alternates and one regular. The judge had ordered everyone to be back in court by 9:30 Tuesday morning. Ten jurors had been selected Monday and Tuesday after both state and defense had interviewed 42 jurors. On October 18, all jurors had been selected and the trial would begin Thursday morning.[16]

Vines had a bad feeling about the trial. If the jury did not believe him about Ashburn's promising him immunity from prosecution, all bets were off. He knew that ATF Agent Tommy Chapman would do all he could to help, but the district attorney carried more weight in Vines' opinion. He could not understand why Ashburn did not just tell them that he had promised not to prosecute him for the kidnapping and murder of Gamboa. Sheriff Waddell had been there and heard Ashburn tell him this.[17]

The first day of the trial was taken up with opening statements made by both attorneys and the testimony of FBI and SBI agents. The district attorney presented first. "I'm Ronald C. Brown, prosecutor in this case." District Attorney Brown stated that he did not give Vines immunity and knew of no one who did. "Duress is not a defense against murder in North Carolina, and I want you to pay special attention to the dates in this case, and the fact that it was thirteen days after the murder occurred before Vines reported the death to anyone."[18]

Gary Cash, defense attorney for Vines, said, "Joseph Vines does not deny being involved in the kidnapping and murder of Gamboa; he does deny being guilty of murder." Cash told the jurors that Vines felt that if he did not push Gamboa into the hole, they both would be killed.[19]

Asheville Detective Ross Robinson took the stand describing Vines now versus then. Vines, tall, clean-shaven, wearing a light blue suit, was calm as Robinson described him as a biker with a bald head, full beard, jeans, boots, rough, mean-looking, using names like Kojak and Satan. Robinson made it clear that he thought Vines should be tried for the murder of Gamboa. Robinson said that the 13-day delay before reporting the murder and the fact that he only went to authorities after Gary Miller was arrested showed that Vines was trying to "get away" with what he had done.[20]

On cross-examination, Defense Attorney Cash brought out the fact that Vines needed to look the part in order to infiltrate the Outlaw Motorcycle Club. Cash told the court, "If you don't play the part of the criminal, your life is in even more danger. He only did what he had to do to stay alive."[21]

District Attorney Brown called the next witness, J. Lawrence Smith of Asheville who was Gamboa's real estate attorney. Smith testified that he talked to Gamboa on December 23, 1981. Gamboa had asked for a transcript of the shootout at Gary Miller's house in November 1981. Gamboa also asked Smith to prepare a property deed for Hattaway. Smith testified that he did not prepare the deed. He did not go into detail as to why he did not prepare the deed.[22]

Brown then called SBI Agent Thomas Frye, who testified next, saying that he went to Sarge's Bar on December 30, 1981, and talked with Vines' wife, telling her to have Vines call him. According to Frye, Vines did not call.[23]

Brown called William Redding, retired FBI agent, next. Redding said Vines had worked for him. He recalled getting a call from Vines on January 1, 1982, in which Vines talked about the criminal characters in the Asheville area. Redding stated, "Vines indicated he had been forced to participate in a murder. I got the impression he was a witness. It seemed to be an old case, something that had happened earlier. On January 7, I called Stan Keel, FBI agent, to let him know Vines had called and wanted to get in touch with him.[24]

Next Brown called William Annarino to the stand. Annarino testified that on January 5, they had received information on Gary Miller and followed him to the U-Haul business where he was arrested for kidnapping Thomas Forester and Betty Callahan. Vines was in the car at the time. Both were asked to get out of the car and were searched. Both had empty holsters, and a knife was found on Vines. At the time, Vines gave his real name to Annarino but said nothing about Gamboa. When Annarino drove him back to Sarge's, Vines told him that he was working for the Indian (Stan Keel) and also needed to get in touch with Tommy Chapman.[25]

On cross-examination, Annarino stated that Miller was dating Rita Jennings, who worked as a secretary for the Asheville Police Department, and that Miller told him that he was on his way to see her when he was picked up. Miller was a suspect at the time in the kidnapping of Forester and Callahan. When questioned about Forester and Callahan, he told Annarino, "If you will get Rita Jennings up here, she will explain everything." Miller continued, "Forester is on a shrimp boat in the Gulf of Mississippi, and Callahan is in a whore house in Atlanta." At that time Miller made bail and was released.[26]

Brown then called SBI Agent Robert Kiser to the stand. He testified about Vines' statement to the SBI, FBI and ATF on January 5, 1982, about the Gamboa kidnapping and murder. Tommy Chapman had called Kiser around midnight and gave him a number to call Vines. Kiser stated that Vines sounded intoxicated to him. He made an appointment to meet Vines the next morning at which time Vines gave the officers a statement about the kidnapping and murder of Lonnie Gamboa.[27]

The next witness called was Ernest Bueker, who gave another account of Vines' statement, giving more details. At that time, according to Tommy Chapman's statement at the Bare trial, no notes were taken at the meeting.[28]

The district attorney called a surprise witness against Vines. Jeffrey Keener was the most damaging witness. He stated that Vines had talked to him about killing Gamboa more than a month before he pushed Gamboa into the Ore Knob Mine. Keener, the last prosecution witness to testify before the state rested its case, said that he met Vines sometime in September, and they were involved in some drug deals together. Keener said Vines had approached him about a contract to kill Lonnie Gamboa shortly after a shoot-out on November 7, 1981, that had occurred in Asheville, involving both Gamboa and Miller. Keener told the court that Vines told him they would be paid for the killing and could take over Gamboa's drug operations. "When he asked me if I would be interested, I turned him down."[29]

Vines' attorney attacked Keener's credibility and asked him if he had ever committed any crimes in Florida. Keener refused to answer, saying it might possibly incriminate him. "Is it true," asked Cash, "that when you first met Vines, your main income was from selling the gold you took from the teeth of corpses in a mausoleum?" Keener again refused to answer on the grounds that it might incriminate him.[30]

The state rested its case.

Vines took the stand after the lunch break, relating the testimony about the Gamboa kidnapping and murder, stressing the fact that he feared for his life when he pushed Gamboa into the mine shaft. Vines also testified that when they were stopped on January 5, 1982, they were on their way back to Wilkes County to do another contract killing. Vines said, "I told Annarino who I was and that I was working with the 'law' and gave him some names to check. I also asked him to help me get in touch with Stan Keel." When asked about Ashburn promising him immunity in 1982 before the Bare trial, Vines testified that Ashburn told him, "You know that I have not promised you anything, but you will not be charged."[31]

When asked about Keener's testimony, Vines, in rebuttal, denied Keener's charges. Vines said Keener told him in September 1981 that he had just come from Cocoa Beach, Florida, where he had knifed a guy in a fight and didn't know if he had killed him or not.[32]

On cross-examination by Brown, Vines replied that he had not heard Gamboa's name until two days before he had been ordered at gunpoint to push him into the mine. Vines said he did not report Gamboa's death until 13 days later because he mistrusted the Asheville police. When Brown asked Vines if he had made a deal to kill Lonnie Gamboa for money and drugs and the chance to take over Gamboa's drug business, Vines denied those charges also.[33]

At the close of court for the weekend, Vines was still being cross-examined by District Attorney Ron Brown. Court was adjourned until Monday at ten o'clock.

The dismal gray fog shrouded the bright fall leaves on Monday morning. It reminded Vines of when he first arrived in Asheville on another foggy morning. He wished now that he had turned around and left after picking up his money. The mountains were like a curse to him. He wished he had never seen them. As Vines entered the courtroom the feelings of impending doom lingered. The district attorney called Vines back to the stand to finish his cross-examination.[34]

Next, ATF Agent Tommy Chapman took the stand for the defense saying that Vines was put into the Witness Protection Program after he received a call saying that if he [Chapman] didn't get Vines off the street, the Hells Angels would kill him. Chapman testified that Vines had helped on cases and went to court for the police in Florida, Chicago, and North Carolina for 11 years prior to June 1981. Chapman seemed to take offense when Brown suggested that Chapman actually had no part in helping with the Ore Knob Mine murder case. Chapman insisted that he had helped with the rope and vehicles that were used to pull up the bodies.[35]

On cross-examination, Brown accused Chapman of trying to protect Vines from prosecution. Chapman defended his actions, saying Vines had done all he could by reporting the murder and, without him, there would have been no case. Agreeing with Chapman, Corkey Miller, former Ashe County sheriff and former U.S. marshal, had suggested putting Vines in the protective custody program. According to Chapman, U.S. District Attorney Charles S. Brewer suggested the Federal Witness Protection Program.[36]

Ashe County Sheriff Richard Waddell testified after Chapman that he had heard Ashburn promise Vines he would not be charged in the Gamboa murder; however, after talking with Ashburn, he [Waddell] later recanted and stated that he must have misunderstood Ashburn and was convinced that Ashburn had not promised Vines immunity.[37]

Next, a Broyhill Furniture security agent testified that Vines had worked for him and helped with many cases.

The district attorney called a rebuttal witness. John Kirkpatrick, while working undercover, said he bought pot from Vines. He also stated that Vines told him that he liked to deal in large amounts of drugs—at least an ounce of cocaine or in lots of a thousand Quaaludes at a time. Ross Robinson was also called in rebuttal.[38]

The defense called Thomas Chapman back to the stand, after which both sides rested their cases. Court was adjourned, and the jury was dismissed for the day with instructions to return on Tuesday at 9:30 A.M. for closing arguments from both sides.[39]

Defense attorney Gary Cash took two hours for his closing argument and tried to convince the jury that Vines had become involved with Bare, Hattaway, and Miller while trying to gather information for law enforcement officers. He stated that Vines should not be held accountable for what Vines testified that he was forced to do. "If you were in Joseph Vines' place that night at the mine, what would you have done?" asked Cash. "What would any man do?"

District Attorney Ronald Brown delivered his closing statement in only 45 minutes. He pointed out that, after three years, it was time Vines was held responsible for his actions. Since Ashe County wouldn't prosecute Vines, it was up to Buncombe County to do it. Brown stated that Vines just found a good deal in the drug business and decided to get in on the big money. Brown closed his argument by asking the jury to bring back first degree kidnapping and first degree murder charges against Vines.[40]

Judge Robert Lewis spoke to the jury for an hour before the jury started its deliberation at 3:00 P.M. Court was adjourned at 6:10 P.M., when the jury came back for additional information. John Shackles of Beaver Creek, the foreman, asked if the jury could stay since they had already completed one of the charges. Judge Lewis told Shackles that it was time to dismiss court, and for him to turn over the jury sheets. The sheets were sealed in an envelope until the next morning. Court was adjourned at 6:10 P.M.

Court reconvened at 9:15 A.M. on Wednesday. The jury reentered the courtroom seven times during the day and a half of deliberation. At 4:00 P.M., after 9½ hours of deliberation, the jury returned guilty verdicts on both the kidnapping and murder charges.[41]

Vines shook his head in disbelief. He felt like this was happening to someone else. When he stood up, his knees were weak. He had done the job for law enforcement and had told the truth under oath. Why did they fail to believe him? As he left the courthouse, he could only hope they wouldn't sentence him to die. He spent a restless night waiting for the next morning because he knew District Attorney Ron Brown was seeking the death penalty. Whether he received the death penalty or life in prison, he felt like his life was over.[42]

The jury returned a recommendation for sentencing Vines to life in prison on Thursday, October 25, 1984. The jury foreman stated that other factors outweighed the cruelty of the murder — that Vines' life was threatened, that he had a good record as an informant, and that none of the other defendants involved had received the death penalty.[43]

After the sentencing, Vines made the following statement:

"I've worked for this state as a government informant and helped put a lot of men in prison. I've heard different things about my chances if I go to prison, plus there was once a price on my head. I don't know if that's off or not. There's really no place in prison to hide."[44]

After the sentencing, word was received at the courthouse that there were some prisoners in the system that would be waiting to deal with Vines. District Attorney Ron Brown admitted that anytime anyone who has a record as an informant goes into the Department of Corrections, there can be security problems. Vines' attorney asked that he be held in the Buncombe County jail until the N.C. Department of Corrections officers were prepared to protect him. Judge Lewis ordered that Vines be held overnight in the jail before being sent to Raleigh. Word was received later that day at the courthouse that Vines would be killed if he was sent to Raleigh. Arrangements were made to relocate him in the prison system under an alias, and he would remain undercover in the system. Vines would be eligible for parole in 17 to 20 years if he could survive.[45]

Vines was the fourth man to be sentenced in that cold mountaintop murder that took place in the wee hours of Christmas Eve of December 1981.

16

Ore Knob Mine History

(Note: This is an article written by the author in 1982 and published first in the Journal-Patriot.*)*

The mining history of Ashe County began with iron and ended with copper. There is no record as to who first discovered iron in the Ashe County mountains, or who set about mining the ore and buying the forges necessary for the production of the iron.

The Ore Knob Mine first opened in the 1800s, and at one time around 1875, the Ore Knob community was the largest incorporated town in Ashe County, although very little evidence of the boom town remains now. The Ore Knob Copper Mine was the largest ore-producing mine in the nation and also had the richest ore in the world. The first ore was mined by hand in 1855 and shipped to Marion, Virginia, by horse-drawn wagons.

One of the most interesting characters recorded among the settlers of Ashe County was a man named Meredith Ballou, born in Amherst County, Virginia. He was among the men who might be classified as pioneers in iron.

Ballou came to Ashe County in the 1800s looking for iron. By buying up large tracts of land for mining, he owned the mining rights for many acres. One of the tracts acquired by Ballou was a tract of about 300 acres that came to be known later as the Ore Knob Mine. Ballou thought he had found promise of iron in the tract but abandoned it after he determined that whatever iron was there was "so badly adulterated with copper that it was useless." Ballou and his sons thought the tract worthless and neglected to pay the taxes on it. The taxes piled up, and the county eventually sold the land for taxes owed. The land brought enough to pay the taxes and cost of sale, leaving an amount of $11 which was divided equally among the 11 surviving children. Later, the Ore Knob Mine came into the possession of Jesse Reeves, who sold it to the Buchannon Company of Virginia four years before the outbreak of the War Between the States. In those early days, the ore was hauled in ox-

The Ore Knob Mine Historic Marker is at the intersection of NC 88 and Little Peak Creek Road, photographed in June 2009 (photograph by Pat Gambill).

drawn wagons to Wytheville, Virginia, where it was smelted. This company operated it as a copper mine until the beginning of the Civil War halted mining operations, and the mine was closed down.

Two men from Baltimore, S.S. and C.E. Clayton, opened the mine again in 1870 after acquiring 500 acres of land around the Ore Knob, a small mountain in southeast Ashe County. The Claytons laid shafts as deep as 300 feet to clean out a belt of rich, black ore. The Claytons also built reducing and refining furnaces on their property, and, using charcoal, smelted their own ore. In a 10-year period from 1873 to 1883, more than 300,000 tons of ore were taken from the mine and transformed into 25 million pounds of copper. In 1883, the ore, which had been averaging 19 percent, was only averaging 3 percent. With the equipment of that day, it wasn't good economics to continue the operation of the mine, so the Claytons closed it down once again.

From 1883 to 1953 the Ore Knob Mine was opened and closed five times. There had been copper, silver, and gold taken from the mine, along with many other sulfides, and, in its most productive years, the ore mine employed 500 men at one time. The pay at that time was 50 cents worth of groceries at the company-owned store for a day's work.

The most recent venture into mining at Ore Knob began in 1953 when Nipissing Mines, Ltd., purchased the mining rights from Rover G. Lassiter, of Oxford, NC. Nipissing started full scale operations that lasted until 1962, when the copper was exhausted.

Residents living in the area around the Ore Knob Mine were shocked when a man went to the authorities claiming he had pushed a man into a mine shaft while he was still alive on Christmas Eve. He was able to retrace the steps with authorities and accurately identify the other persons and places in the sequence of events and prove that he was a free-lance informant working for law enforcement authorities in Asheville, NC. It was a true story of drugs, kidnapping, and murder.

The federal mining authorities were contacted, and they searched the mine shaft area with video cameras in freezing weather, but found no conclusive evidence. The mining authorities called off the search and declared the mine to be too dangerous to enter because of falling dirt. While the police pondered the situation, a volunteer calling himself "The Nashville Flame" offered to enter the mine if authorities would grant him permission.

On January 25, the "Flame" entered the mine, and, on his third descent, a body was spotted; Officer Roger Buckner and Officer Ross Robinson of the Asheville Police Department and Captain Eugene Goss of the Ashe County Sheriff's Department brought up the bodies of two men from an icy grave. They were identified as those of Lonnie Gamboa and Tom Forester, both drug dealers from Asheville, NC. Paul Wilson Bare, a local resident, was tried and convicted in the case and sentenced to life imprisonment. Two other men were convicted for this crime at a later date.

The mine area itself is a desolate looking place in the winter when everything looks bleak except the green pines growing around the area. In the spring, however, the mountain laurel and wild honeysuckle blooming on the edge of the barren waste area caused by the copper by-products makes the dead waste area look like a 10-acre desert on top of a mountain. A pool of water below the waste area is colored golden yellow by sulphur from the mine, and the sulphur smell is very strong. The open air shafts have been filled in now to prevent animals from falling in and to prevent more dumping.

The mountain people say little about the tragedy that occurred in their community, living up to the saying that mountain people mind their own business and don't talk much to strangers. These are a rugged, enduring people, and they know that, in time, the memories will dull and the scars will heal.

The author of the following old mountain ballad about an accident at the Ore Knob Mine could not be determined. Also, a few words of the song are missing. The ballad was transcribed by Fred Hart of Sparta.

THE ORE KNOB SONG

Came blooming youth in the midst of day,
And see how soon some pass away;
There were two men who worked with a share,
And what became of them we soon shall hear.

They worked all day 'til evening time.
Before the ground it made a slide;
It was 50 minutes after five,
These men were healthy and alive.

Before the whistle blew for six,
Their die was cast and doom was fixed;
The rocks and dirt came tumbling down,
And under it these men were found.

They brought them to the top,
Which was a dreadful sight,
(Next line unclear)
They were cold and dead and could not live,
For God had taken the spark He give.

Poor Shirley had a wife and children dear,
And Smith had a mother this sad nears to hear;
We hope they will for consolation,
Read and believe in John's Revelation.

For with the Lord there is nothing strange,
He could their hearts in a moment change;
We hope He did their hearts renew,
And receive them in with Heavenly (word unclear)

Poor Shirley and Smith,
How them we do miss;
Around the Ore Knob today,
There is none of us that dare to say,
But we hope they've gone to a world (unclear).

History of the Ore Knob Mine, 2009–2012 Update

(Adapted from the "Expanded Site Inspection Report" prepared by Black and Veatch Special Projects Corp., courtesy of Terrence Byrd, EPA site manager, 2010.)

The Ore Knob Mine in Ashe County, NC, was first opened in the 1800s. Known as the 19th Century Operation, the mine was first worked for iron ore, but the ore was found to contain too much copper and sulfur. The first copper mining was started four years before the Civil War. The first shaft was sunk in 1855, and black ore was mined between 1855 and 1856. Ore was transported to Wytheville, Virginia, in oxen-drawn wagons. The mine was expanded and operated from 1873 to 1883. This operation sank seven more shafts and deepened the four existing shafts. Two of the new shafts were over 400 feet deep. The other shafts ranged from 30 to 250 feet deep. Originally, the Ore Knob Mine used the Hunt and Douglas process. It was the second mine in the United States to use this process, which was discontinued when the ore was no longer usable. Subsequently, a smelting process was used, involving two reducing furnaces and a refining furnace fueled by charcoal. During this time, about 25,000,000 pounds of copper were processed from over 200,000 tons of ore.

In 1899, four shafts were sunk with a tunnel driven across at the water level. The shafts were 90, 40, 30, and 40 feet deep. In 1896, the number 2 shaft was sunk an additional 25 to 30 feet. In 1897, several carloads of hand-sorted slag were shipped from the most northerly slag dump. In 1913, a carload containing 72,739 pounds of slag and copper bottoms were shipped to New Jersey. This shipment contained 12.9 ounces of gold, 112 ounces of silver, and 12,672 pounds of copper. In 1917 or 1918, the mine was dewatered, and a tunnel was driven under the #4 shaft. Several carloads of ore were mined and shipped at that time. In 1927, the tunnel under the #4 shaft was reopened, and some drifts were opened to the southwest. There is no information on how much ore was mined from this area.

In 1942, the Bureau of Mines conducted an exploration program that involved drilling twenty holes, totaling 4,945 feet along the strike of the vein. Seventy-five feet of drift and cross-cuts were excavated from underground drilling stations, and samples were collected from the drill holes to identify locations of copper ore. During these exploratory activities, adits were cleared based on the Bureau of Mines diagram. The shafts are located from west to east in the areas currently known as the former "1950's Mine and Mill Site" and the "19th Century Operations" area.

Nipissing Mines Company, Ltd., began a new exploration program at the Ore Knob Mine in 1953. This included an electromagnetic survey and 38 drill holes, totaling 27,752 feet. Ore was intercepted in 15 holes, with the deepest holes located at 1,150 feet below land surface. The program delineated reserves of 1,333,300 tons of 3.0 percent copper and 14 percent sulfur.

In 1956, the main shaft (the working shaft) was sunk to a depth of 1,037 feet. The collar was reinforced with concrete down to 55 feet, and six levels were opened for work, starting at a depth of 280 feet. This exploration program led to the reopening of the mine in 1957.

There were 350 tons of ore processed per day, and the contents were fed into two ore bins located in a concrete building. A power station was constructed at the '50s mine site to supply electricity, and water from Peak Creek was pumped into a company-built dam on an acre of land purchased by the company. The processed ore was gravity-loaded into trucks underneath the bins. Both ore bins are still standing at the former '50s mine and mill site. The processed ore was transported three miles to Smethport, near West Jefferson, and shipped by rail to custom smelters.

Through the end of 1961, the Ore Knob Mine had produced over 35,000 tons of copper, 9,400 ounces of gold, and 145,000 ounces of silver. Mining operations at Ore Knob halted in 1962 when the ore body was mined out.

All of the mining activities left the area with toxic waste materials. The first detoxification efforts consisted of placing anoxic limestone drains at the mouths of the adits. The face of the dam was reshaped, and an attempt to re-vegetate the surface of the dam was made. This had little or no effect. A limited number of investigations were conducted by the North Carolina Division of Water Quality through a grant program. A second attempt to re-vegetate the area and create an artificial "wetlands" was marginally successful. Follow-up studies in 1994 revealed improvements in the wetlands above and below the tailings dam. Studies in 1996 showed no fish in the areas below Ore Knob Branch located above Peak Creek, Peak Creek below Ore Knob Branch, and Little Peak Creek. Basically, the reclamation efforts had failed.

"The Toxic Waste Area" photograph was hanging in the EPA on-site manager's office and was photographed by Pat Gambill with permission of the EPA manager in May 2011.

In the late 1990s a joint evaluation made by the Huntington District of the Army Corps of Engineers (USACE) and the North Carolina Department of Environment and Natural Resources (NCDENR). They prepared a detailed report and environmental assessment for Ore Knob. The purpose of the report was to examine alternative strategies for reducing the amount and severity of the toxicity found to still be present in the streams. Recommendations were made for major reclamation projects in the mine area, but everything was put on hold indefinitely due to funding issues.

In July 2007, EPA and Black and Veatch conducted an in-depth assessment at Ore Knob to determine hazardous substances that were still being released from the mine tailings wastes into the area water supply. They found the following hazardous substances being released into water supplies downstream from the Ore Knob properties: arsenic, cadmium, chromium, copper, lead, magnesium, mercury, nickel, selenium, silver, and zinc.

In 2008, the EPA Region 4 Emergency Response and Removal Branch began a time-critical action at the Ore Knob Mine site which has required the total restructuring of the entire area of the dam and tailings area. This has required the use of as many as nine pieces of heavy equipment at one time, crushing and removing huge boulders, layering the run-off area with

Heavy equipment at work, photographed by Pat Gambill while being given a tour of the reclamation site for the old sludge area, May 2011.

Aerial view of the mine area (courtesy EPA).

charcoal, stone, sawdust, and other treatments, and relocating the creek bed of the Ore Knob Creek so that it flows around the mine area.

Recent testing of local wells revealed toxicity. The EPA is providing free bottled water to area residents. Work is continuing at the site now [2011].

The closing chapter is drawing near as the year 2012 ends, spanning 31 years. The Environmental Protection Agency has completed the reclamation project to detoxify the soil and water in the area surrounding the Ore Knob Mine. More information about this project is available online from the EPA. Key into a search engine "Ore Knob Mine NPL Site Summary." This report gives additional information on the site location and background and includes an appendix containing maps and pictures of the reclamation site.

Appendix A:
Official Sworn Statements

These sworn statements have been transcribed verbatim.

PAUL WILSON BARE [1]

Official Sworn Statement of Paul Wilson Bare

(Taken by Officers Absher and Goss at the residence of Paul Wilson Bare on January 8, 1982.)

Paul Wilson Bare
DOB 11–21–39
Laurel Springs, N.C.

Officers Absher and Goss were seated in a patrol car with Paul Wilson Bare. I (Goss) advised Paul Bare of his rights orally and asked him some questions about the kidnapping of Lonnie Gamboa. He (Paul) stated he knew nothing about it and did not know anyone by that name. I (Goss) asked Paul about Gamboa's billfold that he pointed out to a Wilkes County officer some few days earlier. Bare stated that a silver-colored car, he believed to be a Cougar with Florida license, came up behind him on Highway 16 near the top of the mountain in Wilkes County and started blinking the lights and blowing the horn. Bare stated he then pulled over at the church parking lot and that two men got out, there was two or three more in the car, one of which he thought was a female. Paul stated that he was with his girl-friend, Patty. The men that got out of the car told Paul that he was going to drive and deliver some "hot" cars for them and that they were with the "Dixie Mafia." Paul told them that he wouldn't do it. Then one of the men pulled a gun out and Paul kicked him in the groin area. Paul then ran into the woods. The men shot at him two or three times. Paul stated he did not know where Patty got to. Later, he got back with Patty, and they drove down the mountain and flagged a Wilkes County officer and returned to the church parking lot with him. I (Goss) asked him (Paul) if he pointed out the billfold to the Wilkes County deputy and he stated that they both saw it about the same time.

I (Goss) asked Bare to describe the people that he fought with and shot at him. He (Bare) stated one of them had dark hair and he believed he was an Italian. Paul also stated he could tell me that he had dark skin and looked like an Italian. [He said] The other man was real big and was bald, with a chin beard. Paul stated he had never seen either one of the men before. Paul also stated that he could tell me things that would make my hair stand up, when the time was right.

PAUL WILSON BARE

Official Statement #2 — PAUL WILSON BARE
Ashe County Sheriff's Office   January 9, 1982   9:57 A.M.
Taken by SBI Agent Ernest Bueker and Sheriff Waddell

"You boys just don't realize how much is going on. I need to talk to an FBI Agent. There are a lot of Big People involved, and the Dixie Mafia. You know the Dixie Mafia is run by motorcycle gangs. They have been putting pressure on me and on Pattie to get me to work for them. I won't. I have made runs for them as a decoy car, but have never carried any of the stuff. I got shot at in the car a while back in Virginia. As far as the 23rd of December, a big man with a shaved head, I called him Kojak, came to my house, and he had some men with him. I didn't know him, except he is with the Dixie Mafia, and he wanted to use my garage to question this man. I let him use the garage. Also Ronnie Miller or "Red" and Gary Miller were with him. I don't know how long they stayed. Ronnie had a black Mercury and Gary Miller had a brown car. I never went up to the mine with them, if they went. It has been a long time since I have been up there."

Q. How many people have you heard that are in the mine?
A. "Twenty-th —-uh —-twenty-five.

The 44 Magnum in my house belongs to Patty. I gave her $100 to buy it two or three days after Christmas. I think she bought it in Alleghany County or another county close by. I don't know from who. I don't know any Lonnie Gamboa."

"Let me talk to Patty and I may tell you more — all of what I have told you is not the truth.

BARTON, RICHARD

I (Sheriff Waddell) talked to Richard Barton, Detective with the Marin County Police Department. Detective Barton stated that he was familiar with Jo-Jo or Joseph E. Vines, and that Jo-Jo had done undercover work with very good results; that Jo-Jo gave good and truthful statements, and that he did not exaggerate. Detective Barton stated that he knew Jo-Jo had done work in Marin County, Florida on gun running and dope dealers, and that Jo-Jo had to be in court there the last of this month. Detective Barton stated that Jo-Jo had done work for Capt. Robert Crowder and Sgt. Lockwood at the Marin County Florida Sheriff's Department.

BOWLIN, MILDRED — waitress at Stop 'n' Shop
Official Statement of Mildred Bowlin

Several weeks ago, Paul Bare, a red headed man and a bald headed man came in after lunch sometime. I don't remember how many people there was with him. Red headed guy lived in Hiram Bare's house which is an old white house. She appeared very nervous.

CALLAHAN, DARLENE
February 2, 1982
Taken by Sheriff Waddell, Ernest Bueker, Elsie Taylor

Q. What is your full name?
A. Betty Darlene Fie Callahan.

Q. What is your address?
A. Route 2, Box 65 B, Asheville, N.C.

Q. What is your date of birth?
A. 05–01–51

Q. Did you check into the Inn Town Motel in Asheville on December 6, 1981?
A. Yes

Q. What Room?
A. Room 15

Q. Did Tom Forester check in?
A. Yes

Q. The same room?
A. Yes, he had stayed the night before.

Q. Was Tom Forester your boyfriend?
A. Yes

Q. What happened on December 12, 1981 and where did you go?
A. Went to Shoney's about 9:00 A.M. and when I got back Gary Miller and Hattaway and Jay Fagel were standing outside our room.

Q. Did you have food with you?
A. Yes

Q. What happened then?
A. I went up to the door, Hattaway asked me if I had a key to the room and I told him, no. Tom Forester got the door open a little ways, and Hattaway kicked the door in and rushed us in the room. Gary and Hattaway were arguing. Tom had a motorcycle that belonged to Hattaway. The motorcycle was inside the room. They stated saying Tom had stolen the motorcycle and he said he had not. He had the title and they looked at the title and Hattaway said the title had been fixed up and when sell it without him being there. Hattaway and Gary both had pistols and had them pulled the whole time. They shoved me into a seat behind the door and pointed a gun at Tom and wouldn't let me move.

Q. Were you scared?
A. Yes

When Tom was telling them he had not stolen the motorcycle, Gary hit Tom with the pistol on the left side of the head. It was a short barrel pistol and it brought blood from Tom's head. They tore the room up, Gary jerked the telephone out of the wall and checked under the bed to see if Tom had a gun, but he didn't have one. They mentioned that Tom owed Hattaway $2300 in the motel. They stayed in the motel about fifteen to twenty minutes. They made Tom strip and searched him. I had my clothes off and they were going through my clothes. The Asheville Police came up while they were there. After Tom put his clothes back on, the told Tom and Jay to load the motorcycle up and put in a white van outside the room. They took all the things out of our pockets and put them on the table. While Tom and Jay were loading the motorcycle, they had me in the room searching me. Gary came back in and said there was a cruiser out there and for me to hurry. When I came outside, the cruiser was gone. Tom and Jay were already leaving in the van. All of us got into the van. The Police had received a call because of a disturbance. Gary told him he just came to get his motorcycle and he left.

Q. Tom left with Gary, Hattaway, Jay Fagel and his son?

A. Yes, Jay's son's name is Blaine 9–10 years old.

Q. Where did you go then?

A. Went somewhere on Tunnel Road by the Mall on Highway 74 then turned left on Swannanoa River Road and went to a Drive-in.

Q. What's the name of the Drive-in?

A. Park Drive-in.

Gary was driving the van. Hattaway was on the passenger's side with a gun pointed at all of us. Gary stopped at the ticket booth and said something to the woman, he didn't pay anything. Pulled into one of the spaces and Gary got out of the van. I don't know where he went. A Cordoba pulled up beside us. Gary and Hattaway got out and walked toward the concession stand. There was a man driving the car. Then Hattaway opened the sliding door to the van on passenger's side and got Tom out and put him into the back seat of the Cordoba. Hattaway got into the back seat. Gary got me out through the passenger's door and I crawled into the front seat of the car and he drove.

Q. Whose car was this?

A. Gary's car.

Q. What time was this?

A. I guess 10:00 on December 12, 1981.

We left the Park Drive-in and headed west to I-40 to Tennessee into Newport.

Q. While enroute to Newport, what was said?

A. They said I was going up north and work off part of Tom's debt at an Outlaws House in Chicago. They said Tom was to rob a bank or to work on a boat stealing marijuana from others to pay what he owed. They were mad about the motor-cycle more than the money.

Q. Was this when they mentioned Gamboa?

A. Gary and Hattaway were talking about Gamboa talking too much and ratting and he was the next to see. At Newport, they said supposed to be on our way to Chicago. Hattaway said he thought we would go to the other place. Gary knew where they were. Then said we were coming back to North Carolina, I don't know where. I knew when we went through Johnson City. We drove three or four hours and we wound up at this house that I showed you last night.

Q. What time did you get to this house?

A. About 3:00 A.M. on December 13, 1981.

We pulled in next to the house; I saw a house on the left. I saw a car that looked like the one Tom used to have a 1978 Thunderbird, white and white interior with a blue dash and blue pin stripes on side. I knew the car because I had driven it. We pulled up and parked at the house on the left. Passed it just a little bit, there was a wrecker on the right. A drive leading up through a junkyard on each side of the road. Gary and Hattaway got out. Some guy came out and they talked to him. I could tell it was a man. They talked to him a few minutes and came back to the car. Drove up the road between the junk cars and pulled in front of a garage. To the left was an old trailer. Sat there a few minutes and the guy at the house came up and Gary and Hattaway got out of the car and talked to this guy again. They opened the garage door. I think that's where they got the blindfold from. They talked to this guy a while and then got Tom out first and blindfolded and gagged him. They had already tied his feet. They got me out of the car and blindfolded and gagged me. Then we walked back down this road toward the house. Gary and I was in the rear in the automobile. I was sitting on top of Gary and next to the door. Hattaway was next to the driver — five people in all. I assumed it was a truck.

Q. Four that came there and the guy at the house were in the truck.

A. Yes

Q. Did you see the truck when you came in?

A. I can't remember.

The Thunderbird caught my eye, I recognized it. We left and pulled onto the highway to the right. Hattaway said he was taking up to some housing project, and that Tom would go in first and talk to some people and see if they could arrange for him to pay back the money, and that they would take me in after they took him in.

Q. How long a drive was this?

A. About five miles.

Turned off highway into a dirt road, the road had an incline to it and it was rough.

Q. How far was this?

A. About a mile, turned left like facing back out.

Everybody got out but me and Gary said was taking Tom in to talk to these people. Gary told me that they were going to take Tom in and talk to him and see if could make arrangements. He would go steal this pot and if he did not they would kill him. Gary asked me if I had rather stay and take my chances with Tom or take my chances and go on to Chicago and work with the Outlaws as a prostitute. First, he explained Tom's chances, if they worked something out with Tom. If Tom lived, I would live. And which I had rather do to nod my head. I nodded my head yes to going to Chicago.

Q. Did Hattaway and this man come back?

A. They returned and Tom did not.

Q. What did you think happened to Tom?

A. I figured they had killed him or sending him to a boat to work for a while. They left and went back to this house. (The one I just described)

They took my blindfold and gag off. Drove up the road and met guy in truck. He was backed up in there (the guy at the house) Hattaway and Gary got out and talked to him.

Q. What did he look like?

A. Had on a parka, fur on the hood, had a brown dark beard and mustache.

Q. How old was he?

A. 35–40 years old, a white man

Q. They never called him by name?

A. No

Q. What did he say to you?

A. I over-heard this guy telling Hattaway and Gary to take me on to Chicago and that I was to get a job up there and that if I did OK and kept my mouth shut, in a year or two, I could come back home. They talked to this guy about 20–30 minutes, then left about dawn.

Q. What kind of weather was it?

A. Light snow, clear and cold.

Me, Gary, and Hattaway left in Gary's car. They said we were going to Chicago. I remember seeing a sign that said Boone. Went from there into Tennessee, went close to Knoxville then cut up and went through Kentucky, Indiana and into Illinois and Chicago. We checked into a motel. The town was Brookfield and Lyons, the outskirts of Chicago. Checked into motel about 12:00 Sunday night, stayed until Tuesday mid-day and checked into another motel. I met two people that Hattaway knew.

Q. How long did Hattaway and Miller stay?

A. Through Thursday.

Q. While there what did they have you do?

A. Cooking and cleaning.

Q. Did you go to work?

A. No

Q. Why?

A. No proper ID, had to wait until they got me one.

Q. On the last there, how did you manage to get away?

A. I had been staying at two different houses, the guy would leave someone else to watch me. About Friday he checked me into a motel. Came by to get me something to eat, he would stay gone the rest of the time. They had never left me alone like that.

Q. On Monday, January 25, 1982, what happened and what time?

A. About 8:30, we had been in some bars that day, he had made phone calls and he got back and told me he had to go to Wisconsin. All I knew him was by — Jack Daniels. He drank a lot. He said drive was one and half hours each way. I figured I had five hours and that would give me enough time to get to the airport. I hadn't intended to call the police. I called Linda Miller, Gary Miller's wife. Gary gave me the number, she said he was down the road there, and I asked if anywhere I could call him. She said if I left a number he would call me. I called my mother in Asheville. She told me to call the FBI. I told her I didn't want to. She asked if I hadn't heard, they were hunting for Tom and a guy Gamboa and thought they were in a mine. Then I figured it was time to get out. She asked me if I knew about it. I told her I thought he had been dead the whole time. I called the FBI in Chicago. I didn't know where I was at. They had me hold on and they traced the call. Asheville officers came and got me and brought me back here.

Q. Who would you be afraid of after this?

A. Hattaway and Gary, they said if I caused trouble they would kill me and the way they talked, it would not bother them a bit.

When I was in custody in Brookfield Police Department, Captain Beaver didn't know Garth had died. I told Beaver up there that if I made a statement they would be after me and I thought Garth would be next. He owed Hattaway $6000.

I had not met Gary until that night.

Q. Were Gary Miller and Hattaway members of the motorcycle gang?

A. Gary wasn't, Hattaway was or had strong connections.

Q. Did you know Joseph E. Vines?

A. No

Q. Did you know Sarge?

A. No

In Chicago, I heard Sarge ran a bar in Asheville. I knew there was a place called Sarge's, and I thought it probably was the same.

While at the motel in Asheville, Hattaway told Jay Fagel to get the car, a Subaru, which was Hattaway's that Tom had. Tom had painted it for him, just before the shootout on November 7th. After the shootout, didn't see Hattaway until December 12, 1981. Tom had the car parked on a farm in Leicester. Hattaway told Jay to get the car and put everything to Tom's (guns, and stereo) that he might have and put them into the car. They were to get these things from Jay's house and then Jay was to take the car to Sarge's Lounge and park behind, take the keys in and leave them with Sarge.

Q. After you and Tom were taken to Newport, Tenn., or while you were going what happened?

A. Hattaway and Gary were snorting cocaine and drinking white liquor. They offered Tom and I some, but we turned it down.

Q. When Tom was taken from the motel, what was he wearing?

A. Insulated underwear top, pair Levi blue jeans, and Wallaby boots (ankle high, suede). One had a tear in it near the toe, I think the right one.

CHAPMAN, THOMAS

ATF Agent — Official Statement, February 3, 1982

From January 5 through 9, 1982, I participated with Sheriff Richard Waddell and other officers of the Ashe County Sheriff's Department; SBI Agents Robert Kiser, Ernest Bueker, Steve Cabe, Charlie Whitman; Detective Ross Robinson of the Asheville Police Department; and other officers in an investigation into the kidnapping of Lonnie Marshall Gamboa and the execution of a State Search Warrant at the Paul Wilson Bare premises. The search resulted in the seizure of a Sturm Ruger .44 magnum caliber revolver, Model New Super Blackhawk, serial #84-06729, six shot, 7½" barrel length, blue finish, along with other items from the Bare premises located in the Peaks Creek Road Section of Ashe County, Western Judicial District of North Carolina.

On January 5, 1982, I conferred with Joseph E. Vines, known to me as JoJo/Satan, an individual who has in the past worked for ATF, FBI, DEA, and other Federal agencies, Broyhill Industries, Caldwell County Sheriff's Department, North Carolina Bureau of Investigation, Lenoir Police Department, and most recently, for the Florida Department of Law Enforcement. I became acquainted with Vines during the summer of 1981 and the met with him on several occasions, introducing him to State officers who are assigned to the Asheville, NC, area. At no time has Vines worked for me as an informant nor have I instructed him or requested him to do any specific undercover work for me as an informant for me or the Bureau of ATF.

On January 5, 1982, about 10:05 A.M., I, accompanied by SBI Agent Kiser and FBI Special Agent Keel, both assigned to Asheville, NC, met with Vines, who revealed that on December 21, 22, 23, and 24, 1981, he had participated in the abduction of Lonnie Marshall Gamboa at the parking lot of Sarge's Lounge in Asheville, NC, with Gary Hansford Miller and a person known to him as "Red," and known to be Alan Ray Hattaway. Also, Vines revealed that later on the evening of December 23, 1981, they met a person known to him as "Papa Bare" at his residence/garage/junkyard located somewhere in the mountains, now known to be the residence/garage/junkyard owned and operated by Paul Wilson Bare in Ashe County near Laurel Springs, NC. Further, Vines stated that he was ordered at gunpoint by Miller and Bare to shove Gamboa into an open mine shaft located some four to five miles away from the Bare premises about midnight of December 23, 1981. Vines added that Bare remarked that that made 23, referring to the number of persons previously to have been shoved into the mine shaft.

During the interview, Vines stated that one the evening of December 21, 1981, while having supper at the Lonnie Marshall Gamboa residence, located off Towne Mountain Road, Asheville, NC, Gamboa showed him and "Red" an AR-15 rifle that Gamboa stated would fire fully automatic, and a single-action .44 magnum long barrel blue steel revolver and a custom-made leather holster for the revolver.

Vines stated that on December 23, 1981, about 10:00 A.M. he went to the Gamboa residence in Asheville, NC, and there picked up Gamboa who was carrying a .44 magnum long barrel blue steel revolver that appeared to be the one he had observed at Gamboa's residence on December 21, 1981. Vines further stated that Gamboa removed this pistol and laid it on the seat of his car as they drove to the Riverside Lounge in Asheville, NC. Vines stated that while at the Riverside Lounge, he and Gamboa were joined by Hattaway. Vines stated that the three of them then drove to the parking lot at Sarge's Lounge in Hattaway's black 1981 Ford car. Further, Vines stated that Gamboa was still armed with the .44 magnum revolver previously mentioned, and that he had placed it under one of his legs. Vines stated that in the parking lot of Sarge's they were joined by Miller who, after entering the black 1981 Ford, pulled a pistol and pointed it at Gamboa. At the same time, Hattaway pulled his pistol, and they disarmed Gamboa of the .44 magnum caliber revolver he had been carrying. Vines advised that Gamboa was placed in the trunk of the black 1981 Ford car, and the .44 magnum revolver was stuck underneath the driver's seat of the black 1981 Ford by Miller. They proceeded in convoy with Miller to a junkyard in Ashe County, NC, owned and operated by "Papa Bear," Paul Wilson Bare, Vines stated. He also stated that, there, the .44 magnum revolver was removed from beneath the seat of the black 1981

Ford car and left at the Paul Wilson Bare garage, along with Gamboa's pocketbook and other items of identification. To Vines' knowledge, the firearm was still there when he, Miller, and Hattaway left about 2:00 A.M. on the morning of December 24, 1981.

On January 7, 1982, I accompanied Sheriff Richard Waddell to Marion, VA, and, there, about 1:30 P.M. we were joined by Vines. After storing the Vines vehicle, Sheriff Waddell, Vines and I returned to Ashe County, NC. Sheriff Waddell drove past the intersection of U.S. Highway 18 and the Blue Ridge Parkway. Vines identified this intersection as being the intersection he had referred to on January 5, 1982 when he had talked to me, FBI Special Agent Keel, and SBI Agent Kiser. Sheriff Waddell turned around, and we proceeded back to the intersection, there turned onto the Parkway, followed the directions given by Vines to the Peak Creek Road, and continued on the Peak Creek Road passing a white house that Vines pointed out as the house that Hattaway had referred to on December 23, 1981, as being the house where his wife lived, and there I observed several motorcycles parked on the porch as previously mentioned by Vines. We continued, directed by Vines, for about a mile, and came to a point on the Peak Creek Road where Vines indicated that they turned right onto a dirt road on December 23, 1981. Vines stated that they continued on the dirt road to a mailbox having the name Bare, turned right, passing a small house, and continued to the junkyard, and stopped near the Bare garage. I knew this to be the location of the mobile home (residence), garage, and junkyard of Paul Wilson Bare. On December 17 and 18, 1976, I participated with Special Agent

Willie F. Blocker in the execution of a Federal Search Warrant at this location that resulted in the seizure of some distillery equipment, five firearms, an assortment of ammunition, 37½ pounds of Atlas primer high explosives (dynamite), and 19-M-80 type firecrackers. Sheriff Waddell continued for several miles until the Peak Creek Road ended and intersected with NC Highway 88. There we turned left onto the highway, and we continued for several miles, until the Stop and Shop building came into view. Vines identified the Stop and Shop building and stated that, on the evening of December 23, 1981, that he, Hattaway, Miller, and Bare came there and ate supper. Vines further described the young waitress that waited on them. Vines stated that after leaving the hole on or about midnight on December 23, 1981, that he remembered passing the Stop and Shop on their way to the Bare garage. Sheriff Waddell, Vines, and I continued to an abandoned mine shaft near the Ore Knob Mine and Vines indicated that this was definitely the mine shaft that he had been forced at gun point by Miller and Bare to push Lonnie Marshall Gamboa into about midnight on December 23, 1981. Further, Vines pointed out the place in the fence at the gate where he and Gamboa entered into the fenced-in area of the mine shaft. Further, he pointed out the root that Gamboa caught on when first pushed into the hole.

On January 7, 1982, at the Ashe County Sheriff's Office in Jefferson, NC, I was present when Vines again related the events of December 21, 22, 23, and 24, 1981, to SBI Agent Bueker and Ashe County Sheriff's Department Office Deputy Elsie Taylor, who made handwritten notes for preparation of a statement.

On January 8, 1982, I accompanied Sheriff Waddell, SBI Agent Bueker and Vines to the Office of Michael H. Ashburn, District Solicitor, in Wilkesboro, NC. In my presence, Vines again went over the events of December 21, 22, 23, and 24, 1981, relating to the pushing of Lonnie Marshall Gamboa into the mine shaft in Ashe County, with Solicitor Ashburn who made handwritten notes. Later on this date, after returning to the Ashe County Sheriff's Department, I was present when Vines reviewed and made corrections to the statement that had been prepared for his signature. Further, after the corrections were made, I observed Vines as he signed the statement. I was also present when SBI Agent Bueker, SBI Agent Steve Cabe, Detective Robinson, Sheriff Waddell, and others prepared an affidavit and search warrant for the premises of Paul Wilson Bare. An arrest warrant was further issued for the arrest of Bare for his participation in the kidnapping of Lonnie Marshall Gamboa. Bare's arrest was authorized by Michael H. Ashburn, District Solicitor, earlier on this date.

On January 8, 1982, about 8:30 P.M., I was present when a state search warrant was executed at the residence of Paul Wilson Bare as previously described. I first went to an old trash truck that was parked in the junkyard, as described on January 5, 1982, by Vines who stated that on the evening of December 23, 1981, contained a quantity of new metal trash cans full of marijuana. There I observed two empty new metal trash cans, with a vegetable material residue. Shortly, I went to the Bare home. Bare had added to and converted into his residence a vacant white stucco single-story house that I had previously observed on December 17 and 18, 1976, that is located beside and at the beginning of the driveway to his old residence/junkyard and garage. There I observed a concrete mixer still set up in the backyard of the Bare home and further observed that the old stucco house previously mentioned had recently been bricked. Part of the old white stucco structure was still visible on the backside near the top. I entered the back door off the Bare home and Sheriff Waddell handed me an H. Schmidt, .357caliber revolver, model H.S., serial #8848, six shot, 4" barrel length, blue steel. I unloaded the pistol and recorded the identifying information from it. Further, I was present when Detective Robinson found an RG .22 caliber revolver, model RG-23, serial #255993, six shot, 2" barrel length, blue steel, in the purse of Patricia Watson Simmons, who stated that she was living with Bare. I unloaded the pistol and recorded the identifying information from it. Also, beneath the seat cushion of a chair in the bedroom of the Bare home, I located a long barrel pistol. I called Sheriff Waddell to my location and there pointed out to him a Sturm Ruger, .44 magnum revolver, model New Super Blackhawk, serial #84-06729, six shot, 7½" barrel length, blue finish. The firearm was picked up by the handles, still loaded, and placed in two plastic bags by myself and Sheriff Waddell.

At 8:40 P.M., this same date, in the presence of Sheriff Waddell and SBI Agent Whitman, I advised Patricia Watson Simmons, white female, age 20, DOB 2-26-61, POB Detroit, Michigan, of certain of her constitutional rights be reading to her from Sheriff Waddell's rights card. Simmons stated that she understood and waived her rights. Simmons claimed ownership to the three firearms found in the Bare home, as previously described by serial numbers. Simmons stated that she had first received the .22 caliber revolver and then some months later, back in the summer of 1981, the .357 caliber revolver, both from "Pug" Miller. Further, she stated that "Pug" Miller was really Van Miller, Jr., and that his phone number was 919-359-8104; his residence was in Alleghany County, NC; and he is a friend of herself and Bare. Also, Simmons stated that she had a long barrel .22-caliber revolver that she had got from Paul Bare's father, Hiram Bare. The search failed to reveal the hiding place of the long barrel .22-caliber revolver. Simmons stated that she might have left it outside or put it down somewhere. She really did not know where it was. Simmons first lied to SBI Agent Whitman and myself regarding her purchase on February 5, 1981, of the Sturm Ruger, .44 magnum caliber revolver, from a young boy known to her as "Slick" at the Ray parking lot in Sparta, NC, for $150. Later, during the interview, "Pug" Miller came to the Bare residence and the back door looking for Paul Bare. I advised Miller that Bare was under arrest. Van Miller, Jr., told me that he received mail at Route 2, Laurel Springs, NC, and that he was born on February 18, 1925, in Alleghany County, NC. Miller also acknowledged that he had let Patricia Simmons borrow an RG .22-caliber revolver and a .357 magnum caliber revolver. I showed the RG and H. Schmidt revolvers to Miller who claimed ownership of both but did not know or have their serial numbers recorded. Miller stated that he got the .22-caliber revolver from his mother who is now dead and the .357 revolver from a man from California who used to rent his gas station on Hwy. 18 in Wilkes County, NC.

About an hour after we began the interview, Simmons started crying and told me and SBI Agent Whitman that she would be killed if she told us the truth about the Sturm Ruger, .44 magnum caliber revolver. Simmons stated that she did not want to get in trouble over something that she did not do, that she had not done anything wrong. Finally, Simmons stated that the truth of the matter was that, a couple of days after Christmas of 1981, Gary Miller of Asheville, NC, returned to the Bare premises, went by the garage, and talked with Paul Bare. Simmons stated that he stopped by the house on the way out and came in carrying the Sturm Ruger, .44 magnum caliber revolver that I had found beneath the cushion of the chair in the bedroom of the Bare home. Simmons stated that she started pleading for the pistol that Miller had and that he finally agreed to let her keep the revolver. Simmons stated that Gary Miller told her that she could keep the revolver until he wanted it back. Simmons stated that Miller had been to the Bare premises on other occasions and was a friend of Paul Bare when she met Paul Bare. Simmons stated that Bob Miller, a young, large size, white boy, worked for Paul Bare in his shop. Simmons stated that she knew a person that went by the nickname of "Red" and that his name was Ron Miller and he was a friend of Gary Miller, and that they had been together on several occasions. Further, Simmons added that the person she knew as "Red"/Ron Miller used to drive the white Thunderbird car that was parked in the junkyard. Also, Simmons stated that "Red" ... sometimes drove a Chevrolet pickup truck. During the interview, Simmons stated that she had been in Wilkes County on the evening of January 5, 1982, and that she did hear some shots being fired at the parking lot of the Pine Ridge Church and that she later returned the same parking lot along with Paul Bare and some law enforcement officers. Further, that she knew a man from Asheville, NC, by the name of "Sarge," and this person had been at the Bare premises on at least two occasions that she knew about. Simmons stated that she remembered some of the events of December 23, 1981, the day before Christmas Eve. Simmons stated that on December 23, 1981, she, accompanied by some friends, was driving Paul Bare's old model maroon colored Ford car. Further, she stated that she drove up to the garage (Paul Bare's) and there she remembered seeing "Red"/Ron Miller and a bald headed man in a black car parked at the garage. Simmons stated that she had a short conversation with Ron Miller and then left with her friends. Simmons stated that Paul Bare did not return home for the evening meal, and that she knew that he was up at the garage when she went to bed about 11:00 P.M. Simmons said that she started drinking about 5:00 P.M. on the afternoon of December 23, 1981, and that she went to bed before Paul got home because she knew that he did not like for her to drink and would have fussed at her had he known that she was drinking. Later, Sheriff Waddell showed me a heavy blue trash bag that was woven with white string. Vines, in his statement, described bags that appeared to be similar and stated that Paul Bare got two heavy blue bags on the early morning of December 24, 1981, and that he, Miller, Hattaway, and Bare placed the marijuana from the metal trash cans into the bags.

Early on the morning of January 9, 1982, Sheriff Waddell and I picked Vines up from a motel in Jefferson, NC. Just prior to picking up Vines, Sheriff Waddell placed one of the above mentioned blue bags on the front seat of his patrol vehicle. Vines got into the back seat of the vehicle and we drove away from the motel. Vines spotted the bag on the front seat and said, "You found them," referring to the blue bag. Sheriff Waddell, Vines, and I returned to the Bare premises, went inside, and there joined Detective Robinson, SBI Agent Bueker, and Simmons in the kitchen. Vines spoke to Simmons, and she asked if he was the bald headed man that she had seen raise up from the back seat of the car that Ron Miller was in. Vines said that he was, and she immediately asked him if Paul had anything to do with those boys. Vines said, "Yes it's true, they held a gun on me and made me push Gamboa into the mine shaft." Simmons started screaming, crying and cussing at Vines and ran into the living room. I went with Vines to the Bare garage and he identified it as being the place that he came to on December 23, 1981, with Gamboa, Miller, and Hattaway. Vines walked to a point in front of the blue and white trailer where Paul Wilson Bare lived in December 27, 1976. There Vines indicated the area where he and Hattaway took Gamboa from the trunk at gunpoint and cut the tape from his wrists, and there allowed Gamboa to urinate. Vines stated that a handcuff was placed on one of Gamboa's wrists and that he was led up into the woods above the shop and handcuffed to a tree. I accompanied Vines to a wooded area above the shop and there Vines pointed out the tree that Gamboa had been handcuffed to. I used a flashlight to conduct further investigation and observed a piece of fiberglass tape near the tree. I pointed out the tape to Vines and he remarked that it appeared to be the tape that was around the wrists of Gamboa. We left the area of the tree without disturbing the leaves, tape, or a limb, and returned and joined Sheriff Waddell. Sheriff Waddell returned with Vines and myself to the above mentioned tree and further observations were made with our flashlight. Sheriff Waddell left the area as previously observed to wait for daylight to photograph the tree, its surroundings, and tape. I accompanied Vines to the Bare garage and there he identified an old Hudson automobile that he had observed in the shop on December 23 and 24, 1981. Also Vines showed us the air filter that he had previously referred to in his statement along with other items that were there on December 23 and 24, 1981. I found the telephone that had been referred to by Vines on January 5, 1982, to be properly located as were the other items he had referred to such as the maroon colored Hudson with suicide door and a "Fuzz Buster" on the dash as previously referred to by Vines.

On the morning of January 9, 1982, I was present when photographs were made of the tree, tape, and garage previously mentioned and observed Sheriff Waddell as he removed the tape from its location and placed it in a plastic bag.

On January 9, 1982, I initiated an urgent trace of the three firearms found on January 8, 1982 at the Paul Wilson Bare premises.

On January 12, 1982, The Asheville Post of Duty was advised by phone by the Tracing Department of the Bureau of Alcohol, Tobacco, and Firearms, Washington, D.C., that they had traced the above described Sturm Ruger, .44 magnum caliber revolver from its manufacturer, Sturm Ruger, Inc., Southport, Connecticut, to Davidson Supply Company, Greensboro, NC, and that the records of Davidson Supply Company, Greensboro, NC, reflected that they had shipped the above described Sturm Ruger, .44 magnum caliber revolver to Don's Gun Shop, Asheville, NC.

On February 4, 1982, I received a Department of Treasury, Bureau of Alcohol, Tobacco, and Firearms Request for Certification of Firearms Record Search from

Sturm Ruger and Company, Inc., Southport, Connecticut 06497, certifying that the above described Sturm Ruger, .44 magnum caliber revolver had been manufactured and sold by said firm in Southport, Fairfield County, Connecticut, to Davidson Supply Company, Greensboro, NC. The certification was completed and signed by Margaret Kahler, Record Custodian.

On January 31, 1982, I received in the mail a statement that I had prepared earlier and mailed to Sandra Louise Lowdermilk, Bookkeeper, Gun Room, Davidson Supply Company, a Federal Firearms Licensee, 2703 High Point Road, Greensboro, NC, dated 1-28-82, bearing her signature. Her statement reflected the acquisition and disposition of a Sturm Ruger, .44 magnum caliber revolver, model New Super Blackhawk, serial #84-06729, six shot, 7½" barrel length, blue steel finish. Further, the statement reflects that their records show that they received the above described firearm on 4-23-81, under Invoice #31586 from Sturm Ruger, Inc., Southport, Connecticut. Further, the statement reflected that on 5-4-81, they shipped the above described firearm by UPS to Don's Gun Shop, 144 Tunnel Road, Asheville, NC, under Invoice #129605. The statement states that Davidson Supply Company received a check dated 6-8-81 from Don's Gun Shop, check #9636, for payment of the above described firearm.

On February 3, 1982, I witnessed Donald Leroy Brown, a Federal Firearms Licensee, sign a statement that related to his acquisition and disposition of the above described firearm on or about 5-6-81. Further, his statement states that his firearm was picked up by Jerry Hipps, a Federal Firearms Licensee in Canton, NC.

On February 3, 1982, I observed Jerry Ray Hipps, owner and operator of Jerry's Gunsmith Service, Route 3, Box 31, Canton, NC, as he signed and dated a statement that I swore him to, that I had prepared for him related to his acquisition and disposition of a Sturm Ruger, .44 magnum caliber revolver, model New Super Blackhawk, serial #84-06729, six shot, 7½" barrel length, blue steel finish. Further, his statement related that he got the firearm described above from Don's Gun Shop on the date of its delivery by UPS and presently has in his possession the Invoice #129605. Further, his statement states that he let Larry Robinson, a friend and acquaintance, have the pistol and a custom made McKenzie holster several days later.

On February 4, 1982, I observed Larry Ray Robinson sign and date a statement that I swore him to, that I had prepared for him, relating to his acquisition and disposition of the Sturm Ruger, .44 magnum caliber revolver, model Nee Super Blackhawk, serial #84-06729, six shot, 7½" barrel, blue steel. In his statement, Robinson detailed how and when he picked up the firearm and custom made holster, along with an ATF Form 4473, from Jerry Hipps. Further, the statement described its sale on or about May 11, 1981, to Roger Chambers at the Robinson residence on Scarlet Drive, Fletcher, NC, and the filling out of sections of the 4473 [form] relating to the identity of Roger Clyde Chambers, the obtaining of his North Carolina driver's license and the recording of the driver's license number on the 4473, and the return of the 4473 and a permit #4457 to purchase the pistol issue by C. Jack Arrington of Haywood County, NC.

On February 3, 1982, I observed Roger Clyde Chambers sign and date a statement that I swore him to relating to his acquisition and disposition of the only pistol that he had ever owned, being the above described Sturm Ruger, .44 magnum caliber revolver from Larry Robinson in Fletcher, NC, and its sale to Kim Allen at Route 3, Box 613, Canton, NC.

On 2-3-82, I observed David Kim Allen as he signed and dated a statement that I swore him to relating to his acquisition and disposition of the only pistol that he had ever owned, being the above described Sturm Ruger, .44 magnum caliber revolver, model New Super Blackhawk, six shot, 7½" barrel length, blue steel finish from Roger Chambers, several weeks prior to a date in July, 1981, at his residence. The statement also shows the sale of the same revolver at his residence to Lonnie Marshall Gamboa, a friend that he had met at AB Tech in Asheville, NC, some 18 months prior to July, 1981. Further, the statement reflects that Allen was also able to identify a photograph of Lonnie Marshall Gamboa.

On February 11, 1982, I joined Gamboa's attorney, Joel Bond Stevenson, and an associate of Gamboa, George Silver, and accompanied them to the Lonnie Marshall Gamboa residence, 9 Westview Drive, Asheville, NC. There, with their cooperation, a cardboard box used to house a Sturm Ruger Box for the aforementioned .44 magnum caliber revolver, one tan colored soft leather gun case, two boxes of ear protectors, ammunition, spent brass cartridges, and other items were located, retained, and a receipt given for them. On February 18, 1982, the items removed from the Gamboa residence were given to Sheriff Waddell for inclusion in the case.

COLE, DONALD R. [1]

Cole's Official Sworn Statement
Note: Cole refers to Clayton Boggess as "Clifton Boggess."

Moffitt Branch Shootout

On November 7, 1981, Mrs. Taylor, the clerk at the EconoLodge Motel in Asheville, North Carolina, called the Sheriff's Department Communicator saying she had a white male at the desk stating he was looking for Miller and Boggess in room 142. The man had a gun and told the clerk if the officer didn't get there soon he was going to Miller's home on Moffitt Road. Officer Boggess arrived and was told by Mrs. Taylor the subject had left in a blue Cadillac. Minutes later Linda Miller of Moffitt Road called dispatch and said there was a shootout at her home and shooting into her occupied dwelling. Rhew #504 arrived and located a blue Cadillac in the driveway and then circled the residence to locate James Ronald Anthony Jr. armed with a Smith and Wesson hand gun serial number A-685955. Anthony was taken into custody after a short fight in the yard behind the house.

Ronald R. Cole, Criminal Investigator, went into the Gary Miller home where there were Miller, his wife Linda, Paula Jo Anthony, white female, and a two year old child, where he observed two bullet holes in the back door. He also observed three shotgun blasts inside to outside through the wooden front door. When Cole was taken upstairs by Gary Miller, he observed bullet holes and broken windows in both south upstairs bedrooms. Cole also located a Remington model 742 Serial number A-7230524 30-06 caliber with a 2×7 power Redfield scope and expanded casings in the bedroom to right of the stairs at broken window. Also, 12 gauge shells and Remington model 1100 M-532179-V, a stolen firearm from North Kannapolis Police Department. He advised Gary Miller that he was in possession of a stolen firearm. Miller told Cole to follow him into his bedroom. When they entered the back bedroom to the left of the stairs, Miller informed the officer this was the bedroom of him and his wife and that he was afraid for his wife and child due to the involvement with Anthony, Gamboa, and Boggess.

There was an immediate threat to deputies and others in the house at that time of being shot by Lonnie Gamboa and Clifton Boggess. The police had already taken Anthony into custody. Miller's next statement to the officer was of the death and murders of the Durham family in Boone. He then told officers to take the other nickel 9 mm Smith and Wesson Serial number A-606544 that was on the kitchen cabinet for further protection of himself and Miller's family until we all got out of the house or the ones outside were arrested. He also told the officer and the motel verified the before named people were in rooms 142 and 144. The officer sent units to the motel. While the units were at the motel Clifton Boggess was located on Moffitt Road in front of the Miller home. He had an automatic pistol clip in his pocket and a large amount of cash. Officer Hembree and other officers located the people in the motel and an immediate search for weapons was done. They found more weapons and more cocaine, marijuana, and hashish. Gamboa's Ford van was impounded. Anthony's Toyota was searched after a search warrant was obtained. November 8, 1981, more weapons were located, a 6mm model 700 Remington with Weaver scope serial number 6700437 by authority of NCIC showed it to be stolen from Cape Girardeau in Missouri was found in Lonnie Gamboa's van. The officers returned to Miller's residence with permission to search warrant signed by Miller where they located more cocaine, a large amount of cash and another hand gun. Some hours later, Gary Miller told Cole and Herb Deweese there was more Cocaine in the residence and took narcotics officers back to the house and turned more Cocaine over to them.

The officers then interviewed Karen Kirk Young about another weapon that information showed her to have. Young voluntarily turned the weapon over and signed a permission to search. From then she took Officer Cole Hollifield and Smith back to her residence where she turned over a large quantity of drugs including 22 pounds of unwrapped Hashish in Lebanon gauze and approximately 40 pounds of marijuana. When they returned to the courthouse Karen Kirk Young was jailed in lieu of $5,000 secured bond.

Sunday, November 8, 1981, Officer Call, Rickman, Hembree, and Bill Rhew issued search warrants for the James Ronald Anthony trailer where they seized 13 weapons, some bags of ½ oz. marijuana. While they were at the trailer, Anthony's sister, Paula Jo Anthony, arrived and informed the officer of more guns and items left at her trailer by Clifton Boggess when he was staying with her. After getting written permission from the sister, the officer searched and found an assortment of drug cutting equipment and paraphernalia. Items included a .22 caliber handgun being a Colt Huntsman 6" barrel blue steel serial number 51010885. The weapon was reported in NCIC as a stolen weapon from Miami, Florida. A second .22 caliber handgun, a Ruger Mark, serial number 16-23137 which was reported stolen from Waynesville, North Carolina. In phone conversation with detectives the weapon had been stolen during a first degree burglary and involved in an armed robbery in Henderson County, North Carolina. The officer was informed that three black males were arrested and confessed to the crimes and said the weapon was supposed to have been thrown into a river. Further observation of the combined property of the Anthonys showed extensive target practicing and Paula Jo Anthony showed me three bullet holes in the bedroom wall of her trailer and stated that Clifton Boggess had shot at her home. The officer located 2 spent .30 caliber casings on her bed. This was evidence of the .30 caliber combine Gary Miller talked about. The officer in charge had used the same kind of weapon in Viet Nam and knew it to be a fully automatic weapon, records showed that on November 1, 1981 James Roland Anthony Jr. purchased from K-Mart at Skyland, North Carolina. Four boxes of 50 rounds of 9 mm Ruger ammunition, 4 boxes of 50 rounds of .30 caliber carbine as of that date, 11-8-81, the weapon or the ammo for the .30 cal. had not been located while searching the Anthony residence. The officer found safe deposit box keys. Arrangements were made to open the boxes. Before the boxes could be secured, Karen Kirk Young had made bail, already opened the boxes and disappeared and had not been seen or heard from. Her maroon over white Grand Prix contained Anthony's blue coat along with the keys to his car and trailer. Agent David Bossard and ATF Agent Tommy Chapman compiled a complete list of all the weapons seized and Chapman was tracing the weapons for further location and identification of some 59 weapons during searches from the residence of Gary Miller, the Cadillac of James Anthony, the motel room at EconoLodge, the Ford van of Lonnie Gamboa, the residence of Paula Jo Anthony, the sister who lives next door. Agents Call and Deweese interviewed Gary Miller at his request to continue talking about the incident. Miller told about the people involved in the Boone murders in detail and the existence of a .38 caliber revolver that had been buried and dug up by James Anthony and implied the possible connection of this weapon to the double homicide on Haywood Road in Skyland, NC.

COLE, DONALD R. [2]

Note: Cole refers to Clayton Boggess as "Clifton" and "Clifton Clayton."

Moffitt Branch Shootout Investigation at Miller's House (continued)

I then interviewed Karen Kirk Young about another weapon, information showed her to have. I talked with her about the weapon and she voluntarily turned it over to us and signed a Permission to search form, and took myself, Hollifield and Smith back to her residence to surrender her quantity of drugs. We seized some 22 pounds of unwrapped Hashish in Lebanon gauze, approximately forty pounds of Marijuana and returned to the court house. She was jailed in lieu of $5,000 secured bond.

Sunday, 11-8-81, myself, Rickman, Hembree and Bill Rhew, issued search warrants for the Anthony trailer, where we seized 13 weapons, a bag of some ½ ounce of marijuana. While we were at his trailer, his sister arrived, Paula Jo Anthony. She told me of more guns and other items left at her trailer by Clifton Boggess, when he was staying with her. I went to her trailer and she signed inventory and permission to seize those weapons, also confiscated and was an assortment of drug cutting and paraphernalia items. A .22 caliber handgun being a Colt-Huntsman 6" barrel blue steel, serial number S101088-S, this weapon reported in NCIC as a stolen weapon from Miami, Florida a second .22 caliber handgun was located. It is a Ruger Mark 1 Serial number 16-23137. This weapon is NCIC as stolen from Waynesville, North Carolina. As of phone conversation with detectives in Waynesville, this weapon was stolen during a first degree burglary and involved in an armed robbery in Henderson County. Was advised 3 black males were arrested and confessed to these crimes and this weapon was supposed to have been thrown into a river. Further observation of the combined property of the Anthony's showed of extensive target practicing and Paula Jo Anthony showed me 3 bullet holes in the bedroom wall of her trailer, and stated that Clifton Clayton Boggess had shot at her home. I located 2 spent .30 caliber casings on her bed. This is evidence of the .30 caliber carbine Gary Miller told of and being an M-2 type, this officer used this kind of weapon in Viet Nam and knew it to be a fully automatic weapon. Records show that on November 1, 1981 that James Roland Anthony, Jr., purchased from K-Mart at Skyland, North Carolina: 4 boxes of 50 rounds of 9 mm Lugar ammunition, 4 boxes of 50 rounds of .30 caliber carbine ammunition and gave his address of Route 4, Box 143, Arden, North Carolina, Date of birth 06-11-50 N.C. DL# 264653 for positive identification for purchase, and this added evidence of the existence of the .30 caliber carbine at time of this follow-up this weapon not located or the ammunition for the .30 caliber. I have the 4 boxes of 9 mm in my custody. While searching the residence of James Roland Anthony, Jr., I found 2 safe deposit box keys, and Gene Jarvis and defendant with the presence of his attorney are going to enter this deposit box to see contents.

Karen Kirk Young had 2 safe deposit boxes and upon release from jail did in fact go to them, 1 here in Asheville at 9:02 A.M. She has not been seen or heard from since.

Her car a maroon over white Grand Prix contained Anthony's blue coat found that morning on Anthony's mother's car in Skyland, and did contain keys to his trailer and car.

David Bossard and Tommy Chapman of ATF are doing a finalized list of all weapons seized and Chapman is going to trace weapons by his authority for further location and identification of some 59 weapons seized during searches from the residence of Gary Miller, the Cadillac of Anthony, the motel room at EconoLodge, the Ford Van of Lonnie Gamboa, the residence of James Roland Anthony, Jr., and the residence of Paula Jo Anthony, sister who lives next door.

Herb Deweese and myself interviewed Gary Miller, at his request to continue talking to me about the incident. He told of the people involved in the Boone murders in detail, and the existence of a .38 caliber revolver that had been buried and dug up by James Anthony, and implied the possible connection of this weapon to the double homicide on Haywood Road in Skyland.

I have obtained statements of all officers involved, starting with the phone call made to Clarence Aiken, dispatcher from the Taylor female at EconoLodge and James Anthony taking the phone from her and conversation with him. To Anthony going to the Miller residence, shots fired into the dwelling, evidence located, Bill Rhew first officer at the Miller house and arrested Anthony. Riddle locating the drugs and weapons in the Cadillac of Anthony and other officers involved and what was located or they were told or observed.

Further investigation is to follow due to the in-depth involvement of these people in Cocaine trafficking in Western North Carolina. Information obtained shows that Boggess has a brother in Marathon, Florida to these people. Herb Deweese talked with authorities in Marathon and confirmed this information.

Investigation Continues   Donald R. Cole, Criminal Investigator
                                           — November 9, 1981

FAGEL, JAY

Jay Fagel's Official Sworn Statement

On December 30, 1981, at 11:40 P.M., Detectives R.R. Robinson, V.H. Smith, Lt. W.R. Annarino, interviewed John Charles Fagel, "Jay," of Rt. 3, Leicester, white male, DOB 3-26-48, NC operator's license no. 5924205, in reference to the kidnapping of Tom Forester and Darlene Callahan. The interview took place in person at the Asheville Police Department.

208-H-1 (pp. 7–10) from the Asheville Police Department

On Wednesday, December 30, 1981, at 11:40 P.M. , Detective Ross Robinson of the Asheville Police Department, interviewed John Charles Fagel, reference this investigation.

Mr. Fagel related that he had received a phone call on December 12, 1981 at approximately 4:00 P.M. from Tom Forester, who wanted him (Fagel) to come to the market on Lexington Avenue and help him jump off the motorcycle, which he had been riding. Mr. Fagel and his son, Blaine, met Fagel's girlfriend at Bojangle's on Patton Avenue at 5:30 P.M. for dinner, and it was about 6:00 P.M. before he and his son arrived at the Lexington Avenue Market. Someone at the market told Mr. Fagel that Forester had already left. Mr. Fagel and his son, followed by Fagel's girlfriend, went to the In-Town Motel, where Tom Forester and Darlene Callahan were staying in room 15.

Fagel's girlfriend was following him, in order that he leave Forester's vehicle at the motel. Arriving at the motel, Fagel could see a black, older model pickup truck, parked near Tom and Darlene's room, and Forester was standing outside the room. Mr. Forester was drunk and told him that some "good ole boys" from Sandy Mush had helped him to get the motorcycle in the room. Several men were standing outside the room, and when he opened the door to Forester's and Callahan's room, he could see Callahan inside, naked, with a couple of guys in the room. Mr. Fagel shielded his son's view and closed the door. Mr. Fagel left, arriving home between 6:30 and 7:00 P.M. Around 8:00 P.M., he put his son to bed and he went to sleep. Mr.

Fagel was awakened at 8:40 P.M., by a knock on the door. He answered the door, and found "RED" (ALAN HATTAWAY) and GARY MILLER, and a short, dark haired, white male in his forties, at the door. "RED" asked, "Where's the bike, and where's Tom?" Mr. Fagel told "RED" that his house had been broken into, and the bike had been stolen. Mr. Fagel had been keeping "RED's" black Harley-Davidson Motorcycle in his home, until about one (1) month prior to this time. Mr. Forester had wanted the motorcycle, and along with Mr. Fagel, had contrived the story that the house had been broken into, and the motorcycle stolen. Mr. Fagel related this to "RED." "RED" obviously did not believe this story, and they came into the house and turned the lights on. Mr. MILLER went to the room where the motorcycle had been stored, then cocked his pistol and stuck it in Mr. Fagel's ear. Mr. Fagel described the pistol as being a .38 caliber revolver, blue steel, with a short barrel. Mr. Fagel was then again asked where Mr. Forester and the bike were. Mr. Fagel told them that the motorcycle and Tom Forester were at the In-Town Motel. Mr. MILLER and "RED" told him to get in the van and come with them Mr. Fagel told them that his son was in the house, and he was not leaving him there alone. They waited for Mr. Fagel to awaken his son. "RED" instructed him to bring his son with them because they did not want anything (implying phone call to Forester or the Police while they were en route to the motel). Mr. MILLER told him that it would be better if his son accompanied them because if anything did happen, they knew who he and his son were, and could prevent anything from happening to them. During this time, "RED" kept his hand on the grip of his pistol, which he carried in a shoulder holster, in a ready manner. Mr. Fagel and his son got into an off-white or beige colored van, parked outside their house, with "RED," GARY MILLER, and the unknown white male, who was operating the vehicle. They traveled Leicester Highway, Patton Avenue, to Interstate 240, exiting onto Highway 70, traveling east to the light, near Bell School, turning right, and finally stopping at Sarge's Lounge. The white male, who was operating the vehicle, got out, and Mr. MILLER drove the vehicle to the In-Town Motel. During the trip, "RED" asked Mr. Fagel where his nine (9) millimeter was. Mr. Fagel told him it was at his house. Mr. MILLER parked the vehicle, and they got out and approached room number 15. As they approached the room, Darlene Callahan walked around the corner, carrying food. Ms. Callahan stated "he's probably not here." "RED" asked her where her key was and Ms. Callahan did not reply, but shook her head no. "RED" instructed her to knock on the door. After a long time, Mr. Forester finally pulled back the curtain, with a puzzled look on his face, and barely cracked the door. "RED" forced the door open and Mr. MILLER entered the room, followed by "RED," Darlene, and Mr. Fagel. "RED" kept his hand in a ready position on the handle of his gun, in the shoulder holster. Mr. MILLER checked the room to see if anyone else was inside. "RED" put Darlene in a chair, directly behind the door, which was now closed. "RED" then saw the motorcycle, which was damaged, and examined the spot where a mural had been painted on the tank. "RED" told them that the bike was the bike his dead brother had painted. Mr. Fagel told them that Forester had removed this mural, so that the bike could not be easily recognized. Mr. Forester asked what was going on, at which time, GARY MILLER struck him in the ear with his handgun.

Mr. Forester was standing at the foot of the bed, wearing underpants and an insulated undershirt, when he was struck, and blood ran down onto the insulated undershirt. "RED" stated "I haven't been this mad in a long time." "RED" then looked at Tom and asked where his money was. Mr. Forester made a gesture with his empty hands, indicating that he did not have the money. "RED" then asked "how'd the bike get smashed?" Mr. Forester replied "I wrecked it." Mr. MILLER then asked Ms Callahan if she was still using needles. Ms. Callahan told him no, she was on Methadone. Mr. MILLER then replied "that's worse." Mr. MILLER then ordered Mr. Fagel to sit down in a chair, and "RED" told Mr. Forester he ought to take him to the clubhouse. Mr. Fagel later overheard "RED" say that he was going to take Ms. Callahan to Chicago to work off Tom's debt. Mr. Fagel then asked Mr. Forester "tell them I did not have anything to do with this." Mr. Forester explained to "RED" and Mr. MILLER that Mr. Fagel did not have anything to do with the motorcycle. Mr. Fagel then went outside and saw an Asheville Police Cruiser arrive. Mr. Fagel was afraid that the surprise of Police Officer would prompt shooting, so he stuck his head back inside the motel room, and told them that a Police Officer was there. Mr. MILLER came out of the room and walked directly to the officer and told him that he was visiting friends and they would be leaving shortly. The officer appeared satisfied and left. Mr. MILLER then walked to Mr. Fagel and told him how important it was for him to keep his mouth shut, and they "knew who he was and who his son was." Mr. Fagel then went to the room and asked "RED" to let he and his son go. Mr. MILLER said that they had a back-up and it was necessary for he and his son to accompany them, in the event that something happened, such as an automobile accident or being stopped by the Police, and nothing would happen to Mr. Fagel and his son.

Mr. Fagel and "RED" then loaded the motorcycle into the van, and he and his son got into the van to support the vehicle. Mr. Forester and Ms. Callahan were placed into the van to support the motorcycle. Mr. MILLER then drove the van down Highway 70 to the Park Drive-in, where he pulled up to the ticket booth. Someone approached the van and Mr. MILLER told them to get away from the van. He then said "get Virginia."

Someone came to the ticket window, and Mr. MILLER said "we're going in for a few minutes." Mr. MILLER is a former employee of the Park Drive-In. Mr. MILLER drove the van to one corner of the lot and got out. "RED" then ordered Mr. Fagel and his son to sit in the driver's seat. They sat there for a long time in total silence, for about an hour. Mr. Forester asked about Lonnie. "RED" told him that "Jay" (Mr. Fagel) "doesn't know anything about that, and we'll talk about that later." "RED" then told him "you stick your arm out to help someone, and they cut it off." After a lengthy wait, a large black car pulled up beside the van operated by GARY MILLER. Ms. Callahan and Mr. Forester were moved from the van and placed in the car. Mr. Forester was placed in the rear seat with "RED," and Ms. Callahan was placed in the front seat with Mr. MILLER, who drove the vehicle away. Mr. Fagel overheard Mr. MILLER make some remark about chaining her to the front seat. Mr. MILLER told Mr. Fagel to keep quiet or else, and asked "is that fair enough?" Mr. Fagel was told to remain in the van and remain there for a short time.

He was getting out of the van to walk away with his son, when a small car, probably foreign, drove up with two (2) white males in it. He did not see the second (2nd) occupant of the vehicle, but the man who got out was the same man who had come to his house with "RED" and Mr. MILLER. Mr. Fagel was given instructions that he was to drive a small foreign car, parked near his car, on the following day, to Sarge's Lounge, and leave it there with the keys in it.

Arriving at his home, Mr. Fagel was followed into the house by the white male, who was still holding a gun on him. Once inside, the white male requested Fagel's nine (9) millimeter handgun. He gave him the gun and the man held both guns on him, while exiting. Mr. Fagel then left with his son and drove to his girlfriend's house, because he was afraid to stay at home.

The next day, he drove the small foreign car to Sarge's Lounge on NC 81, as instructed, and left it parked with the keys in it. He was picked up by a friend and driven back home.

About two (2) days later, Mr. Fagel decided the best thing he could do was to abandon the vehicle, belonging to Forester at Quincy's Steakhouse, on Henderson Road, because he realized Forester's vehicle carried the tag from a van formerly owned by Forester, and was thereby improperly registered.

Please refer to enclosure number two (2).

Note: A second partial accounting of Fagel's statement was included in the papers submitted to Sheriff Waddell but has been omitted from this book.

GOSS, CAPTAIN EUGENE [1] — Body Recovery
Official Statement from Captain Gene Goss
January 25, 1982

On January 25, 1982, at approximately 3:30 P.M., I (Goss) along with Officer Bueker of the Asheville Police Department and the "Nashville Flame" were lowered by crane into the air shaft at Ore Knob Mine. They were lowered approximately 230 feet to where they were able to set down on solid ground and anchor to two pilings — a passageway led off to two sides. Goss shined a spotlight further off to the right and observed part of a body lying in a semi-fetal position. They unhooked from the crane and hooked onto a life-line. They worked their way down near where the body was lying and observed a leg sticking out of the debris to the left of the other body. Goss held a light and Officer Bueker made photographs of what they observed. After photos were taken, Bueker and Goss went on to where the bodies lay and began to try to retrieve the bodies. The bodies were frozen and could not be moved. They dug with pick and shovel around the body on top. The body was clothed with a tan colored coat, a blue shirt with red stripes, a pair of denim pants, a tan belt, and a cowboy type boot on one foot. Goss also observed that the other body had a thermal top and denim type pants and one shoe and also had dark hair. At this point, they were able to loosen the frozen body from the ground. Officer Bueker placed a shovel under the hip of the body. They returned to the point where the "Nashville Flame" had the crane anchor, hooked up and were pulled back to the surface along with the first body.

At approximately 5:30 P.M., Goss along with Officer Bueker and Officer Ross Robinson of the Asheville Police Department descended back down to the shaft and used the same procedure to remove the other body believed to be Thomas Forester. They searched the entire area finding no evidence of any other bodies anywhere in the shaft.

GOSS, CAPTAIN EUGENE [2]

Official Statement on Arrest of Gary Miller

On June 10, 1982, at approximately 12:45 I (Goss) received a call from Detective Hutches of the Caldwell County Sheriff's Office that they thought Gary Miller was living in a camper in Caldwell County. Sheriff Waddell and myself left for Caldwell County and along with officers from Asheville, SBI, Caldwell County, ATF and SBI Officers. Miller was arrested at approximately 4:30 P.M. A .357 Mag., 38 cal and a .22 Beretta were taken from Miller's camper. Miller was transported to the Caldwell County Jail and from there to the Ashe County Detention Center. Gary Miller was advised of his rights at approximately 4:50 P.M. by Sheriff Waddell in my presence. Gary Miller made a statement to Sheriff Waddell and myself on the way back and at the Ashe County Detention Center.

LOCKWOOD, SGT.

Official Statement of Sgt. Lockwood

Sgt. Lockwood stated that he knew Jo-Jo (Joseph E. Vines) and that he was a very truthful person and was an excellent undercover man. Sgt. Lockwood stated that Jo-Jo's mother lives in Marin county, Florida and that he and known Jo-Jo since 1977. In 1977, Jo-Jo had been working undercover and was involved in a ten-pound buy-bust which also led to the recovery of $20,000 worth of stolen property and cleared fifty (50) breaking and enterings. if Jo-Jo tells you he will be in court, he will. Jo-Jo has no criminal record that I know of. Sgt. Lockwood stated that Richard Barton of the Lenoir, North Carolina Police Department knew Jo-Jo and that Richard Burton was a Deputy in Martin County at one time and had used Jo-Jo then.

MILLER, BOBBY WAYNE

Official Statement of Bobby Wayne Miller

DOB 04-19-47

Bobby Miller stated that on December 23, 1981, he was working in Paul Bare's garage in Laurel Springs. That Paul Bare was the only person in the garage with him. At approximately 1:30–2:00 P.M., someone knocked on the door and a red haired man that he knew as Al told Paul that someone wanted to see him outside. That Al stayed inside and Paul Bare went outside and closed the door. Bare was gone approximately 10 minutes. He (Bare) came back inside and started working, and a short time later, he (Bobby) started to leave [and noticed] that down near the trailer just below the garage two men were talking. They had some papers in their hands. One was a real big man with a cap pulled down low over his eyes. The other man was holding a bottle of liquor and offered him a drink that he declined, walked on down to his truck and left to go home. That he went to his house in Glendale and while he was there, he saw no one taken from the trunk of a car that when he left, he saw two cars, one a black car, he thought was a Mercury, the other was a tan or yellow car, wasn't sure what kind it was. Later that evening he received a call from his wife that she was at Paul Bare's house. That she had been in Wilkes County with Patti Simmons, Bare's girlfriend, Christmas shopping. That he told her he would pick her up as he was going by Sam Kern's house to look at some calves he was trying to buy. He in fact did pick up his wife there late that evening. Paul Bare did not borrow his pickup that night or any other time. Miller stated that he did not know either of the two men that was standing outside when he left, that he did not pay very much attention to them. He did notice that one of them was a very big man that kept his cap pulled low down to his eyes, and that the other was slim build with brown hair; there was another man there on the outside working on a tractor, and that he left about the same time that he did.

MILLER, GARY

Official Sworn Statement of Gary Hansford Miller
Ashe County Detention Center
June 10, 1982 7:10 P.M.

Gary Hansford Miller was advised of his rights by Sheriff Waddell immediately after being arrested in Caldwell County. Miller talked to us for some length of time about the Gamboa and Forester murders. Miller stated that he had been dealing in drugs for several years in Asheville but quit when he wife became pregnant. That he was paid a visit at his home in Asheville by Boggess and others that they brought fifty pounds of marijuana and told him they knew he could get rid of it, that he had a wife and daughter and he took it as a threat. Miller stated that he did get rid of the fifty pounds of marijuana and put in his basement. Also, a man by the name of "Whiskers" moved in his house. They were various dealings in marijuana and cocaine.

Hattaway was mad at Tommy Forester for wrecking his motorcycle but he did not believe that he was mad enough to kill him over that. Miller believed that it was over money owed to the Tennessee people. That on the night Tommy Forester and Darlene Callahan was brought to Paul Bare's residence it was late in the morning hours. When they arrived there he got out of the car and knocked on the door at Paul Bare's residence. Paul came to the door immediately, and there was some moving of cars around because a car had the driveway blocked. Then they drove on up to the garage at Paul's residence, the people that he knew was there was himself (Miller) Allen Hattaway known as "Red," Darlene Callahan. Paul Bare and a man from Tennessee (that he declined to name at this time), but did state that he was driving a Ford LTD, blue with a black vinyl top with a Tennessee tag. This man was from Tennessee was connected with the "Dixie Mafia." They stated they were going for a ride. Also, that he knew that Tommy Forester would not be coming back. Miller felt that he had saved Darlene Callahan's life that they were going to take her too, but he asked her if she wanted to go with them or stay with him. He asked them to let him take care of her, and was told if anything happened that he (Miller) would be held responsible. Then Bare, Hattaway, and Forester left, along with the Tennessee man who was in his car by himself. It was common for car to block the road down at the highway where you went up to the mine shaft. Miller and Darlene waited in a truck parked in front of a mobile home at Bare's house. He (Miller) did not know how long they were gone but it seemed a long time. When they returned the man from Tennessee was not with them, also Tommy Forester was not with them. Darlene asked where Tommy was, and was told by either Bare or Hattaway that he had to go talk over some matters with someone, but he knew where Forester was taken, but did not see anyone push him in the hole. Miller had been up to the hole several times before and said that he was put down in the hole on one occasion from a rope on the back of a wrecker. Miller later heard Bare and Hattaway discuss what happened, and he believed that Forester owed the people in Tennessee money. I (Goss) asked Miller if he knew anything about any more bodies at the Ore Knob Mine or anywhere else. He (Miller) stated that he wouldn't be surprised but he did not know of any more bodies at the Ore Knob, but he knew of several holes around. I (Goss) asked him where and he stated that there was several holes on property that his people owned in Watauga County, that connected with Ashe County and Long Hope Falls. They would be better for use than the Ore Knob Mine, they were old mica mines. We, Sheriff Waddell and Goss, asked Miller about taking Darlene Callahan to Chicago. He (Miller) stated that her only objection to going was that she did not like the cold weather. When they left her, they left a loaded gun in her room. Miller also stated that on December 23rd, when Lonnie Gamboa was brought to Paul Bare's residence in Ashe County, that it was over $35,000 that they came up short on a drug transaction, and that was when it became a situation where he or Gamboa one had to come up with some answers or the missing money. The reason Gamboa went into the hole instead of him was that he was able to back up his story, and that Gamboa was not. He (Miller) stated that there were seven people present when Lonnie Gamboa was brought to Paul Bare's residence on December 23, 1981.

We (Waddell and Goss) asked Miller who all was present that he knew. Miller stated that he, Hattaway, Vines, Bare and Gamboa was all that he knew by name. We asked if Paul Bare's girlfriend was present, and Miller stated that she was not, that he remembered someone saying she was Christmas shopping. When she returned, there was another girl with her; the other people there did not know her name. Miller was asked why Gamboa would be taken from a car trunk, tied up in front of people. Miller stated he did not believe they would do this in front of people not involved or people that could not be trusted. Miller was asked what happened up at the hole on the night Gamboa was thrown in the Ore Knob. Miller declined to say except that Jo-Jo vines was a hired killer and he believed the reason Vines told was, he was afraid that they would find out he was working on the law's side. He stated that Paul Bare could get information on anyone within five minutes by phone, through the Police Information Network, they had a station set up where the signals could be intercepted. The PIN system was through the telephone company which was controlled by satellites and could be intercepted that way.

Miller stated Vines seemed really worried after he gave Paul a name and he made a phone call and received information. Vines thought he would be found out.

Gary Miller also stated that he was in the Long Horn Bar on 421 in Wilkes County some short time before Christmas and heard Claude Vickers make the statement that anyone that would do away with Sheriff Waddell could come by and pick up $30,000 Miller could not remember if it was before or after Forester and Gamboa disappeared or in between their disappearance.

Miller also stated that Paul Bare was really big in the marijuana business including plane loads and boat loads. That Paul Bare was shot by Jim Anthony sometime back, but that "Red" Hattaway nursed him back to health. Miller stated that Jim Anthony was trying to take over Paul Bare's business and Jim Anthony had thought he had killed Paul Bare.

PARSONS, J.D. — Ashe County Deputy
Official sworn statement of J.D. Parsons

I, J.D. Parsons, Deputy Sheriff of Ashe County listened to a conversation between Paul Wilson Bare and Patricia Simmons in the hallway of the Ashe County Jail. Patricia Simmons and Paul Wilson Bare were visiting in the visiting room. I heard the following: Paul and Patricia were discussing the Federal subpoena which had been served on her by Tommy Chapman earlier in the day. Paul asked Patricia are you under arrest? Patricia answered no. Paul then said, just go get in your car and drive away. Patricia stated that she had been brought into the jail and did not have a car. Paul then said, just slip away without them seeing you. Then Paul stated tell the truth in the Grand Jury, tell them about my personal problem with Tommy Chapman, tell them it is over my ex-wife. Then Atlanta was brought up in the conversation, between Paul and Patricia. Paul said that you might be able to slip away in Atlanta.

POWELL, CHARLIE
Official Statement of Charlie Powell
Director of Security for Broyhill Industries in Lenoir

Charlie Powell stated that he knew Jo-Jo or Joseph E. Vines and that Jo-Jo had done undercover operations for them involving stolen guns and dope about two or three years ago. That Jo-Jo had done an excellent job in all but one of the cases. Mr. Powell stated that the one case was put off many times in court and during that time, Jo-Jo became involved in undercover cases in Florida and that Jo-Jo could not get back for the court action in the last case. All in all, Mr. Powell was pleased with Jo-Jo's work. Charlie Powell stated that Det. Richard Barton with Lenoir Police Department was the one that introduced Jo-Jo to them. That Richard Barton knew Jo-Jo in Florida, where he (Barton) used to be an Officer.

ROBERTS, DANNY OREN

Official Sworn Statement of Danny Oren Roberts

On January 5, 1982, at 5:50 P.M., Detective Ross R. Robinson and C. M. Calloway interviewed Danny Oren Roberts, 39 Pleasant Ridge, in Asheville, NC — white male — in reference to the kidnapping of Betty Darlene Callahan and Thomas Eugene Forester. The interview took place in person at the Asheville Police Criminal Investigation (CIB) Department where Mr. Roberts was represented by an attorney, Grover Mooneyham, who is also his brother-in-law. Roberts had been questioned on an earlier occasion by Detective Calloway regarding the possible involvement of his Ford van, color off-white to beige, being involved in the kidnapping of Callahan and Forester. At that time, Roberts insisted that no one other than himself operated the van and that he had no knowledge of this alleged use. Mr. Roberts was again contacted on this date by officers and agreed to come into the CIB office for additional interview. Detective Robinson questioned Roberts as to whether or not he recalled where he might have been on December 12, 1981. Roberts replied that he had not recalled at the time he had spoken with Detective Calloway on a prior occasion, but since then had given it some thought and now recalled his whereabouts and the whereabouts of his van on that date. Mr. Roberts went on to say that on December 12, 1981, between the hours of 7:30 and 8:00 P.M., he was at Sarge's Lounge when he was approached by Gary Miller and a subject known as "Red." Miller requested to borrow Roberts' van. Roberts had given the keys to Miller, and, according to Roberts, Miller returned alone approximately one hour later with the keys. At this time, Miller told Roberts that the van was parked at the drive-in up on the left, referring to the Park Drive-In, and further instructed Roberts to take the motorcycle in the van to Sarge's (Paul D. Harris) residence, which is located on Hawthorne Lane near Sarge's Lounge.

Miller went on to say that the motorcycle belonged to "Red" (Alan Ray Hattaway). Roberts told the officers that he walked to his van which was parked in the area described by Miller. When he arrived at the van, Roberts saw a man and a boy in the van with the door partly open. Inside the van, Roberts saw a black motorcycle. Roberts stated that he drove the man and boy, whom he did not know, to their residence in the Leicester area. During this time, Roberts said the man told him that at one time he had kept this motorcycle for "Red." Roberts said that there was other idle talk about the motorcycle, etc., and upon arriving at the man's and boy's residence, he went inside briefly to use the bathroom. Roberts was questioned by the officers as to whether or not he was armed at the time he entered the man and boy's residence. Roberts replied that he was, and that he had a handgun stuck down in his belt, and always carried a gun when he was at Sarge's. The officer questioned Roberts as to whether or not he had been to this man and boy's residence any time prior to this one occasion, and Roberts stated that he had not. Roberts was questioned as to whether or not and any time he held the weapon in his hand or if he took any weapon from the man and boy's residence while there. Roberts replied that he never held any gun in his hand while at the man and boy's residence nor did he leave with any weapon that was not his own. Roberts stated after a brief conversation with the man, he left, and that the man followed him out the driveway in what Roberts believed to be a 1963 Chevrolet. Roberts was then questioned as to what he did with the motorcycle in his van. He replied that he took the motorcycle as instructed by Miller to Sarge's residence where Sarge (Paul D. Harris) helped him unload the motorcycle and store it in his basement. Roberts refused to make any written statement of this transaction or any recorded statement but was well aware, as was his attorney, the officer made notes during this interview. Roberts told the officer that he would testify as to what he had told the officer, and Roberts' attorney told him that he would be witness to what Roberts had said in this matter.

Investigator's Notes:

#1— The above described motorcycle was seized at Sarge's residence on Hawthorne Lane, January 5, 1982. It had on it at the time, a North Carolina license plate No. 218997, listed by P.I.N. as a 1952 Harley Davidson belonging to Harold Ray Hattaway, Rt. 2, Briarwood Terrace, Salisbury, NC.

#2 — Paul Harris was present at the time the motorcycle was seized, voluntarily gave up the motorcycle, and stated that Gary Miller had asked him to let the motorcycle be stored at his residence, as it belonged to a friend. Harris went on to say that Gary Miller's wife and he had been staying with him and that Herbert Deweese and Donnie Cole of the Buncombe County Sheriff's Department had told Harris that it would be a good idea for the Millers to stay with him since all of the trouble on Moffitt Branch.

#3 — The Roberts van was seen at the In Town Motel by Pat Annas during the kidnapping of Callahan and Forester while he was answering a suspicious vehicle call reported by the manager of the In Town Motel, and the tag number of the Roberts van was recorded at that time on departmental records at 2230 hours on December 12, 1981. Gary Miller did converse with Patrolman Annas at that time regarding the parking location of the van, etc. (See Statements of Jay Fagel and Gary Miller.)

ROBERTS, CAPTAIN MELVIN

Official Statement of Captain Melvin Roberts
At Piney Ridge Church — January 7, 1982–11:45 P.M.

The Wilkes County Sheriff's Office received a call from an unknown caller at about 9:30 P.M. on January 5, 1982 of shots being fired from a car on NC 16 near the Piney Ridge Baptist Church. This call was given to the Highway Patrol. A short time later, I was going up 421 and met a car blinking its lights. I turned onto NC 16 and was going toward Miller's Creek. Then a car started blinking its lights behind me, so I pulled over to see what they wanted. It was Paul Bare. Paul told me about a shooting incident at Piney Ridge Church and insisted I follow him up there, and I did. At the church, Paul showed me where a man was standing that had pulled a gun on him. Paul Bare told me he kicked the man in the groin and that shots rang out as Paul Bare ran to the woods. Paul Bare spotted something on the ground and went over and picked up this wallet and handed it to me. I asked Paul Bare to describe the man and Paul said, "He was a Mexican or an Indian, but like an Italian." I also found two spent 9mm shell casings near the wallet.

SIMMONS, PATRICIA WATSON

Official Statement of Patricia Watson Simmons— January 9, 1982
12:42 A.M.   By Ernest Bueker
(Patricia Watson Simmons was advised of her rights by ATF Agent Tommy Chapman.)

On December 23, 1981, Paul had made me go to Wilkesboro about 11:00 A.M. with Sue Miller. Bob and Paul were at the shop working. Went in the burgundy Mercury. Went to

K-Mart and Pizza Hut and arrived home about 3:30 [to] 4:00 A.M. Drove to shop, Bob's truck wasn't there. Red got out of the car. Red came over and asked, "how doing," and said Bob had left and came back down. Sue called Bob. Didn't see Paul. A black car was sitting down at the trailer, thought saw someone in the car.

Didn't see Gary Miller. Nothing unusual around the shop. Bob came over and got Sue and kids. I stayed at the house. Paul came down about the time Bob came. I stayed at the house. Paul came down about the time Bob came, [and] stayed a few minutes and talked with Bob. Then went back to the shop. Heard cars coming in and out. Paul came back down at 7:00 P.M. and ate supper. He stayed until 8:00 P.M.— were wrapping Christmas presents. Made PJ about 9:00 P.M., started drinking it. I don't remember if the phone rang. I was listening to the radio. Got pretty blitzed. A little before or a little after 12:00 P.M., Paul came home. He passed out from drinking. He doesn't like for me to drink or smoke. Paul didn't act abnormal. Was pretty blitzed and didn't pick up any vibes. He was wearing old work clothes, jeans and old jacket, and work boots. It wasn't muddy, but was chilly. Don't remember exactly how long stayed up, about one- half hour. Didn't hear anything. Paul got up about 7:00 A.M. and I got up about 7:30 A.M. I fixed breakfast. Bob Miller came over about 8:30 or 9:00 A.M.— they went to the garage. Paul acted just as usual. I have never seen a transcript. I went to the garage around 12:00 to 1:00 P.M. Paul and Bob were the only ones at the garage. I cannot remember if any cars went up. I didn't see any keys. Paul hasn't brought any keys to the house. I didn't see Gary, Red, or Sarge that day. The last of November was the first time Sarge came to the house. He was with Gary Miller. Miller introduced him. They talked at the house with me and Paul. They didn't talk about drugs or a shootout.

Sarge had a turquoise ring with red in the center. They talked about how big it was. Red tried on the ring. Sarge was proud of it. Gary's wife was staying at Sarge's. Paul wondered about a place where she would be safe. Red was there and he sized and tried on Red's ring.

The second and last time I saw Sarge was around January 2, 1982. Gary and Sarge came in the night. Gary brought a Christmas present, a blue Nigger hat [golf hat] to Paul. They talked about Gary getting a car real cheap. I was wanting a car, the car had been wrecked and he could get it cheap. I don't know where Gary or Sarge lives, Sarge runs a bar. One of the times, Gary and Sarge was up they talked about getting some expensive jewelry back. Apparently someone stole it. They talked in riddles about getting the jewelry. They had gone to Florida — hasn't seen Sarge since.

Gary came up a couple of days after Christmas, by himself. Driving "spot." He stopped at the house and stayed fifteen minutes. Gary showed me a .44 blue revolver, the gun in the chair that he got out of the car and brought it inside the house. He asked if Paul was here. He knew I liked guns. I tried to get him to give the gun to me. He told me I could have it, but I would have to give it back if he ever wanted it. He asked about Christmas. Then he went up to the garage. He left without stopping at the house. Gary hasn't been back since. I haven't seen Red since the 23rd of December, but think I saw his car.... I have never heard anyone talk about the family and never heard the name Gamboa. Sometime before November, Gary said someone had shot into his house and his wife and baby were there. This is all I know, he didn't mention any names. I haven't heard the name of Darlene Callahan or Tom Forester. Red wears a big gold skull and crossbones with four diamonds and I'm not sure if it has a ruby.

About March of 1981, I started getting threatening calls. Our trailer was ransacked, etc. the dog was gone. We live in a trailer near Ore Knob Road. My girlfriend, Terry Baggatta, narced on Sam Henderson on stuff (pot) that belonged to him in North Wilkesboro. I moved in with Paul in September of 1981. We have been living together. I have known Paul all of my life. I lived in North Carolina seven or eight years and before I lived in Detroit. I know Paul from grandparents in Alleghany County. Paul is employed, received VA benefits and is a self-employed mechanic. Paul has never talked about the mine. I don't know where it is. Paul and a guy talked about caffeine pills when up north in Ohio last year. Paul's property is probably in Alva Miller Bare's name.

Paul met Gary through Red, Sarge through Gary. Red showed me an automatic a long time ago. Gary never showed me any other guns.

We were at home on Monday and Tuesday of this week on January 4 and 5, 1982. I asked Paul if we were going any place. He said he didn't know. I got ready. He said he had to go see a fellow. We left a little after 7:00 P.M. we stopped at the drink machine and got drinks and drove to the church. A silver or gray car, about the size of a Fairmont (not shaped that way) was parked next to the tree line. I didn't see how many people was in the car, two white males got out of the car. This was about 8:00 or 8:30 P.M. One got out on the driver's side, with gray short hair and beard, same height as Paul, but slimmer. One got out on the passenger's side, he had dark short hair, clean shaven. They walked to the side and stood in the grass, the car was running. Paul was talking to two men that was standing next to the gray car. I heard three or four shots. I ducked down didn't see anything, but the other car pulled out fast. Paul got back in the car and said, they wanted him to do something he wouldn't do and kicked one of them and the gun went off. They were trying to put me in the car. Paul drove to KOA and set there a few minutes. Then drove to Wilkesboro and saw a deputy. Paul told him about what happened and they went to the scene. Two of the deputies picked up two shells. I saw a deputy with a wallet and I looked at a photo. I had never seen him before — eyes closed. I didn't notice the name. Paul asked me if I thought it was the guy. I didn't think he was any of the men out there. Kojak was not at the scene — didn't see him. Then we came back home.

Paul got a phone call Wednesday afternoon, something to do with me going back up north. I was not around the trash cans or any marijuana. I called the FBI and told them about the Henderson threats. They said, it wasn't under the jurisdiction of the FBI and told me to call the SBI. I tried to call John Foster (Big John).

A lock was put on the shed a week ago. Paul knew where the keys were. He had put a lock on because he had put some tires in the shed. I borrowed a pump shotgun from Paul's father, who lives near the Parkway, Hiram Bare, during squirrel season and I kept it a week. It is a new pump shotgun, possibly a 12 gauge. Finished interview at 3:07 A.M.

JOSEPH EUGENE VINES

Official Sworn Statement of Joseph E. Vines

Joseph E. Vines was advised of his rights by Sheriff Richard R. Waddell and also signed a waiver of his rights.

Q. You are willing to make a statement, is that correct?
A. Yes

Q. What is your full name?
A. Joseph Eugene Vines.

Q. Your date of birth?
A. January 9, 1950

Q. Where were you born?
A. Baltimore, Maryland

Q. Are you married?
A. Yes

Q. What is your wife's name?
A. Janet Lorraine Vines

Q. What is her maiden name?
A. Koert

Q. What is your permanent address?
A. Not had one, since I left Asheville.

Q. What is your occupation?

A. Last ten years has been professional undercover work for the Federal Bureau of Investigation, Alcohol, Tobacco, and Firearms, Florida Division of Law Enforcement, and numerous sheriff's departments.

Q. You do this for money and personal satisfaction?

A. Yes, mostly when I go into a town. I go on my own working at odd jobs on the side, anything I can get a hold of.

Q. Do you have a criminal record?

A. Not that I know of, may have been a bad check and assault on police officer when I was 17 years old, this was in Michigan. Worthless check was in Rutherford County, about $60. Then when I went back to Florida and when I came back, I sent money to cover the check that had been returned due to insufficient funds, but the man didn't pay it off.

Q. You lived there until when?

A. Until yesterday, I was living in Asheville, since June or July.

Q. While in Asheville, your undercover work was what?

A. Mostly gathering information on Motorcycle Gangs. On December 20, 1981, Sarge introduced me to a white male named Red. He's about 6'1" to 6'2", probably 230–240 pounds, long bright red hair, full red beard. Sarge's first name is Paul, last name is Harris.

Q. When was this?

A. In June or July, I met Paul Harris at Sarge's Bar.

Q. Where is Sarge's Bar located?

A. On Road 84, Swannanoa River Road. Sarge introduced Red and a Gary Miller that I had seen around the bar. Gary Miller is a white male, 5'9" to 5'10", slender, 130–140, black curly hair, black mustache and drives a brownish-tan car with sides rubbed down to repaint. It is a large car. Maybe a Pontiac.

Q. How old is Miller?

A. Middle 30s.

Q. How old is Sarge?

A. Middle 40s.

At this time, Sarge introduced me to them and said I would be working with Gary Miller and Red. It was getting [him] into their family business. I had been working on Sarge since June. Earlier in the summer I had seen Sarge on two occasions with suitcases containing guns and automatic weapons with silencers.

At that time, he told me he was importing guns by tractor trailers to a plane and flying [them] to South America.

Q. How were you working on Sarge?

A. I got in town; I contacted ATF Agent Tommy Chapman. I knew Tommy from before. Tommy brought an SBI agent with him. The SBI agent asked me to set up a drug deal. At that time, I called Bill Redding with the FBI stationed in

Hickory. I had worked with Bill on a four-wheel-drive truck. At that time, Bill asked me to do some work on Sarge and motorcycle clubs.

Sarge also at another time, mentioned about stealing new Cadillac and taking them to Charleston, South Carolina. Sarge got my wife a job in a factory. Then the factory shut down. After that, then Sarge put my wife to work in his bar, the bar is called Sarge's. He also put me to work on weekends as a bouncer and doorman, plus I cleaned the bar from time to time. Then I started running with motorcycle clubs called Ghost Riders. At that time I was asked by Bill Redding, FBI, to look for some persons that were out on wanted posters that he knew hung around with motorcycle clubs and partied with the Ghost Riders.

Q. What kind of car did Red have?
A. A black Monte Carlo in '70s model. Gary Miller also drove this. When I met Red, we sat around and drank at the bar. At that time, I was asked about two rings (1) a gold skull with cross-bones, which had diamond chips up and down each cross-bone, plus two large diamonds for eyes and a large ruby in the mouth. (2) a silver blazing cross that was supposed to be in Hendersonville. I was told if I found the rings, it would be worth a lot of money to me, that they had been stolen from Red.

On the night of December 21, 1981, I first met Lonnie Gamboa, he was of Italian descent, black hair, black mustache, 5'6" tall, 135 pounds. in his mid 20s. Red and Gary Miller had me drive the Monte Carlo to the Pizza Hut in the shopping center on [U.S.] 70 in East Asheville. We had been there earlier and went around the parking lot to see if any police officers were there. Then we went to Sarge's.

This was around 4:00 P.M. Gamboa was to meet Red at the Pizza Hut at 4:00 P.M. I was to drive the Monte Carlo that belonged to Red to the Pizza Hut and park on the back side near the door. I was to go inside [instructed by Gary and Red]. I ordered something to eat and drink and waited for Gamboa. At this time, I didn't even know Gamboa.

Red and Gary Miller sat in the brownish-tan car which was backed up in the parking lot. Gary drove the car and Red was with him. There was an automatic weapon in the back seat rolled in a leather type jacket with a long magazine, a machine gun. The reason I was to go in was to make sure it wasn't a set. They were going to watch and when Red saw Gamboa go in, he was to join us. They told me to tell Gamboa that Red had to make a phone call and would be in, in five to ten minutes. I sat in there by myself until 5:30 which at that time, Red came in and sat in the booth with me. About ten minutes later, after Red came in, Gamboa came in and he sat with us. Then they were talking, Gamboa said, he knew he owed Red a lot of money, but not as much as Gary Miller had told Red. Red's figure was $120,000. Gamboa said he only owed $30,000, because he had been turning money over to someone named Anthony. At this time, Red told him the family was out $380,000 and that the drugs had been delivered, but the money had not been brought back. Gamboa told Red that he would try to pay him somehow. He also told him where he could pick up about 4500 Canadian blues to give back to Red. Red then asked how much money he could give him. Gamboa stated that he had put $2,000 out on a house he had bought, but would try to pay so much a month. Red asked him, if he had any property. Gamboa said yes, he had two acres paid for and he would sign it over to him. He also told him he had a trailer and would sign the title over to him and if he wanted it, he would sign title to his van over to him. Then Gamboa started talking about Gary Miller, stating Gary Miller was the one that was telling the cops everything and telling lies on him. Then Red asked him (Gamboa) where the skull ring was. Red explained why he had given him the ring along with a turquoise ring. He had given him the turquoise ring because it fit Red's finger. The ring with the skull was to be cut down to fit. He asked him if he knew where the rings were. Gamboa said they were in Atlanta, that Kathy still had them. Kathy is the female that was caught in the motel room with Gamboa at the time of his arrest. Red asked him if we could go to Atlanta and get the rings. Gamboa said, yes. It was an icy night and we didn't go. After that we left the Pizza Hut around 6:00. We got into Gamboa's light blue, four-wheel-drive vehicle. Red got in front and Gamboa drove and I sat in the back.

Q. Did they resolve anything about the land?
A. Said that he would.

We went to two different locations in the Candler area where we picked Up 4500 Canadian blues (valium). Picked up 500 at one spot and 4000 at another. I couldn't find the house again, because it is out in the country. I went back to Gamboa's house, I don't know the address in Asheville, but is near the courthouse on Town Mountain Road. His wife was there. We got there around 8:00 P.M. Went inside, his wife was ready to have a child, she set the table and had dinner with them. We sat around and discussed the same thing we had discussed at the Pizza Hut. Gamboa put the blame on Miller about everything. Red asked Gamboa if he was stupid or something. Gamboa asked him, why "Red couldn't you see that Anthony was going to rip everybody off for the drugs and kill everybody." Gamboa brought out a 44 Magnum Ruger pistol. He also showed us an AR-15 rifle which had been changed to fully automatic. (Gamboa's wife still has AR-15 unless he had gotten rid of.)

We left Gamboa's house about 10:00–10:30. They made an arrangement [that] he would sign over the trailer and two acres of land. This was done the next day before going to Atlanta. At that time, Gamboa called Atlanta, a girl named Kathy, and told her we would be down to get the rings the next day. That should have been December 22, 1981. Red and I waited around the next day until about 12:00 and Gamboa said that he couldn't get the trailer or land signed over, that he had called the lawyer and he was in court.

We went to Atlanta, to a place that sells hams. Red, Gamboa, and me went in Red's Monte Carlo, it was on the outskirts of Atlanta. Two police officers were directing traffic that day, it was busy in and out of the parking lot. Gamboa went into a ham shop and returned with this young white female, 18–19 years old, shoulder-length brown hair and a little chunky. Red and I stayed in the car, Kathy got in the back seat with me. Gamboa was on the driver's side in front. Kathy handed him (Red) the two rings, the skull and cross-bones and also the turquoise ring. At that time, Red told Kathy not to come back to Asheville to go to court, that they wouldn't extradite her.

Q. What court action was this?
A. Concerning the shootout at Gary Miller's house.

Kathy told him she had to come back, because she had signed a waiver of extradition. Red told her again not to come back. Then Gamboa asked Kathy if she had any girlfriends, because he planned to stay and party. She told Gamboa she had a date that night and could not break it. This must have been around 3:00 or 4:00 when we were talking to her. Then we drove back to Gamboa's house, we got there at exactly 8:30. Gamboa's wife made Red and Gamboa something to eat and made me a cup of coffee. We sat around until about 9:00 or 10:00. At this time, Gamboa told Red that he could get a transcript of the trial and he would have the two acres of land signed over to any name that he wanted, and that he would sign title to trailer and give it to him the next day, which would have been the 23rd. Red told Gamboa he had to go out of town tonight to Virginia and that he would have me (Jo-Jo) call him the next morning about 11:00 and give him a name to give to his lawyer to put the land in. Then we left; Red took me to Sarge's. On the way down to Sarge's, Red told me that the reason he wanted me to call back up was to make sure that Gamboa wasn't going to try and set him up for the police department to pick him up. We met with Gary Miller at Sarge's. We sat at a table in the back, and Red discussed everything that was said and what happened to Gary Miller.

The next morning I got a call from Red about 9:30 A.M. telling me to call Gamboa and give him a name and address in North Carolina. (Gamboa's lawyer has name and address, his wife will know) he also told me to make sure that Gamboa got a copy of the transcript. I called Gamboa and gave him the name Red had given me and also told him to make sure he got a copy of the transcript. About 9:30 – 10:00 I called Gamboa back. Gamboa said he had a copy of the transcript and that it had cost him $370 to get it, but that the lawyer said he couldn't transfer the deed because the courthouse was closed. Red called me back at the house shortly after that from Sarge's house. At that time, Gary Miller was with him because I could hear Gary Miller in the background. Red told me to go up to Gamboa's house in my car and pick him and the transcript up, this was around 10:00 or 11:00 and bring them up to the River Lounge located on Highway 84 East in Asheville also called Swannanoa River Road. Red said he was just going to read the transcript and talk some more to Gamboa. I drove to Gamboa's house in my '68 Dodge, blue in color. When I got there, there was a white van I hadn't seen before, later found out it belonged to Gamboa, it was parked in front and Gamboa's light blue four-wheel-drive was there. I blew the horn and waited a couple of minutes and started to get out of the car and Gamboa's door opened and he said wait a minute. He went back inside, his wife came to the door and saw it was me and went back into the house. Gamboa got out and got in my car. At this time, he pulled a 44 Magnum Ruger Pistol out of back of his pants and laid it on the seat beside him. We drove from Gamboa's house to River Lounge.

Red's black Monte Carlo was parked outside in the parking lot, but Red wasn't in it. So Gamboa put the gun back in his pants, took transcript in brown manila envelope and he and I went into the River Lounge. The bartender's name was Dick, who was the prior owner at one time. Red wasn't inside. Gamboa and I ordered a beer. As soon as we got it, Red came through the door. I started to sit in a booth with Gamboa and Red said, let's leave, I don't want to read the transcript in here. When we got outside the door, Red gave me the key and told me to drive the black Monte Carlo. I was driving, Gamboa behind me in the back seat and Red in the back with Gamboa. Gamboa at that time, took the .44 Magnum Ruger pistol and stuck it up under his left leg. We rode from River Lounge to Sarge's about one and half to two miles. At that time, Red told me to pull into Sarge's by front door. Sarge's was closed. We stopped and parked in front of the front door at Sarge's. At that time, Gary Miller came from the other side of parking lot and pulled up next to us, got out and came around and got in the passenger side of front seat. He was driving his brownish-tan car of his. He looked at Gamboa and told him he shouldn't be telling the things he was telling. Gary then asked him why he was trying to blame everything on him. At that time, Gary pulled an automatic pistol, 9mm or 45 automatic. At the same time Red pulled his gun, it was an automatic. Gary Miller reached into the back seat and took a .44 Magnum Ruger pistol out from under Gamboa's leg. Red held his automatic pistol on Gamboa and Gary Miller told me to hold Gamboa's hands, which I didn't have to, Gamboa held them together. Gary Miller got out of the Monte Carlo and went to his car and got a roll of silver duct tape and a roll of clear fiberglass tape. Gary then taped Gamboa's hands together. Gary then had Gamboa get out of the car. He took keys out of the ignition, opened the trunk and helped Gamboa into the trunk of the black Monte Carlo.

Q. Where was Red?
A. He walked to the trunk and I got out also. Red was going to drive. Gary told Gamboa he was taking him to the big man, so he could talk to him. Red and I left Sarge's in the black Monte Carlo with Gamboa in the trunk. Red was driving. Gary was following in his brownish-tan car. Before we left, Gary took an automatic weapon which was lying over the seat wrapped in a black leather jacket and laid it in the front seat of his car. We proceeded on Interstate 40 toward Morganton where we got on Highway 18.

Q. From the time you left Sarge's, all this occurred between 10:30 and 11:30?
A. Yes

We took Highway 18 out of Morganton, stopped for gas outside Morganton at a self-service and filled up both cars. We followed 18 North until we came to the [Blue Ridge] Parkway, then turned left off 18 and onto the Parkway. Then went about five or ten minutes and made a right off the Parkway onto a rural, paved, rough road. We rode down that road until came to a muddy dirt road and turned right. We passed a big wooden house, three motorcycles were on the porch.

Q. Is this the same house you showed us today [Sheriff Waddell and ATF Agent Tommy Chapman]?
A. Yes

Q. Can you describe the entrance?

A. We passed this house, Red said he used to live there and had to move and a friend moved in. On down, we passed two little mail boxes, turned right. On the left side, a small house, I think it was a stucco or concrete, passed that house on a rough road and there was a junk yard all around, junk cars on both sides and an armored half-track on the right hand side. Across from that, was an old light blue two-bedroom trailer in a run-down condition, behind that was a shed or garage.

We parked beside the trailer. Red got out and told me to just sit in the black Monte Carlo. Miller got out of his car also and went back to this shed or garage. This was about 3:30 P.M. They stood back there for two or three minutes. I didn't look around. Red and Gary came back to the car and told me to get out. Gary got the key out of the ignition, this was the black Monte Carlo, and went around to the back of the Monte Carlo. Gary told me to get my 38 Blue Smith and Wesson revolver out. Red gave me the gun about the 21st. At that time, Red held his gun out. I had my gun to my side, Red pulled his automatic and Gary pulled his out. Then they unlocked the trunk of the car. Gary got Gamboa out of the trunk. We unwrapped the fiberglass tape from his hands and put a handcuff on one of his hands. Then he told me to hold the gun on Gamboa and he took him by the handcuff and went to the left of shed, up a hill about 100 yards or so, then left back into the woods and went into the woods a little ways. Gary handcuffed Gamboa's hands around a tree; he was facing the tree and arms around it. Gary Miller and me went to the tree. We then go back down the hill to the shed or garage. At that time, Red introduced me to a guy named Papa Bare, a white male, 5'8", dark black hair, receding hair line, dark black beard, 140–150 pounds, in his late 40s.

Q. Is this the same individual you picked out of a book of many pictures that Sheriff Waddell showed to you?

A. As soon as I saw the picture, I knew it was Papa Bare. There was two other white males there. I was introduced to them at Papa Bare's residence and garage. An older man with glasses in his mid 50s, short man and skinny with Papa Bare. There was another white male, 6' or taller real heavy, 200 pounds or more, short dark brown hair in his late 20s.

Q. Did they see them get the man out of the trunk and take him to the tree, guns and all?

A. Yes, they watched everything.

Back at Papa Bare's, he got on the phone. Gary asked him to check out some names. This was at the garage. There is a phone in the garage on the left side. There was an old maroon car there and Gary Miller said it used to belong to Delinger's. In front of that was a yellow wrecker. On right hand side of wrecker was an old black car with rumble seat, boxes and stuff piled all over it. Back in the far right corner of the shop was a stove (boiler type) and had a blower, the switch was on the wall and turned the blower on. A drill press on the left side and also a saw on table with junk on it and an air filter on top. There was a 750 Honda covered with a tarp. We got back outside, there was a flatbed truck there and Red, Gary and the old man with glasses looked at it. We sat for a while, Red told Papa Bare we needed to get something to eat. Papa Bare said, go talk to Gamboa, so he wouldn't start hollering. Gary Miller and Papa Bare went to the area where Gamboa was in the woods. They came back down in about ten minutes. Me and Papa Bare, Gary and Red then went to get something to eat. Came out of driveway, turned left onto asphalt road, then right to a stop sign, two or three miles and turned left, went to a little restaurant and gas station building. (I previously today, pointed this out to ATF Agent Chapman and Sheriff Waddell.) There was a tall, slender, blond-headed waitress in her late 30s that waited on us. She knew Papa Bare and seemed to know Red, because she was joking around with him. We got through eating, went back to garage behind Papa Bare's house, close to 6:00 P.M. when we got there. At that time Papa Bare and Gary Miller left — said they were going to collect some money or take care of some business, I had a real bad cold or flu. Red and I stayed in the Monte Carlo and slept. Before they left, there was an old car; I think Papa Bare's Mercury pulled in. Patty was driving it. About 6:00 P.M. Gary and Papa Bare left, I was talking to Red about why they had blocked the road with an old car. They got back about 9:30 P.M. At this time Gary told me to go with him. He had a flashlight, a small black tube type, it was weak. He went back up the hill to where Gamboa was handcuffed to the tree. Gary Miller uncuffed Gamboa from the tree, he kicked some leaves out of the way and told me to pick up Gamboa's wallet which was on the ground and a set of car keys, one one-ounce bag of pot, with a chunk of hashish in it. I picked them up and put them in my pocket. Then they led Gamboa back to the garage, where Papa Bare took him by the stove, where he had built a fire. Miller removed the handcuffs from Gamboa.

Q. Did Gamboa make any statements?
A. Said, Gary am I going to get out of this alive?
   Gary didn't answer at all.

   They had a paper bag with milk, Pepsi, candy bars and I think some brownies in it. Papa Bare asked Gamboa what he wanted to eat or drink out of the bag. After he had warmed up and ate, Gary asked him where his list of people that had gotten drugs from him was. He told him they were in his wallet. At this time, Papa Bare told me to take everything out of my pockets and lay it on the floor. Gary told me a big guy that was there earlier was in the woods with a machine gun protecting the road earlier when we came in, I am positive I saw it sitting there. Then Gary asked Gamboa to get the list and Gamboa did. Then Gary asked Gamboa how much he had paid for his house and Gamboa told him $2,000.

Q. What did the list look like?
A. Pieces of white paper, note paper torn in half. Then he asked Gamboa about the shootout. Gary said Gamboa was in on it with this Anthony character. Gary asked Gamboa if there was any way he could come up with the drugs that were missing. Gamboa told him there was fifty pounds at somebody's house in back of a Jeep and that he had the key to Jeep on his key ring. Then Gary Miller and Papa Bare and Red went to the door and were talking real low among each other. They came back over to where Gamboa was and Gary Miller told Gamboa to

call his wife and tell her to go to the place in Candler and get the fifty pounds from the Jeep and have his [Gamboa's] wife deliver it to the Country Food Store next to Holiday Inn West off Candler exit and go inside to ladies room leave the van unlocked and wait ten minutes, and then two girls would pick the pot up and transfer it from Gamboa's wife's vehicle to another vehicle. Gamboa's wife then was supposed to go out and go home. Gamboa agreed to make the phone call. Gary Miller dialed Gamboa's number and handed the phone to Gamboa and he told his wife exactly what Gary had told him to tell her. Gary and Gamboa stayed in the garage. Papa Bare went somewhere for about five minutes in a truck. He came back, I think he had a white towel or rag, he told Gamboa he was going to take him to the big man's house, but had to go the back way and had to blindfold Gamboa, because the big man didn't want Gamboa to know where he lived. Took him outside, Papa Bare warmed the truck up. It was very dark. Papa Bare blindfolded Gamboa. All got into the truck, Papa Bare was driving, Gary Miller was sitting next to Papa Bare, Gamboa was next to Gary Miller and I was next to the door. Papa Bare told Red to sit at the bottom of the road to meet the two girls. We got in the truck and Papa Bare told me to pull my hat down over my eyes, so I couldn't see and I did this. So we drove until he told me to pull my hat up, the truck had stopped. Then he told me to get out and bring Gamboa out on same side of truck. I had a hard time opening the door, there was briars all around. I got Gamboa out with me. Gary Miller got right out after Papa Bare.

Q. What shape was Gamboa in at this time?
A. Like a drunk, messed up on the drugs.

We got out and went to the rear of the truck, stated walking through the woods where some small pine trees and little seedlings were. Papa Bare got a pump shotgun out from the floorboard under seat.

Q. Who was helping Gamboa walk?
A. I was. Papa Bare led the way, he had a big square flashlight and shot gun. Gamboa and I followed him, Gary Miller was behind me. Been searching around three or four minutes, then came to a fence. I thought a fence to a house.

Q. How high was the fence?
A. Seven feet, it was above my head.

Q. What kind of material was the chain?
A. Chain link fence, a big hole was ripped in it. (This was the same hole I showed ATF Agent Tommy Chapman and Sheriff Waddell today.)

Papa Bare took Gamboa by the arm, told him to duck down and helped him through a hole in the fence.

Q. Where was the flashlight?
A. It was on the ground. I was standing beside Papa Bare and Gamboa.

Q. Could you see what was inside the fence?
A. A huge hole. After he helped Gamboa through the fence, Papa Bare tapped me

on the back with the gun and told me to go through too. I was scared; I thought they were going to kill me. At that time, I knew what was going on.

Q. Prior to the arrival at the fence, did you have any idea what was going on?

A. I thought we were going to a house. Then Gary Miller and Papa Bare were outside the fence. Papa Bare still had a shotgun on me and Gamboa. Gary Miller had his gun the same way and motioned for me to push him. This motion was made with his left hand, the gun was in his right hand.

Q. Was Gamboa blindfolded at this time?

A. Yes. Gamboa was on the edge of the hole. I took my fingertips and just pushed him enough to take a step forward. Gamboa took a step and about two or three feet there was a log sticking out (about 6" in diameter). (The one I showed ATF Agent Tommy Chapman and Sheriff Waddell today.) Gamboa's leg went down behind the limb and the limb caught him about the ankle, his left leg. Papa Bare told me to lean over and help him up. I told him I couldn't reach him. Then Papa Bare went out into the woods and found a limb (about 5" in diameter and 6' long), dried out and told me to take the limb and help him get back up. Gamboa didn't say a word. Gary Miller didn't say anything. I handed the limb to Gamboa. Papa Bare told him to take hold of the limb and I would help him up. He told Gamboa it was a steep hill. So I did, he was hollering that his leg was broken, he grabbed the limb. Papa Bare told him to try and he did. I pulled him to the edge of the hole and at that time, Papa Bare made a pushing motion with the shotgun, which I did. I came back out of the fence, real quick. Gamboa sounded like he hit a couple of times. I was hurrying to get out. I thought I would be next. Papa Bare then threw the stick in the hole. Then he told me and Gary to pick up some rock, good size and throw them in the hole. Papa Bare threw some in too. We threw about two each. Took a minute or two to hit the bottom, then sounded like it hit tin. Papa Bare looked around with the flashlight to see if we had missed anything.

Q. How long were you there?

A. Ten to fifteen minutes, after we got out of truck. Then got back in truck. Papa Bare told me to pull my hat back down over my eyes, and I eased my hat up just as we were coming on asphalt road. Then went back to Papa Bare's house. We got to the road by the stop sign; Red in black Monte Carlo was sitting in it. Red followed us back. While at the hole, Papa Bare turned to Gary Miller and said that made twenty-three bodies in there now. Then we got back to the shop and laid the wallet out, all phone numbers, cards, and papers out. Gary and Red did this. Spread them out over a filter. Some names recognized and some didn't.

Q. Did they make any statement about him being dead? I mentioned that he didn't holler. Red said that he had a heart condition, probably dead before reached the bottom. Red said Gamboa went in a lot easier than the guy that went two weeks before, he had to fight him. Then Papa Bare told us all to wash our boots off when we got home, soles real good. Then after looking at cards, Papa Bare burned the insurance cards, Master Charge, and pictures. Gary Miller turned the business cards with the names and numbers over to Sarge (that was what Sarge told).

Q. Do you know the time you all were at the hole?
A. 12:00 Midnight

Gamboa's wallet, driver's license, Social Security card, keys and the court transcript were left at Papa Bare's. All that was taken was just the cards with the numbers. Gary Miller said, want to see something. Papa Bare and he took me back up the hill on left side of garage past where Gamboa was handcuffed up a hill a good distance and there was a cleared field, a big, huge airplane sitting there. Papa Bare said it was a DC-10 and said that was how they got drugs in.

Q. This field was large enough to land a plane?
A. Large enough to land a plane. Then brought me back down the hill, went to this big metal truck, like a garbage truck. On the right hand side in front, had a big metal door. Five or six silver metal garbage cans inside the truck. Then Papa Bare got into the truck and slid two of the garbage cans to back of truck to me and Gary. We carried them back inside garage, they were not too heavy. Went back inside, Papa Bare came out with two large light blue bags, he opened garbage cans up and they were full of pot, then he put blue bag on top of cans and dumped pot into blue bags. Then Gary put blue bags inside green garbage bags. Gary asked Red what he wanted to do with the stuff that was left, bag of pot, chunk of hashish and about $60. Red said give Jo-Jo the money, which they did. He told me they were short of money and after this I would be getting some money after first of year. Then we took the pot to Gary's car, put in the trunk, the brownish-tan car then Red took automatic weapon from the front seat of Gary's car and put it in the seat next to him, still wrapped up. Red told Gary and me he was going to stop at Myers Motel and spend the night, because he was too sick to drive to Charlotte. Then he told Gary to trade 38s (weapon) with me, because it was too hot and the other could go back to the "Outlaws." Then me and Gary, Gary driving, left at 2:00 A.M., came back another way through Boone, stopped in Boone at Gary's brick home, he owns. There was a red Grand Prix with white top and a Jeep with eagle on it, was light brown. Left pot in the trunk of the brownish-tan car and got in the Jeep. Gary drove Jeep back to Asheville, at my house, which at that time was Apartment 13C, Oak Knoll apartments in East Asheville. Gary handed me another $50 bill and told me at that time, that the Gamboa money and $50 extra was to buy my wife some Christmas presents.

The day after, Sarge kissed me on both cheeks, this was Christmas Eve, and he told me I was part of the family, and I would be making a lot of money from then on. This was about 6:30 P.M. That's when he told me he had the cards.

WADDELL, SHERIFF RICHARD [1]

Waddell's Official Sworn Statement

At 11:00 on January 6, 1982, three SBI agents arrived at the office of Sheriff Richard Waddell in Jefferson, NC. They were Charlie Chambers of the Hickory SBI office, Bob Kiser of the Asheville office, and Ernest Bueker of the Raleigh office.

Agent Chambers told Sheriff Waddell the visit concerned some kidnapping that had recently occurred in Asheville and that Bob Kiser and ATF agent Tommy Chapman would fill me in when Chapman arrived to the office. Agent Chambers offered Waddell the full support of the North Carolina SBI agency.

At noon on January 6, 1982, Waddell met Tommy Chapman and officers from the Asheville police department at Eldreth's Restaurant, where Chapman related to him the following events:

1. There had been two kidnappings from a motel in Asheville on December 13, 1981, a man and a woman
2. That Lonnie Gamboa, a young Italian male, was kidnapped around 10:00 A.M. on December 23, 1981
3. That he (Chapman) had an informant named Jo-Jo that had brought Lonnie Gamboa in the trunk of a car to Paul Wilson Bare's residence in Ashe County, NC, at 3:30 P.M. on December 23, 1981
4. That Gary Miller and Red (Alan Hattaway) had assisted in the kidnapping and bringing Gamboa to Bare's residence
5. That Jo-Jo's name was Joseph E. Vines
6. That Jo-Jo was hiding out in Virginia
7. That Jo-Jo had described to him Paul Bare's premises and other houses and landmarks in the nearby community of Paul Wilson Bare's
8. That Jo-Jo had described a mine shaft near Paul Bare's house as having a chain-link fence around it with a tear in it
9. On the inside of the tear were logs and roots at the edge of the shaft
10. That Jo-Jo had described the vegetation around the immediate area of the mine.
11. That [Jo-Jo] Paul W. Bare and Gary Miller took Lonnie Gamboa to the mine shaft around midnight on December 23, 1981, or the early morning hours of December 24, 1981
12. That Paul Bare forced Jo-Jo to push Lonnie Gamboa in the mine shaft while Bare held him at gunpoint
13. That Jo-Jo first pushed Gamboa into the shaft at which time Gamboa's foot caught on a tree root at the rim of the mine shaft
14. That Paul Bare gave Jo-Jo a limb and ordered him to pull Gamboa back out of the mine shaft, and that Jo-Jo was ordered to push him in again
15. That Paul Bare said, "Lonnie Gamboa went in easier than the one did two weeks ago."
16. That Paul Bare said that Gamboa made number 23 in the shaft
17. That Lonnie Gamboa was alive when he was pushed in by Jo-Jo
18. That the Asheville Police Department had arrested Gary Miller for the two kidnappings at the motel on December 13, 1981, and that they were looking for Red (Alan Hattaway)
19. That Jo-Jo described Red's house in Ashe County as being near Paul Bare's house and having four motorcycles on the porch.

Also Ross Robinson of the Asheville Police Department related much [the same] information concerning the kidnappings in Asheville.

At approximately 2:00 P.M. on January 6, 1982, ATF Agent Tommy Chapman, Bob Kiser, Deputy Gene Goss, and myself [Waddell] went to the old mine shaft at the Ore Knob Mine. I [Waddell] observed that the shaft was approximately 60' across the top and 100' deep; the fence was a chain-link and had a tear in it on the west side [and] that there were roots and a log on the rim of the mine shaft just inside at the tear. Also, there were also numerous small white pine trees near the shaft and fence [just as Jo-Jo had described it to Chapman].

At approximately 3:00 P.M. on January 6, 1982, the Ashe County Rescue Squad was at the Ore Knob Mine shaft to be of assistance in looking into the shaft. At 4:30 P.M. the Blue Ridge Electric basket truck came, and Ross Robinson got into the basket. Robinson was put out over the mine shaft and took pictures and tried to look into the mine shaft with spotlights. It became obvious to everyone that we would need some professional help in getting to the bottom of the mine to see what was there.

At 7:00 P.M. on January 6, 1982, I [Waddell] contacted the mining rescue and people with MSHA and the North Carolina Bureau of Mines, and they agreed to send their people at approximately 2:00 P.M. on January 7, 1982, to make an assessment of the mine shaft and see what we would need to get to the bottom of the shaft. At 8:00 P.M. on January 6, 1982, Chapman contacted Jo-Jo by telephone to set up a meeting with me [Waddell] so I could obtain a statement from Vines and so Vines could show me the area of the mine and the area of Paul Bare's house. Tommy Chapman set up a meeting of myself [Waddell], himself [Chapman], and Jo-Jo at 1:30 P.M. on January 7, 1982, at the John Deere Tractor place in Marion, Virginia.

At 1:50 P.M. on January 7, 1982, Tommy Chapman and myself [Waddell] met Jo-Jo in Marion, Virginia, at which time I advised Vines of his rights, and he gave me an oral statement concerning Lonnie M. Gamboa's kidnapping on December 23, 1981. Jo-Jo told me much of what he had told Tommy Chapman earlier, but in greater detail. In such detail, I knew he had been to Paul W. Bare's and that he had been to the mine shaft. Jo-Jo guided me into the mine area by his own direction and told me where to park at the mine — the same place he, Paul Bare, Gary Miller, and Lonnie Gamboa had parked on December 23, 1981. Jo-Jo walked directly to the mine shaft and said, "That's it." Jo-Jo showed me the tear in the fence, the roots and the pine trees around the area of the mine shaft, just as he had previously described. We arrived at the mine at 3:00 P.M. on January 7, 1982. Also at 3:00 P.M. on January 7, 1982, two men from MSHA were present at the mine shaft making an evaluation of the scene.

On January 7, 1982, at approximately 5:00 P.M., Joseph E. Vines began giving me a written statement at my office in Jefferson concerning the kidnapping of Lonnie Gamboa on December 23, 1981. Present at the taking of the statement were myself [Waddell], Elsie Taylor, Ernest Bueker, and Tommy Chapman. The interview of Joseph E. Vines ended January 7, 1982, at 8:30 P.M. The statement was typed and [was] signed by Joseph Vines on January 8, 1982, at 8:00 P.M. after he was sworn to it by Magistrate Jerry Roten. Among the highlights of the statement was an intense description of Lonnie Gamboa's wallet that Paul Bare had kept the night of the murder.

At 9:00 P.M. on January 7, 1982, I [Waddell] received information from Captain Gene Goss that Captain Melvin Roberts of the Wilkes County Sheriff's Department had Lonnie Gamboa's wallet. I [Waddell] set up a meeting with Captain Roberts at the Pine Ridge Baptist Church in Wilkes County — the site where the wallet was found — and met Captain Melvin Roberts there at 11:45 P.M. on January 7, 1982, and took a statement from Captain Roberts concerning the wallet (see statement). I took possession at 11:50 P.M. of a light brown nylon wallet with Velcro sticking sides which contained Lonnie Gamboa's North Carolina driving license, two Buncombe County Technical Institute ID cards, a bank card, a Master Charge card, and two spent 9mm shell casings.

On January 8, 1982, at 10:30 A.M., Waddell, Chapman, Bueker, and Vines went to the office of District Attorney Michael Ashburn in Wilkesboro, NC, where Ashburn interviewed Joseph Vines. After the interview, Ashburn advised them to charge Paul Wilson Bare with the kidnapping of Lonnie Gamboa and to search the premises.

Search Warrant Results

On January 8, 1982, at 8:00 P.M., myself [Waddell], Captain Goss, J.D. Parsons, James Absher, Eugene Greer, Steve Cabe, Charles Whitman, Ernest Bueker, and Tommy Chapman went to the Paul Wilson Bare residence armed with an arrest warrant, and a search warrant. The following items were seized:

1. .357 Caliber Pistol — Serial Number 3845 — found under seat of sofa
2. .22 Caliber RG23 Pistol — Serial Number 255993 — found in Patty Simmons' purse
3. Two Quaalude pills — found in Patty Simmons' purse
4. Plastic film container containing marijuana — found in Patty Simmons' purse
5. Pack of firecrackers — found in Patty Simmons' purse
6. 44 Magnum Ruger Super Black Hawk Pistol — Serial #84-06727 — found under cushion of a chair in bedroom
7. Plastic sandwich bag containing marijuana seed — found in a suitcase in back bedroom
8. One-half carton firecrackers — found in a pillowcase in back bedroom
9. Two Roman candles
10. Three pieces of scrap paper with telephone numbers — found on the phone table
11. One quart can of marijuana seeds
12. A Mead notebook with telephone numbers in it
13. A 20-gallon garbage can with marijuana residue in bottom — found on the back of an old garbage truck
14. One box of blue garbage bags — found in the dryer in house trailer (14 of those bags, blue in color and reinforced with fiberglass, described to me before the search by Joseph E. Vines)
15. One pair of work boots — from the living room of Paul W. Bare

16. Several cans of black powder and rifle shells—found in the closet of Paul W. Bare's house.

At approximately 11:00 P.M. on January 8, 1982, me and the officers left the Paul Bare residence and transported Paul Bare to the Ashe County Jail for booking. However, SBI Agents Ernest Bueker and Ross Robinson stayed on the scene and continued the search pursuant to the search warrant and continued to interview Patricia Simmons at the Paul Bare residence.

At 12:05 A.M. on January 9, 1982, Tommy Chapman [and I] went to Eldreth's Motel to pick up Joseph E. Vines. When Joseph Vines got into the car, I had one of the blue reinforced garbage bags lying in the front seat, and I never mentioned any reference to Joseph E. Vines concerning the garbage bag, at which time Joseph Vines said, "That is the same kind of bag that Paul Bare put the marijuana into that we took back to Boone after Gamboa was thrown into the mine."

At approximately 12:20 A.M. on January 9, 1982, Tommy Chapman, Joseph E. Vines, and myself (Waddell) arrived at the Paul Bare residence. All three of us went into the residence where Patricia Simmons, Ernest Bueker, and Ross Robinson were present, at which time Joseph Vines told Patricia Simmons that it was good to see her again, and Patricia Simmons said, "Do I know you?" Joseph Vines said, "I was in the back seat with Red and Gary," and she said, "I remember you, you stuck your head over from the back seat." At this time, Patricia Simmons called Joseph Vines a "son-of-a-bitch" and began crying.

At this time, Agent Tommy Chapman and myself (Waddell) asked Joseph Vines to show us the location of the garbage truck that marijuana had been removed from on December 23, 1981, and he did. The old garbage truck contained two new twenty-gallon garbage cans as Joseph Vines had described earlier, and these two new garbage cans contained marijuana residue. At this time I asked Joseph Vines if he thought he could show me the tree that Lonnie Marshall Gamboa was handcuffed to, and Joseph Vines said he thought that he could and believed it was near the old garbage truck that contained garbage cans. Approximately 30 feet inside the woods from the old garbage truck, Joseph E. Vines pointed out to me a tree where Lonnie Marshall Gamboa had been handcuffed to on December 23, 1981. I observed that the tree was a tree approximately 12 inches in diameter, a dead locust tree that the bark about waist high had been scuffed off all the way around the tree at that height. There was a cut out path on the ground around the tree, and on the ground approximately 3 feet from the tree was wrinkled up fiberglass tape (which was obtained as evidence). Also the area of the tree and the garbage truck were photographed at 7:30 A.M. on January 9, 1982, by SBI Agent Ernest Bueker.

At approximately 8:00 A.M. on January 9, 1982, Patricia Simmons was arrested at the Paul Bare residence for felonious possession of marijuana, and the search was terminated. The Paul Bare residence was secured by Patricia Simmons before she was taken to the Ashe County Jail.

On January 9, 1981, at 9:57 A.M., Paul Wilson Bare was advised of his rights and made a statement at the Ashe County Sheriff's Office in the presence of myself (Waddell) and SBI Agent Ernest Bueker. (See attached statement.)

On January 8, 1982, the Ore Knob Mine was secured by personnel of the Ashe County Sheriff's Department and the Asheville Police Department with a constant vigil over the alleged crime scene, and arrangements were made with the North Carolina Division of Mine Inquiries and the Federal Mining Safety and Health Administration to probe the abandoned mine shaft with a TV monitor camera. Also on Friday, January 8, 1982, the area of the Ore Knob Mine was checked by members of the MSHA, and the James R. Vannoy Construction Company crane removed a cement cap from an adjacent mine shaft.

On January 12, 1982, with the aid of the James R. Vannoy Construction Company crane, the MSHA video equipment was lowered into the mine shaft in question, and a video survey of the inner mine shaft was begun and continued through January 13, 1982. During this video examination, of the mine shaft in question, two objects were viewed that appeared to be bodies. Video tapes of the examination of the mine shaft in question were turned over to the Ashe County Sheriff's Department and the Asheville Police Department for further review. The scene of the mine shaft was kept under constant observation by the Ashe County Sheriff's Department and the Asheville Police Department until 11:00 A.M. on January 25, 1982.

On January 25, 1982, a self-proclaimed stunt man known as the "Nashville Flame" was lowered into the mine shaft in question by the James R. Vannoy Construction Company crane. The operation was aided by the Ashe County Sheriff's Department, the Ashe County Rescue Squad, the Asheville Police Department, the Buncombe County Rescue Squad, the North Carolina Bureau of Investigation, and the Bureau of Alcohol, Tobacco, and Firearms.

The "Nashville Flame" was lowered into the mine shaft in question on several occasions to a depth of approximately 200 feet to check the area out for gases and other hazards which one might encounter. After making these assessments, the "Nashville Flame" found the area at the bottom of the mine shaft to be suitable to sustain life in a safe manner.

At approximately 2:00 P.M. on January 25, 1982, the "Nashville Flame" and Officer Roger Buckner were rigged onto the boom of the crane and lowered to the bottom of the mine shaft at which time they advised the crew on top of the ground that they had found two bodies at the bottom of the shaft. Roger Buckner and the "Nashville Flame" were brought back to the surface of the mine shaft, and tools were obtained to remove the frozen bodies from the earth below. When this was done, the "Nashville Flame," Roger Buckner, and Eugene Goss were rigged to the boom of the crane, along with the necessary tools, and lowered to the bottom of the mine shaft.

At 3:07 P.M. on January 25, 1982, the body of Lonnie Marshall Gamboa was brought to the top of the ground. The body was viewed on top of the ground and appeared to be frozen; was wearing one cowboy boot; was blindfolded with a white cloth; was wearing a tan parka, which had previously been described by Joseph E. Vines.

The medical examiner, Dr. E.J. Miller, came to the scene, and the body of Lonnie Marshall Gamboa was taken to the morgue at the Ashe Memorial Hospital and arrangements made for a subsequent autopsy at Chapel Hill on January 26, 1982.

At 3:07 P.M. on January 25, 1982, warrants were drawn for the arrest of Paul Wilson Bare, Gary Hansford Miller, and Alan Ray Hattaway, charging them with murder, and a search was begun by Lt. Parsons and others for Paul Wilson Bare.

At 5:45 P.M. on January 25, 1982, the "Nashville Flame," Roger Buckner, and Eugene Goss were lowered back into the mine to retrieve the suspected body of Thomas Forester.

At approximately 7:15 P.M. on January 25, 1982, the second body was retrieved from the bottom of the mine shaft and tentatively identified as Thomas Forester by members of the Asheville Police Department who had previously known him. The body of Thomas Forester was transported to the morgue at the Ashe Memorial Hospital by the Ashe County Rescue Squad, and arrangements were made to transport the body of Thomas Forester along with the body of Lonnie Marshall Gamboa to Chapel Hill for an autopsy on January 26, 1982.

During the recovery of the two above bodies, the crime scene inside the mine shaft was photographed and other photographs made on the surface of the victims.

At 7:45 P.M. on January 25, 1982, the crime scene search at the Ore Knob Mine was concluded with the removal of all equipment and personnel.

At approximately 6:30 P.M. on January 25, Paul Wilson Bare was taken into custody for the murder of Lonnie Marshall Gamboa through the aid of Attorney John Siskind and Lt. J.D. Parsons.

On February 1, 1982, Ernest Bueker, SBI Agent, and myself (Waddell) went to the Police Department and interviewed Darlene Fie Callahan and took her statement. (See attached statement.)

After obtaining a protective custody for Darlene Callahan, Ernest Bueker and myself returned to Ashe County on February 1, 1982, at 9:30 P.M. and asked Darlene Callahan to participate in a junkyard lineup to see if she could pick out the type of surroundings when she was taken to by Gary Miller and Alan Ray Hattaway during the early morning hours of December 13, 1981.

Darlene Callahan was first taken to the Calloway Garage in Jefferson, North Carolina, and she advised that this was not the place that she had been taken on December 13, 1981.

Next Darlene Callahan was taken to the Ed Jones Garage in Lansing, North Carolina, and she advised that this was not the place she had been taken on December 13, 1981.

Darlene Callahan was then taken to the Alonzo Phipps Garage in Crumpler, North Carolina, and she advised that this was not the place she had been taken by Gary Miller and Alan Ray Hattaway on December 13, 1981.

Note: John Siskind, Attorney for Paul Wilson Bare, was also present.

Then we took Darlene Callahan to the Fred Hart Junkyard in Laurel Springs, and Darlene Callahan advised that this was not the place she had been taken.

From there, Darlene Callahan was taken to the garage and residence of Van Miller, Jr., and she advised that this was not the place she had been taken on December 13, 1981.

From there we drove into the drive at the Paul Wilson Bare residence and garage, at which time the road in front of the house was blocked with an old Mercury automobile, but we could pull around barely, and passed the house by a few feet, at which time, Darlene Callahan made the statement, "This is the place that I was brought, I am sure, I am positive." Directly in front of a trailer, a wrecker was blocking the road between Bare's house and garage, thus blocking the view from the house trailer and the garage. At this time, Darlene Callahan said that the house trailer and garage are up above the wrecker, and that was the wrecker she had seen on December 13, 1981.

We got out of the car and walked past the wrecker toward the house trailer and garage, and, when Darlene Callahan saw the house trailer and garage by flashlight, she advised that this was also the place she had been taken on December, 13, 1981, by Gary Miller and Alan Ray Hattaway. We left at approximately 11:10 P.M. on February 1, 1982.

On February 2, 1982, a lineup was prepared at the Ashe County Jail for the benefit of Darlene Callahan. The lineup consisted of six men, who are:

Ronnie Hopkins	Ray Roark
Bernard McNeill	James Gentry
John Able	Paul Wilson Bare

Each was given a number and a toboggan and a phrase to say — "Take her up there."

The lineup was photographed by Ernest Bueker. Also present were John Siskind (Paul Bare's attorney), Eugene Goss, J.D. Parsons, and myself (Waddell).

At 10:30 A.M. on February 2, Darlene Callahan was brought into the presence of the lineup, and after the lineup had completed their assigned task, Darlene Callahan was returned to my office and advised that she could not pick out any one for sure that she thought was the man that she had seen at the junkyard that she had been taken to by me at 11:00 P.M. on February 1, 1982.

Waddell, Sheriff Richard [2]
The Capture of Gary Miller
June 10, 1982

As a result of information developed by the Caldwell County Sheriff's Department in Lenoir, North Carolina, federal, state, and local officials raided a camper at 4:30 P.M. on 6-10-82 at the Burke County and Caldwell County at the Catawba River. Gary Hansford Miller was taken into custody by myself (Waddell) after being placed under arrest for murder. Gary Hansford Miller gave an oral and written consent to search the camper. The following items were seized:

1. Note pad and phone numbers.
2. One .38 special, S&W pistol serial # D759238 (loaded)
3. One .357 Mag. Colt trooper III pistol serial # ground off (loaded)
4. One black wallet
5. $630 in cash
6. One .22 cal. Berretta pistol serial # 41626T (loaded)
7. Assorted ammunition
8. $1.67 in change

Gary H. Miller was advised of his rights orally; he said he understood them and that he would talk to me. Gary H. Miller continued to make a statement from 6:00 P.M. until 10:00 P.M. 6/10/82 in the presence of myself (Waddell) and Gene Goss.

Miller also stated that he knew who did the Durham murders in Boone. He stated that Cassada, who was arrested and turned loose, was one of the people and there was two colored men from Wilkes County helped him. That one of the colored men was now living in California and the other one was living in Wilkes County. Miller stated that Durham was one of the largest drug dealers in the area, that he (Miller) himself had bought hundreds of pounds of marijuana from him.

On June 12, 1982, at 3:00 P.M., Tommy Chapman and myself (Waddell) went to the Knox County Jail in Knoxville, Tennessee, and talked to Alan Ray Hattaway and his lawyer, Ben Hooper. Alan Ray Hattaway and his lawyer, Ben Hooper, did not wish to make a statement concerning the Gamboa murder, but wanted to read Joe Vines' statement. I, (Waddell) let them read the statement and Alan Ray Hattaway's only statement was that Joe Vines was a "fink" or "rat fink."

Alan Ray Hattaway wanted to trade certain information to the U.S. attorney in Chicago for slack in the cases against him in Chicago. Alan Ray Hattaway mentioned information on the 5 murdered "Outlaws" in Charlotte, North Carolina, on July 4, 1979, and the two outlaws in the trunk of the car in Randolph County some time back.

Appendix B: Forester
and Gamboa Autopsies

DEPARTMENT OF HUMAN RESOURCES
DIVISION OF HEALTH SERVICES
OFFICE OF THE CHIEF MEDICAL EXAMINER
CHAPEL HILL, NORTH CAROLINA 27514

ME-82- 9

REPORT OF AUTOPSY

DECEDENT   THOMAS   EUGENE   FORESTER   Autopsy authorized by: E.J. Miller, M.D., M.E.
      First name   Middle name   Last name   Name Ashe County Official Title

TYPE OF DEATH:		
Violent or Unnatural ☒	Unattended by a physician ☐	
Means: Trauma	Sudden in apparent health ☐	
	Unusual ☐ In prison ☐	
	Suspicious ☐	

RIGOR — JAW ☐ ARMS ☐ NECK ☐ CHEST ☐ BACK ☐ ABDOMEN ☐ LEGS ☐

LIVOR — COLOR ____ ANTERIOR POSTERIOR ☐ LATERAL ☐ REGIONAL

Body Identified by: Papers, law enforcement personnel

PERSONS PRESENT AT AUTOPSY

AGE 22 RACE White SEX Male LENGTH 70" WEIGHT 150 EYES ____ PUPILS: R ____ OPACITIES, ETC.
HAIR Br/long BEARD No MUSTACHE Yes CIRCUMCISED No BODY HEAT 26° F L ____

Mr. Boone
Mr. Alston
Dr. Hudson
Mr. Brinkhous
Mr. Robinson
Mr. Bucker
Mr. Calloway

NON FATAL WOUNDS, SCARS, TATTOOING, OTHER FEATURES: The body is received wrapped in
a sheet and is that of a young white male. He is clothed in a pair of blue
jeans, long-sleeved thermal undershirt, white socks. He has a Clark-type
boot on the left foot. He is wearing brief underpants. The body is frozen
and lies in a flexed-at-the-waist position on the left side with the right
arm pulled back and flexed at the elbow so that the right hand lies on the lateral chest. The
left arm is slightly flexed to bring the left arm up to approximately the same area as the

PATHOLOGICAL DIAGNOSIS   (Continued on next page)

1. Blunt trauma
    a. Multiple fractures of the ribs, left; laceration of left lung, spleen, left kidney,
        tear of left diaphragm
    b. Left hemothorax
    c. Hemoperitoneum
    d. Laceration of scalp
    e. Diffuse subarachnoid hemorrhage, mild
    f. Multiple abrasions and lacerations

TOXICOLOGY: Blood Ethanol - Negative

Probable cause of death: Massive blunt trauma

PROVISIONAL REPORT ☐
FINAL REPORT ☒

A true copy:

The facts stated herein are true and correct to the best
of my knowledge and belief.
John D. Butts, M.D.
                Signature of Pathologist
01-27-82; 11:00 AM   OCME

Chief Medical Examiner   Date
          Date and time of autopsy   Place of autopsy

DHS FORM...(74)

Thomas Forester — Report of Autopsy, page 1

DECEDENT:　　　　THOMAS EUGENE FORESTER

CASE NUMBER:　　ME-82-069

NON FATAL WOUNDS, SCARS, TATTOOING, OTHER FEATURES, continued

right hand. Both legs are extended. A considerable amount of dirt and rock is present
on the body and clothing. A tag from the Asheville Police Department signed by
R. Robinson is present on the right shoulder. The clothing is removed -- in some
instances it needed to be cut to be removed -- and the body washed and then allowed to
lie for twenty-four hours in the autopsy facility in order to let it thaw out so that
further examination could be performed. On the morning of the twenty-seventh, the
autopsy was continued.

There are multiple abrasions present on the body as indicated in the accompanying
diagram. They consist of numerous abrasions on the back, base of the left buttock,
backs of both upper arms. A 1 1/2" laceration is present on the back of the right
wrist. There is a 3" laceration on the right forehead. A gaping laceration has torn
off the right ear. A 3/4" laceration is present in the left parietal region of the
scalp and there is a 3" laceration posterior and inferior to this one in the parieto-
occipital region of the scalp. There are some recent cuts of the right lower lip and
chin and an abraded flap of the bridge of the nose. No blood is noted around these
latter injuries. A number of abrasions are present on the knuckles of both hands and
there is some abrasion of the backs of the hands as well. There has been some drying
of the body and some venous marbling of the arms is noted. The eyes are sunken and
their color cannot be determined. Teeth are present in both upper and lower jaw and
show evidence of restorations.

GROSS DESCRIPTION, continued

RIBS, continued: fractured lateral-posteriorly. Rib four is also fractured anteriorly,
　　　　　　　　as is rib five. Ribs six and seven are fractured anteriorly and
　　　　　　　　laterally. Ribs eight and nine are fractured laterally and poster-
　　　　　　　　iorly and rib number ten is fractured posteriorly. A number of
　　　　　　　　these fractures extend into the left pleural cavity. There is con-
　　　　　　　　siderable surrounding hemorrhage.

　　　　PELVIS: Intact.

Thomas Forester — Report of Autopsy, page 2

DEPARTMENT OF HUMAN RESOURCES
DIVISION OF HEALTH SERVICES
OFFICE OF THE CHIEF MEDICAL EXAMINER
CHAPEL HILL, NORTH CAROLINA 27514

S U M M A R Y A N D C O M M E N T

This was a 22 year old white male, who was allegedly, on or about 12-13-81, pushed into a mine shaft in Ashe County. The body was subsequently recovered, along with that of another young man, on January 25, 1982.

At autopsy the body was noted to be in a generally good state of preservation, although frozen. After thawing, internal examination revealed multiple traumatic injuries including fractures of ribs, tears of the lungs, spleen, kidney, tear of the diaphragm leading to herniation of abdominal contents into the left chest cavity, injuries to the scalp with mild bleeding over the brain. These injuries are compatible with the blunt trauma that might have been incurred in the fall. In my opinion death is the result of these injuries and it is also my opinion that the injuries were received while the decedent was still alive.

Probable Cause
Death: Massive blunt trauma

- -

Decedent: THOMAS EUGENE FORESTER   Autopsy No. ME-82-069   Date: 01-27-82

Prosector: John D. Butts, M.D.   Slides Read By: _____   Date: _____

Reviewed By: _____

Form 1915 (Rev. 3-76)
Medical Examiner

Thomas Forester — Summary and Comment

NORTH CAROLINA DEPARTMENT OF HUMAN RESOURCES
DIVISION OF HEALTH SERVICES — VITAL RECORDS BRANCH
MEDICAL EXAMINER'S CERTIFICATE OF DEATH — 50-A

REGISTRATION DISTRICT NO. ___ LOCAL NO. ___

NAME OF DECEASED: **Thomas** (first) **Eugene** (middle) **Forester** (last)

SEX: Male — DATE OF DEATH: December 13, 1981

COLOR OR RACE: Cauc. — STATE OF BIRTH: N.C. — COUNTY OF BIRTH: Madison — DATE OF BIRTH: November 13, 1952 — AGE: 29

PLACE OF DEATH COUNTY: Ashe — CITY OR TOWN: Laurel Springs — INSIDE CITY LIMITS: No

RESIDENCE—STATE: N.C. — COUNTY: Buncombe — CITY OR TOWN: Asheville — STREET AND NUMBER OR RFD NO.: 1003 Riverside Drive — INSIDE CITY LIMITS: Yes

CITIZEN OF WHAT COUNTRY?: USA — MARRIED, NEVER MARRIED, WIDOWED, DIVORCED: Married — SURVIVING SPOUSE: Brenda Drake

SOCIAL SECURITY NUMBER: 246-86-9150 — USUAL OCCUPATION: Mechanic — KIND OF BUSINESS OR INDUSTRY: Self Employed — WAS DECEDENT EVER IN U.S. ARMED FORCES?: No

FATHER'S NAME: Morris Forester — MOTHER'S MAIDEN NAME: Helen Wilson

INFORMANT'S NAME AND ADDRESS: Brenda D. Forester, 18 B. Oak Knoll Apts., Asheville, N.C. — RELATION TO DECEASED: Widow

PART 1 DEATH CAUSED BY:

(a) IMMEDIATE CAUSE: Pending

PART II OTHER SIGNIFICANT CONDITIONS:

AUTOPSY: yes — M.E.

ACCIDENT, SUICIDE, HOMICIDE, UNDETERMINED, NATURAL CAUSES, OR PENDING: Homicide

DESCRIBE HOW INJURY OCCURRED: Pushed into mine shaft

TIME OF INJURY: 12 13 81 P. — INJURY AT WORK: no — PLACE OF INJURY: mine shaft — CITY OR RFD: Laurel Springs — COUNTY: Ashe — STATE: N.C.

MEDICAL EXAMINER CERTIFICATION — DEATH OCCURRED: P. 01 25 82 10 — DATE SIGNED: 01-25-82

SIGNATURE: Edward J. McC. — ADDRESS: P. O. Box 27, Jefferson, N. C. 28640 — MEDICAL EXAMINER OF: Ashe

BURIAL, CREMATION, OTHER: Burial — DATE: 1/30/82 — NAME OF CEMETERY: Bowman Rector Cemetery — LOCATION: Marshall, N.C.

FUNERAL HOME: Bowman — Marshall, N.C. — SIGNATURE OF FUNERAL DIRECTOR: Clyde B. Shook — LICENSE NO.: 3549

DATE REC'D BY LOCAL REG.: 2-04-82 — SIGNATURE OF REGISTRAR: Cary D. Tuttle — No Embalming

Thomas Forester — Medical Examiner's Certificate of Death

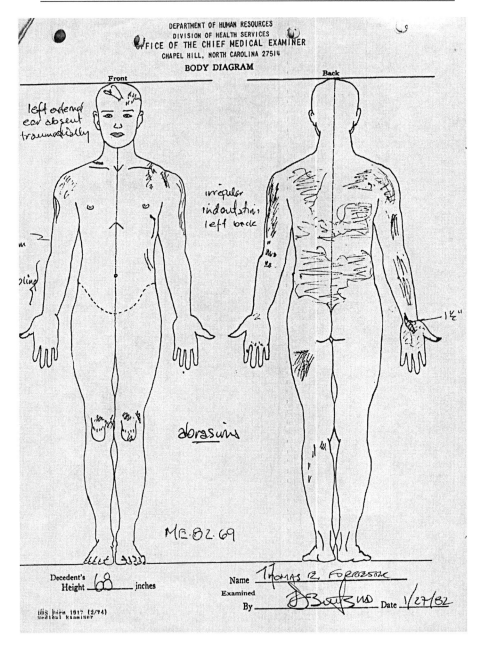

Thomas Forester — Whole Body Diagram

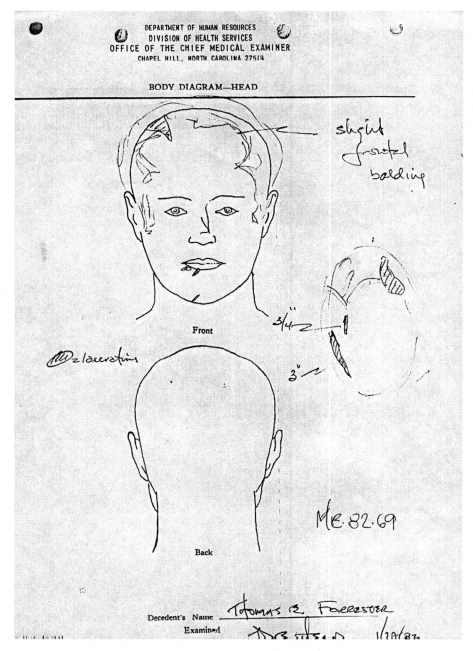

Thomas Forester — Body Diagram (Head, Frontal/Posterior)

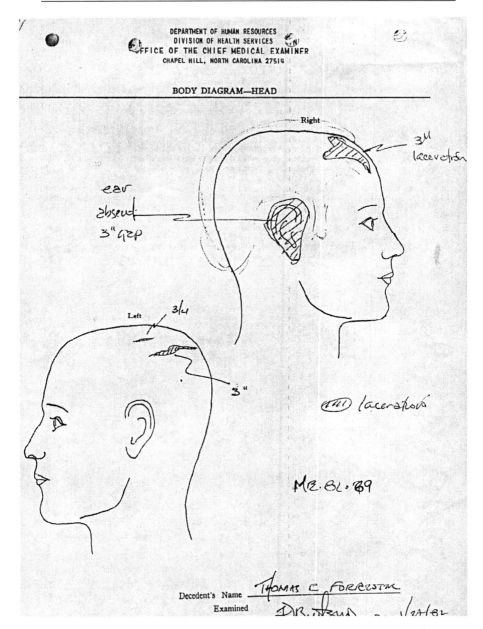

Thomas Forester — Body Diagram (Head, Lateral, Right/Left)

DEPARTMENT OF HUMAN RESOURCES
DIVISION OF HEALTH SERVICES
OFFICE OF THE CHIEF MEDICAL EXAMINER
CHAPEL HILL, NORTH CAROLINA 27514

Received 3-11-86
ME-82-

REPORT OF AUTOPSY

DECEDENT LONNIE   MARSHALL   GAMBOA   Autopsy authorized by: E.J. Miller, M.D., M.E.
    First name   Middle name   Last name   Name Ashe County Official Title

TYPE OF DEATH:		RIGOR	LIVOR	Body Identified by:
Violent or Unnatural ☒ Unattended by a physician ☐		JAW ☐ ARMS ☐	COLOR _____	Law enforcement officers, papers, wrist tag
Means: Fall Sudden in apparent health ☐		NECK ☐ CHEST ☐	ANTERIOR POSTERIOR ☐	
Unusual ☐ In prison ☐		BACK ☐ ABDOMEN ☐	LATERAL ☐ Mixed	PERSONS PRESENT AT AUTOPSY
Suspicious ☐		LEGS ☐ Frozen REGIONAL		Messrs. Robinson

28 RACE White SEX Male LENGTH 68" WEIGHT 154 EYES Brown PUPILS: R 7mm OPACITIES, ETC. & Calloway,
Black BEARD No MUSTACHE No CIRCUMCISED Yes BODY HEAT Frozen L 7mm Dull Asheville P.D.,

ON FATAL WOUNDS, SCARS, TATTOOING, OTHER FEATURES: Blue mid-length sleeved shirt
with red, white and blue sleeve stripes, blue corduroy trousers, brown belt,
left boot, athletic socks, down jacket on wrists. ID tag
on right wrist. Tattoo featuring snake on back of lower right arm. Gold
crowns on teeth #15 and #30. Chipping of teeth #7 and #8. Tooth #9 is peg-shaped.

Mr. Busker, SBI,
Messrs Boone &
Brinkhous,
Dr. Butts

PATHOLOGICAL DIAGNOSIS

Blunt force injury to head
  Large laceration, right parieto-temporal area
  Massive fracturing of skull
  Subarachnoid hemorrhage, brain
Blunt trauma of right chest
  Fractures of clavicle and ribs 1-8, right
  Hemothorax, right
  Pulmonary contusion and tear, right lower lobe
  Filling of lower tracheobronchial tree with blood
  Slight aspiration of blood, left lower lobe
  Subcapsular hematoma, dome of right lobe of liver

TOXICOLOGY: Blood Alcohol - Negative for ethanol and other similar volatiles
            Blood Diazepam - Less than 0.03mgs%, if present
                 Urine - Negative for opiates, benzodiazepines, cocaine, amphetamines
                   and barbiturates

Probable
Cause of death: Blunt injury of head and chest

PROVISIONAL REPORT ☐
FINAL REPORT ☒

Blue copy:

Chief Medical Examiner   Date

The facts stated herein are true and correct to the best of my knowledge and belief.
Page Hudson, M.D. _____
               Signature of Pathologist
01-26-82; 10:30   OCME
Date and time of autopsy   Place of autopsy

Lonnie Gamboa — Report of Autopsy, page 1

SEROUS CAVITIES:	Internal organ are still largely frozen.
PLEURA:	Left pleural cavity contains a considerable quantity of frozen blood. A portion of bowel is present extending through torn diaphragm into the left pleural cavity.
PERITONEUM:	Contains some frozen bloody fluid.
PERICARDIUM:	Frozen blood is present.
HEART:	Weighs 340 grams. The coronaries show normal distribution and no atherosclerosis. The myocardium is unremarkable. The aortic valves shows partial fusion of two cusps to give partially bicuspid valve. The aorta and its major branches are intact with minimal atherosclerotic plaquing. There is some tears in the inferior vena cava at its entrance into the pericardial sac.
LUNGS:	The left lung weighs 390 grams, the right 550. Several tears are noted in the lateral portions of the left upper and lower lobes secondary to fractured ribs. Some bloody fluid is present in the bronchi.
LIVER:	Weighs 1,400 grams. It is reddish-brown. The gallbladder contains liquid bile. The extrahepatic system is intact.
SPLEEN:	Weighs 100 grams. It is torn in several places.
PANCREAS:	Autolyzed.
ADRENAL GLANDS:	Unremarkable.
G. I. TRACT:	Intact throughout its length. The appendix is present. The stomach contains several tablespoonsful of pinkish frozen fluid.
KIDNEYS:	The left kidney weighs 140 grams, the right 120. There is a considerable amount of hemorrhage present around of the hilum of the left kidney and there are some tears extending through the substance of the kidney. Ureters intact.
BLADDER:	Contains frozen urine.
INTERNAL GENITALIA:	Normal adult male.
NECK ORGANS:	Larynx is clear. Thyroid normal in size and configuration.
BRAIN AND MENINGES:	The brain weighs 1,340 grams. It is somewhat decomposed. Gyri are flattened and there is a diffuse veneer of subarachnoid hemorrhage present over both hemispheres and at the base. Multiple cross sections reveal freezing artifact but no internal hemorrhage.
SKULL:	There is a small area of depressed fracture of the frontal bone on the right beneath the large laceration in that area, approximately 7mm in diameter, and does not extend to the inner table. No other fractures are noted. Subgaleal hemorrhage is present especially over the right parietal and temporal regions involving the two lacerations in that area. The larger laceration posteriorly shows considerable avulsion as well.
VERTEBRAE:	Intact.
RIBS:	Multiple rib fractures are present on the left and the clavicle is fractured at mid-shaft as well. Rib one is fractured laterally, ribs three and four are

OTHER LABORATORY PROCEDURES: TOXICOLOGY ☒   BACTERIOLOGY ☐   SEROLOGY ☐   NONE ☐

DISPOSITION OF EVIDENCE

TYPE (Clothing, Bullets, Etc.)	NAME OF RECIPIENT	ADDRESS	OFFICIAL TITLE	DATE

Lonnie Gamboa — Report of Autopsy, page 2

DEPARTMENT OF HUMAN RESOURCES
DIVISION OF HEALTH SERVICES
OFFICE OF THE CHIEF MEDICAL EXAMINER
CHAPEL HILL, NORTH CAROLINA 27514

SUMMARY AND COMMENT

History indicates that the deceased was forced down a mine shaft in December. The body, as well as another one (ME-82-069), were removed 01-25-82. As the deaths appeared suspicious and violent, jurisdiction was assumed by Ashe County Medical Examiner, Dr. E.J. Miller, in cooperation with the Ashe County Sheriff's Department. Dr. Miller authorized autopsy.

There were numerous superficial abrasions as indicated in the diagram. There was a massive blunt force impact site on the right side of the skull. This caused extensive skull fracturing and brain damage. In addition there was blunt force impact on the right upper chest with extensive rib fracturing. There was a tear of the right lower lobe of the lung and some aspiration of blood into the left lower lobe. This would only have taken a breath or two after the impact.

Autopsy presents me with no definitive evidence that this person was beaten before going into the mine shaft. All of the injuries I found could have been and probably were inflicted upon impact. The head injury could represent one severe blow with a heavy relatively narrow instrument, but is at least as likely to have been caused by impacting with something quite hard such as a rock or piece of wood at the bottom of the mine shaft. In view of the severity of the head wound and the one or two breaths that were taken after the chest injury, it is virtually inconceivable that there was significant time if any between head and chest impacts.

Probable Cause
of Death:
    Blunt injury of head and chest

Decedent: LONNIE MARSHALL GAMBOA   Autopsy No. ME-82-070   Date: 01-26-82

Prosector: Page Hudson, M.D.   Slides Read By: _____   Date: _____

Reviewed By: _PH_

DHS Form 1915 (Rev. 3-76)

Lonnie Gamboa — Summary and Comment

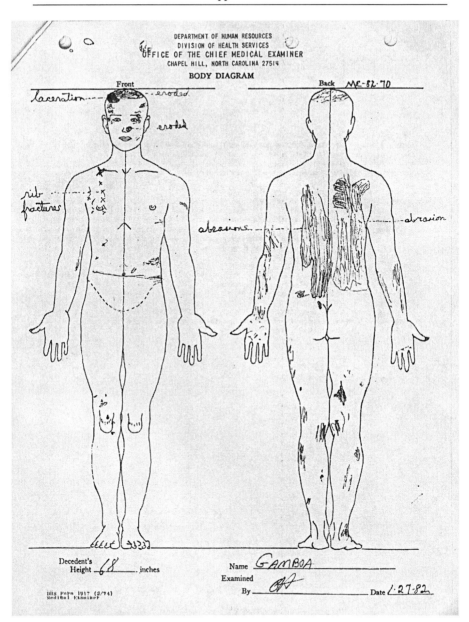

Lonnie Gamboa — Whole Body Diagram

Chapter Notes

Chapter 1

1. Weather report, TV station WXII, Winston-Salem, North Carolina, December 23, 1981.
2. Joseph Vines, "Testimony Given during the Paul Wilson Bare Trial for the Kidnapping and Murder of Lonnie Marshall Gamboa," June 2–11, 1982 (Paul Wilson Bare Trial Official Transcript hand-copied by Rose M. Haynes, 1983–1984) and verified during personal interview with Rose M. Haynes (audiotape and handwritten notes) in an undisclosed prison location, July 14, 1986.
3. Joseph Vines, personal interview with Rose M. Haynes at an undisclosed location, July 14, 1986.
4. Official Court Transcript of Paul Wilson Bare Trial for the Kidnapping and Murder of Lonnie M. Gamboa, June 2–11, 1982 (Paul Wilson Bare Official Trial Transcript hand-copied by Rose M. Haynes — original transcript destroyed, 1983–1984).
5. Official Court Transcript of Paul Wilson Bare Trial for the Kidnapping and Murder of Lonnie Marshall Gamboa, June 2–11, 1982 (handwritten copy by Rose M. Haynes, 1983–1984).
6. Official Court Transcript of Paul Wilson Bare Trial for the Kidnapping and Murder of Lonnie Marshall Gamboa, June 2–11, 1982 (handwritten copy by Rose M. Haynes, 1983–1984).
7. Vines, personal interview with author, July 14, 1986.
8. Vines, personal interview with author, July 14, 1986.

Chapter 2

1. Joseph Vines, "Testimony Given during the Paul Wilson Bare Trial for the Kidnapping and Murder of Lonnie Marshall Gamboa," June 2–11, 1982 (Paul Wilson Bare Trial Official Transcript hand-copied by Rose M. Haynes, 1983–1984), and verified during personal interview with the author in an undisclosed prison location on July 14, 1986.
2. Vines, "Testimony Given at Bare Trial," and prison interview, 1986.
3. Vines, "Testimony Given at Bare Trial," and prison interview, 1986.
4. Vines, interview with Haynes, 1986.
5. Paul Wilson Bare Trial Official Court Transcript, Haynes' handwritten copy, 1984.
6. Vines interview, 1986.
7. Vines interview, 1986.
8. Paul Wilson Bare Trial Official Court Transcript, Haynes' handwritten copy, 1984.
9. Vines interview, 1986.
10. Vines interview, 1986.
11. Vines interview, 1986.
12. Paul Wilson Bare Trial Official Court Transcript, Haynes' handwritten copy, 1984.
13. Paul Wilson Bare Trial Official Court Transcript, Haynes' handwritten copy, 1984.
14. Vines interview, 1986.
15. Paul Wilson Bare Trial Official Court Transcript, Haynes' handwritten copy, 1984.
16. Paul Wilson Bare Trial Official Court Transcript, Haynes' handwritten copy, 1984.
17. Paul Wilson Bare Trial Official Court Transcript, Haynes' handwritten copy, 1984.
18. Paul Wilson Bare Trial Official Court Transcript, Haynes' handwritten copy, 1984.

19. Vines interview, 1986.
20. Paul Wilson Bare Trial Official Court Transcript, Haynes' handwritten copy, 1984.

Chapter 3

1. Joseph Vines, personal interview with Rose M. Haynes, July 14, 1986; telephone interviews with Rose M. Haynes, 2009–2012.
2. Vines, interview with Haynes, July 14, 1986.
3. Vines, interview with Haynes, July 14, 1986.
4. Vines, interview with Haynes, July 14, 1986.
5. Vines, interview with Haynes, July 14, 1986.
6. Joseph Vines, "Testimony Given during the Paul Wilson Bare Trial for the Kidnapping and Murder of Lonnie Marshall Gamboa" (handwritten copy of Official Transcript by Rose M. Haynes), 1984.
7. Vines, interview with Haynes, July 14, 1986.

Chapter 4

1. Joseph Vines, interview with Rose M. Haynes (audiotape and handwritten notes) at an undisclosed location, July 14, 1986.
2. Official Court Transcript of Paul Wilson Bare Trial for the Kidnapping and Murder of Lonnie Marshall Gamboa," June 2–11, 1982 (handwritten copy by Rose M. Haynes, original transcript destroyed, 1983–1984).
3. Joseph Vines, interview with Rose M. Haynes (audiotape and handwritten notes) at an undisclosed location, July 14, 1986.
4. Vines interview by the author, July 14, 1986; telephone interviews, 2009–2012.
5. Vines interview by the author, July 14, 1986; telephone interviews, 2009–2012.
6. Joseph Vines, "Testimony Given during the Paul Wilson Bare Trial for the Kidnapping and Murder of Lonnie Marshall Gamboa," June 2–11, 1982. (Official Court Transcript of Paul Wilson Bare Trial for the Kidnapping and Murder of Lonnie M. Gamboa, hand-copied by Rose M. Haynes, 1983–1984.)
7. Vines, interview by the author, July 14, 1986; telephone interviews, 2009–2012.
8. Vines, interview by the author, July 14, 1986; telephone interviews, 2009–2012.
9. Vines interview by the author, July 14, 1986; telephone interviews, 2009–2012.
10. Vines, interview by the author, July 14, 1986.
11. Vines, interview by the author, July 14, 1986; telephone interviews, 2009–2012.

Chapter 5

1. Ashe County Sheriff's Department Archives. Paul Wilson Bare Trial Records, "Official Sworn Statement of Thomas L. Chapman," June 1, 1982.
2. Ashe County Sheriff's Department Archives. Paul Wilson Bare Trial Records, "Official Sworn Statement of Joseph E. Vines," June 1, 1982.
3. Ashe County Sheriff's Department Archives. Paul Wilson Bare Trial Records, "Official Sworn Statement of Sheriff Richard Waddell," June 1, 1982.
4. Waddell, "Official Sworn Statement," June 1, 1982.
5. Waddell, "Official Sworn Statement," June 1, 1982.
6. Chapman, "Official Sworn Statement," June 1, 1982.
7. Chapman, "Official Sworn Statement," June 1, 1982.
8. Sharon Gamboa, Ashe County Sheriff's Department Archives, "Official Sworn Statement of Sharon Gamboa," June 2, 1982.
9. Melvin Roberts, Ashe County Sheriff's Department Archives, Paul Wilson Bare Trial Records, "Official Sworn Statement of Captain Melvin Roberts," June 1, 1982.
10. Waddell, "Official Sworn Statement," June 1, 1982.
11. Chapman, "Official Sworn Statement," June 1, 1982.
12. Chapman, "Official Sworn Statement," June 1, 1982.
13. Chapman, "Official Sworn Statement," June 1, 1982.
14. Chapman, "Official Sworn Statement," June 1, 1982.

15. Waddell, "Official Sworn Statement," June 1, 1982.
16. Waddell, "Official Sworn Statement," June 1, 1982.
17. Terry Henry, "Bare Bound Over," *Jefferson Times*, January 15, 1982.
18. Terry Henry, "Probable Cause Found on Kidnap," *Jefferson Times*, January 21, 1982.

Chapter 6

1. Richard Waddell, Ashe County Sheriff's Department Archives. Paul Wilson Bare Trial Records, "Official Sworn Statement of Sheriff Richard Waddell," June 1, 1982.
2. Terry Henry, "Search of Mine Yields Nothing," *Jefferson Times*, January 14, 1982.
3. Waddell, "Official Sworn Statement," June 1, 1982.
4. Elsie Taylor, Ashe County Sheriff's Department Archives. Paul Wilson Bare Trial Records, "Official Sworn Statement of Elsie Taylor," June 1, 1982.
5. Eugene Goss, Ashe County Sheriff's Department Archives. Paul Wilson Bare Trial Records, "Official Sworn Statement of Deputy Eugene Goss," June 1, 1982.
6. Waddell, "Official Sworn Statement," June 1, 1982.
7. Eugene Goss, interview by the author, Jefferson, NC, May 9, 2012.
8. Goss interview, May 9, 2012.
9. Waddell, "Official Sworn Statement," June 1, 1982.
10. Terry Henry, "Bare Bound Over to Superior Court," *Jefferson Times*, February 8, 1982.
11. Terry Henry, "Bare Bound Over to Superior Court," *Jefferson Times*, February 11, 1982.
12. Henry, February 11, 1982.
13. Henry, February 11, 1982.
14. Henry, February 8, 1982.
15. Eugene Goss, telephone interview with author, August 29, 2012.

Chapter 7

1. *United States v. Thomas Stimac, also known as West Side Tommy; Robert George Burroughs, also known as Snoopy; Allan Ray Hattaway, also known as Red; Ron Miller; Marty Curran, also known as Scarface; and Gary Miller.* 82 CR 308, United States District Court Northern District of Illinois Eastern Division, "Government's Memorandum of Evidence in Aggravation of Sentence." Dan K. Webb, United States Attorney (1982), p. 31.
2. *United States v. Thomas Stimac et al.* (1982), pp. 7–8.
3. *United States v. Thomas Stimac et al.* (1982), pp. 8–9.
4. *United States v. Thomas Stimac et al.* (1982), p. 11.
5. Donald Cole, Criminal Investigative Bureau — Investigative Follow-up Report, Case File #81-26-0079, Asheville, NC, January 1982.
6. Cole, Investigative Follow-up Report, January 1982.
7. Donald Cole's Official Statement, Asheville, November 7, 1981.
8. Donald Cole, "Moffitt Branch Shoot-out," interview of Gary Miller, November 7, 1981.
9. *United States v. Thomas Stimac et al.* (1982), p. 14.
10. *United States v. Thomas Stimac et al.* pp. 14–15.
11. Jay Fagel, Statement — Asheville Police Department, Investigative Follow-up Report, Case File #81-26-0079, #81-26-0080, "Callahan/Forester — Missing Persons," December 30, 1981.
12. Darlene Callahan, Ashe County Sheriff's Department Archives, "Official Statement of Darlene Callahan taken by Sheriff Waddell and Ernest Bueker," February 2, 1982.
13. Jay Fagel, "Official Statement of Jay Fagel," Asheville Police Department Investigative Report, December 30, 1981.
14. Jay Fagel, Statement, Asheville Police Department Investigative Follow-up Report, December 30, 1981.
15. Callahan, "Official Statement," February 2, 1982.

Chapter 8

1. Betty Darlene Callahan, Ashe County Sheriff's Department Archives. Paul Wilson Bare Trial Records, "Official Sworn Statement of Betty Darlene Callahan," June 1, 1982.

2. Callahan, "Official Sworn Statement," June 2, 1982.

3. *United States v. Thomas Stimac, also known as West Side Tommy; Robert George Burroughs, also known as Snoopy; Allan Ray Hattaway, also known as Red; Ron Miller; Marty Curran, also known as Scarface; and Gary Miller.* 82 CR 308, United States District Court, Northern District of Illinois Eastern Division, "Government's Memorandum of Evidence in Aggravation of Sentence." Dan K. Webb, United States Attorney (1982), pp. 8–9.

4. Callahan, "Official Sworn Statement," June 2, 1982.

5. *United States v. Thomas Stimac et al. (1982)*, p.17–21.

6. *United States v. Thomas Stimac et al. (1982)*, p. 23.

7. Callahan, "Official Sworn Statement," June 2, 1982.

8. Richard Waddell, Ashe County Sheriff's Department Archives. Paul Wilson Bare Trial Records, "Official Sworn Statement of Sheriff Richard Waddell," June 1, 1982.

9. *United States v. Thomas Stimac et al. (1982)*, pp. 23–24.

10. *United States v. Thomas Stimac et al. (1982)*, pp. 26–28.

11. Terry Henry, "Bare Surrenders to Authorities: Woman Found," *Jefferson Times*, January 28, 1982.

12. *United States v. Thomas Stimac et al. (1982)*, p. 32.

13. *United States v. Thomas Stimac et al. (1982)*, p. 16.

14. Callahan, "Official Sworn Statement," June 2, 1982.

15. *United States v. Thomas Stimac et al. (1982)*, p. 17.

16. Gary Miller, Ashe County Sheriff's Department Archives. Paul Wilson Bare Trial Records, "Official Sworn Statement of Gary Miller," June 2, 1982.

17. Waddell, "Official Sworn Statement," June 2, 1982.

Chapter 9

1. Gene Goss, interview with Rose M. Haynes in Jefferson, NC, on August 8, 2009.

2. John Downey, "Bare's Attorney Met First Defeat in Small Town," *Winston-Salem Journal*, June 13, 1982.

3. Gene Goss, telephone interviews and personal interviews in Jefferson, NC, with Rose M. Haynes, 2009–2012.

4. Thomas Chapman, "Testimony Given during the Paul Wilson Bare Trial for the Kidnapping and Murder of Lonnie Marshall Gamboa," June 2–11, 1982 (Paul Wilson Bare Trial Official Court Transcript hand-copied by Rose M. Haynes—original transcript destroyed, 1983–1984).

5. Official Court Transcript of the Paul Wilson Bare Trial for the Kidnapping and Murder of Lonnie Marshall Gamboa (hand copied by Rose M. Haynes, 1983–1984).

Chapter 10

1. Eugene Goss, personal interview with Rose M. Haynes on August 8, 2012.

2. Sharon Gamboa, "Testimony Given during the Paul Wilson Bare Trial for the Kidnapping and Murder of Lonnie Marshall Gamboa," June 2–11, 1982 (Paul Wilson Bare Trial Official Transcript, hand-copied by Rose M. Haynes, 1983–1984).

3. Sharon Gamboa, "Cross-examination of Sharon Gamboa," June 2–10, 1982.

Chapter 11

1. Susan Pardue, *The Journal-Patriot*, "Testimony Continues about Informant," June, 1982.

2. Official Court Transcript of Paul Wilson Bare Trial for the Kidnapping and Murder of Lonnie Marshall Gamboa, June, 2–10, 1982 (hand-copied by Rose M. Haynes, 1983–1984).

3. Official Court Transcript of Paul Wilson Bare Trial for the Kidnapping and Murder of Lonnie Marshall Gamboa, June 2–10, 1982 (hand-copied by Rose M. Haynes,1983–1984).

Chapter 12

1. Associated Press. "Spectators Face Search," June 7, 1982 (scrapbook of Eugene Goss, no newspaper name included).

2. Joseph Vines, Official Court Transcript of Paul Wilson Bare Trial for the Kidnapping and Murder of Lonnie Marshall Gamboa, June 2–1982 (handwritten copy by Rose M. Haynes— Official Transcript destroyed, 1983–1984).

3. Susan Pardue, "Vines Says He Was Forced," *The Journal-Patriot*, June 3, 1982.

4. Pardue, June 3, 1982.

5. Pardue, June 3, 1982.

6. Pardue, June 3, 1982.

7. Bruce Henderson, "Witness Not Informant on December 23," *Catawba Valley Observer*, June 1982.

8. Susan Pardue, "Testimony Continues about Informer," *Journal Patriot*, June 7, 1982.

9. Pardue, June 7, 1982.

10. Pardue, June 7, 1982.

11. Susan Pardue, "Bare Eligible for Parole in 20 Years," *The Journal-Patriot*, June 14, 1982.

12. John Downey, "Bare's Attorney Met First Defeat in Small Town," *Winston-Salem Journal*, June 13, 1982.

Chapter 13

1. Eugene Goss, interview by the author, August 2012.

2. Van Denton, "Murder Suspect Captured," *Lenoir News*, June 11, 1982.

3. Associated Press, "Gunfire Wounds Two Deputies," June 6, 1982.

4. Goss interview, August 2012.

5. Goss interview, August 2012.

Chapter 14

1. Joseph Vines, personal interview with Rose M. Haynes at an undisclosed prison location, July 14, 1986.

2. *United States v. Thomas Stimac, also known as West Side Tommy; Robert George Burroughs, also known as Snoopy; Allan Ray Hattaway, also known as Red; Ron Miller; Marty Curran, also known as Scarface; and Gary Miller.* 82 CR 308, United States District Court, Northern District of Illinois Eastern Division, "Government's Memorandum of Evidence in Aggravation of Sentence." Dan K. Webb, United States Attorney (1982), p. 5.

3. *United States v. Thomas Stimac et al. (1982)*, p. 6.

4. *United States v. Thomas Stimac et al. (1982)*, p. 6.

5. *United States v. Thomas Stimac et al. (1982)*, p. 7.

6. *United States v. Thomas Stimac et al. (1982)*, p. 7.

7. *United States v. Thomas Stimac et al. (1982)*, p. 7.

8. *United States v. Thomas Stimac et al. (1982)*, p. 10.

9. *United States v. Thomas Stimac et al. (1982)*, p. 24.

10. *United States v. Thomas Stimac et al. (1982)*, pp. 28–29.

11. *United States v. Thomas Stimac et al. (1982)*, p. 32.

12. *United States v. Thomas Stimac et al. (1982)*, pp. 33–34.

13. *United States v. Thomas Stimac et al. (1982)*, p. 34.

14. *United States v. Thomas Stimac et al. (1982)*, p. 35.

15. *United States v. Thomas Stimac et al. (1982)*, p. 37.

16. *United States v. Thomas Stimac et al. (1982)*, p. 37.

17. *United States v. Thomas Stimac et al. (1982)*, p. 38.

18. *United States v. Thomas Stimac et al. (1982)*, p. 41.

19. *United States v. Thomas Stimac et al. (1982)*, p. 42.

20. *United States v. Thomas Stimac et al. (1982)*, pp. 44–45.

21. *United States v. Thomas Stimac et al. (1982)*, p. 46.

22. *United States v. Thomas Stimac et al. (1982)*, p. 48.

23. *United States v. Thomas Stimac et al. (1982)*, p. 48.

24. Joseph Vines, interview by Rose M. Haynes, at an undisclosed prison location, July 14, 1986.

25. Interview by Rose M. Haynes, at an undisclosed prison location, July 14, 1986.

Chapter 15

1. Joseph Vines, interview by Rose M. Haynes in an undisclosed location, July 14, 1986.

2. Lynn Worth, "Attorneys Want New Trial for Paul Wilson Bare, *Jefferson Times*, July 12, 1984.

3. Lynn Worth, "Vines Murder Trial Set for October 15 in Buncombe County," *Jefferson Times*, September 20, 1984.

4. Lynn Worth, "Vines to Be Tried for Murder," *Jefferson Times*, July 16, 1984.

5. Vines interview, July 14, 1986.

6. Lynn Worth, "Vines Murder Trial Set," *Jefferson Times*, September 20, 1984.

7. Worth, September 20, 1984.

8. Worth, September 20, 1984.

9. Lynn Worth, "Vines Murder Trial Began Monday," *Jefferson Times*, October 20, 1984.

10. Lynn Worth, "Vines to Fight Extradition to North Carolina for Murder Trial," *Jefferson Times*, March 19, 1984.

11. Lynn Worth, "Vines Murder Trial Set for October 15 in Buncombe County," *Jefferson Times*, September 20, 1984.

12. Lynn Worth, "Vines Claims Ashburn Promised Him Immunity," *Jefferson Times*, July 9, 1984.

13. Lynn Worth, *Jefferson Times*, July 12, 1984.

14. Vines interview in Prison, 1986.

15. "Vines Murder Trial Opened Monday," newspaper (no name), October 18, 1984.

16. Rose M. Haynes, Personal Notes from Joseph Vines Trial in Asheville, October 17–29, 1984.

17. Vines interview, Haynes, 1986.

18. Haynes, Personal Notes from Vines Trial Attendance, October 17–29, 1984.

19. Haynes, Personal Notes, October 17–29, 1984.

20. Haynes, Personal Notes, October 17–29, 1984.

21. Haynes, Personal Notes, October 17–29, 1984.

22. Sharon Gamboa, Ashe County Sheriff's Department Archives. Paul Wilson Bare Trial Records, "Official Sworn Statement of Detective Ross Robinson," Interview of Sharon Gamboa, June 1, 1982.

23. Haynes, Personal Notes, October 17–29, 1984.

24. Haynes, Personal Notes, October 17–29, 1984.

25. William Annarino, Ashe County Sheriff's Department Archives. Paul Wilson Bare Trial Records, "Official Sworn Statement of Detective William Annarino," June 1, 1982.

26. Gary Miller, Ashe County Sheriff's Department Archives. Paul Wilson Bare Trial Records, "Official Sworn Statement of Gary Miller made to Asheville Police Department," June 1, 1982.

27. Haynes, Personal Notes, October 17–29, 1984.

28. Thomas Chapman, Ashe County Sheriff's Department Archives. Paul Wilson Bare Trial Records, "Official Sworn Statement of Thomas Chapman," June 1, 1982.

29. Haynes, Personal Notes, October 17–29, 1984.

30. Haynes, Personal Notes, October 17–29, 1984.

31. Sharon Gamboa, Ashe County Sheriff's Department Archives. Paul Wilson Bare Trial Records, "Official Sworn Statement of Joseph E. Vines," June 1, 1982.

32. Haynes, Personal Notes, October 17–29, 1984.

33. Haynes, Personal Notes, October 17–29, 1984.

34. Vines interview, Haynes, 1986.

35. Haynes, Personal Notes, October 17–29, 1984.

36. Haynes, Personal Notes, October 17–29, 1984.

37. Haynes, Personal Notes, October 17–29, 1984.

38. John Downey, "Officer Says Vines Sold Marijuana, Bragged of Deals," *Winston-Salem Journal*, October 23, 1984.

39. Haynes, Personal Notes, October 17–29, 1984.

40. Haynes, Personal Notes, October 17–29, 1984.

41. Lynn Worth, "Vines Convicted, Sentenced to Life in Prison for Murder," *Jefferson Times*, October 29, 1984.

42. Vines interview, Haynes, 1986.

43. Worth, October 29, 1984.

44. Worth, October 29, 1984.

45. John Downey, "Informant Gets Life in Prison for Ashe Murder," *Winston-Salem Journal*, October 29, 1984.

References

Court Records

Chapman, Thomas L. "Testimony Given During the Paul Wilson Bare Trial for the Kidnapping and Murder of Lonnie Marshall Gamboa," June 2–11, 1982. (Paul Wilson Bare Trial Official Transcript hand-copied by Rose M. Haynes, 1983–1984.)

Gamboa, Sharon. "Testimony Given During the Paul Wilson Bare Trial for the Kidnapping and Murder of Lonnie Marshall Gamboa," June 2–11, 1982. (Paul Wilson Bare Trial Official Transcript hand-copied by Rose M. Haynes, 1983–1984.)

Gamboa, Sharon. "Cross-Examination of Sharon Gamboa," Paul Wilson Bare Trial for the Kidnapping and Murder of Lonnie M. Gamboa," June 2–11, 1982. (Paul Wilson Bare Trial Official Transcript hand-copied by Rose M. Haynes, 1983–1984.)

Haynes, Rose M. Personal Notes from Joseph Vines Trial in Asheville, October 17–29, 1984.

Official Court Transcript of Paul Wilson Bare Trial for the Kidnapping and Murder of Lonnie M. Gamboa, June 2–11, 1982. (Paul Wilson Bare Official Trial Transcript hand-written copy by Rose M. Haynes — original transcript destroyed, 1983–1984.)

Webb, Dan K. "*United States v. Thomas Stimac, also known as West Side Tommy; Robert George Burroughs, also known as Snoopy; Allan Ray Hattaway, also known as Red; Ron Miller; Marty Curran, also known as Scarface; and Gary Miller.*" 82 CR 308, United States District Court Northern District of Illinois Eastern Division, "Government's Memorandum of Evidence in Aggravation of Sentence," 1982, pp. 3–31.

Vines, Joseph. "Testimony Given during the Paul Wilson Bare Trial for the Kidnapping and Murder of Lonnie Marshall Gamboa," June 2–11, 1982. (Paul Wilson Bare Trial Official Transcript hand-copied by Rose M. Haynes, 1983–1984.)

Ashe County Sheriff's Department Archives

Annarino, William. Paul Wilson Bare Trial Records, "Official Sworn Statement of Detective William Annarino," June 1, 1982.

Callahan, Darlene. Paul Wilson Bare Trial Records, "Official Sworn Statement of Darlene Callahan," taken by Sheriff Richard Waddell and Ernest Bueker, February 2, 1982.

Chapman, Thomas L. Paul Wilson Bare Trial Records, "Official Sworn Statement of Thomas L. Chapman," June 1, 1982.

Cole, Donald. "Moffitt Branch Shoot-out," Interview of Gary Miller, in Asheville, NC, November 7, 1981.

Cole, Donald. Criminal Investigative Bureau — Investigative Follow-up Report, Case File #81-26-0079, Asheville, NC, January 1982.

Fagel, Jay. "Official Statement" — Asheville Police Department, Investigative Follow-up Report, Case File #81-26-0079, #81-26-0080, "Callahan/Forester — Missing Persons," December 30, 1981.

Gamboa, Sharon. Paul Wilson Bare Trial Records, "Official Sworn Statement of Sharon Gamboa," June 2, 1982.

Goss, Eugene. Paul Wilson Bare Trial Records, "Official Sworn Statement of Deputy Eugene Goss," June 1, 1982.

Miller, Gary. Paul Wilson Bare Trial Records, "Official Sworn Statement of Gary Miller," made to Asheville Police Department, June 1, 1982.
Roberts, Melvin. Paul Wilson Bare Trial Records, "Official Sworn Statement of Captain Melvin Roberts," June 1, 1982.
Robinson, Ross. Paul Wilson Bare Trial Records, "Official Sworn Statement of Detective Ross Robinson," iterview of Sharon Gamboa, June 1, 1982.
Taylor, Elsie. Paul Wilson Bare Trial Records, "Official Sworn Statement of Elsie Taylor," June 1, 1982.
Vines, Joseph E. Paul Wilson Bare Trial Records, "Official Sworn Statement of Joseph E. Vines," June 1, 1982.
Vines, Joseph. "Testimony Given During the Paul Wilson Bare Trial for the Kidnapping and Murder of Lonnie Marshall Gamboa," June 2–11, 1982. (Paul Wilson Bare Trial Official Transcript hand-copied by Rose M. Haynes, 1983–1984.)
Waddell, Richard R. Paul Wilson Bare Trial Records, "Official Sworn Statement of Sheriff Richard Waddell," June 1, 1982.

Television Reports

Weather report, WXII, Winston-Salem, North Carolina, December 23, 1981.

Newspaper Articles

Associated Press. "Gunfire Wounds Two Deputies." June 6, 1982.
Associated Press. "Spectators Face Search." June 7, 1982 (scrapbook of Eugene Goss, no newspaper name included).
Denton, Van. "Murder Suspect Captured." *Lenoir News*, June 11, 1982.
Downey, John. "Bare's Attorney Met First Defeat in Small Town." *Winston-Salem Journal*, June 13, 1982.
Downey, John. "Officer Says Vines Sold Marijuana, Bragged of Deals." *Winston-Salem Journal*, October 23, 1984.
Downey, John. "Informant Gets Life in Prison for Ashe Murder." *Winston-Salem Journal*, October 29, 1984.
Henderson, Bruce. "Witness Not Informant on December 23." *Catawba Valley Observer*, June 7, 1982.
Henry, Terry. "Search of Mine Yields Nothing." *Jefferson Times*, January 14, 1982.
Henry, Terry. "Bare Bound Over." *Jefferson Times*, January 15, 1982.
Henry, Terry. "Probable Cause Found on Kidnap." *Jefferson Times*, January 21, 1982.
Henry, Terry. "Bare Surrenders to Authorities: Woman Found." *Jefferson Times*, January 28, 1982.
Henry, Terry. "Bare Bound Over to Superior Court." *Jefferson Times*, February 8, 1982.
Henry, Terry. "Bare Bound Over to Superior Court." *Jefferson Times*, February 11, 1982.
Pardue, Susan. "Vines Says He Was Forced." *The Journal-Patriot*, June 3, 1982.
Pardue, Susan. "Testimony Continues about Informant." *The Journal-Patriot*, June 7, 1982.
Pardue, Susan. "Bare Eligible for Parole in 20 Years." *The Journal-Patriot*, June 14, 1982.
"Vines Murder Trial Opened Monday." Newspaper, no name, October 18, 1984.
Worth, Lynn. "Vines to Fight Extradition to North Carolina for Murder Trial." *Jefferson Times*, March 19, 1984.
Worth, Lynn. "Vines Claims Ashburn Promised Him Immunity." *Jefferson Times*, July 9, 1984.
Worth, Lynn. "Attorneys Want New Trial for Paul Wilson Bare." *Jefferson Times*, July 12, 1984.
Worth, Lynn. "Vines to Be Tried for Murder." *Jefferson Times*, July 16, 1984.
Worth, Lynn. "Vines Murder Trial Set for October 15 in Buncombe County." *Jefferson Times*, September 10, 1984.
Worth, Lynn. "Vines Murder Trial Set for October 15 in Buncombe County." *Jefferson Times*, September 20, 1984.
Worth, Lynn. "Vines' Murder Trial Began Monday." *Jefferson Times*, October 20, 1984.
Worth, Lynn. "Vines Convicted, Sentenced to Life in Prison for Murder." *Jefferson Times,* October 29, 1984.

Interviews

Goss, Eugene, personal interview with Rose M. Haynes in Jefferson, NC, June 12, 1985.

Goss, Eugene, personal interview with Rose M. Haynes in Jefferson, NC, on August 8, 2009.

Goss, Eugene, personal interview with Rose M. Haynes in Jefferson, NC, October 2009.

Goss, Eugene, personal interview with Rose M. Haynes in Jefferson, NC, May 9, 2012.

Goss, Eugene, telephone interview with Rose Haynes, August 29, 2012.

Goss, Eugene, telephone interviews and personal interviews in Jefferson, NC, with Rose M. Haynes, 2009–2012.

Vines, Joseph, personal interview with Rose M. Haynes at an undisclosed location, July 14, 1986.

Vines, Joseph, personal interviews by telephone with Rose M. Haynes, 2009–2012.

Index